Interactive Mathematics Program®

IMP

Integrated High School Mathematics

YEAR 3

Dan Fendel and Diane Resek
with
Lynne Alper and Sherry Fraser

Key Curriculum Press
Innovators in Mathematics Education

This material is based upon work supported by the National Science Foundation under award number ESI-9255262. Any opinions, findings, and conclusions or recommendations expressed in this publication are those of the authors and do not necessarily reflect the views of the National Science Foundation.

Key Curriculum Press
1150 65th Street
Emeryville, California 94608

10 9 8 7   06 05
ISBN 1-55953-293-9
Printed in the
United States of America

Project Editor
Casey FitzSimons

Editorial Assistant
Jeff Gammon

Additional Editorial Development
Masha Albrecht, Mary Jo Cittadino

Art Developer
Ellen Silva

Production Editor
Caroline Ayres

Cover and Interior Design
Terry Lockman
Lumina Designworks

Production Management
Diana Jean Parks, Steve Rogers

Art Editor
Laura Murray

Technical Graphics
Laurel Technical Services

Illustration
Taylor Bruce, Deborah Drummond, Tom Fowler, Evangelia Philippidis, Sara Swan, Diane Varner, Martha Weston, April Goodman Willy

Publisher
Steven Rasmussen

Editorial Director
John Bergez

MATHEMATICS REVIEW
Rick Marks, Ph.D., Sonoma State University,
    Rohnert Park, California

MULTICULTURAL REVIEWS
Genevieve Lau, Ph.D., Skyline College,
    San Bruno, California
Arthur Ramirez, Ph.D., Sonoma State University,
    Rohnert Park, California
Marilyn Strutchens, Ph.D., University of Maryland,
    College Park, Maryland

TEACHER REVIEWS
Daniel R. Bennett, Hoolehua, Hawaii
Maureen Burkhart, North Hollywood, California
Dwight Fuller, Shingle Springs, California
Daniel Johnson, San Jose, California
Brian Lawler, Aurora, Colorado
Brent McClain, Hillsboro, Oregon
Susan Miller, Philadelphia, Pennsylvania
Amy C. Roszak, Cottage Grove, Oregon
Carmen Rubino, Aurora, Colorado
Barbara Schallau, San Jose, California
Kathleen H. Spivack, New Haven, Connecticut
Wendy Tokumine, Honolulu, Hawaii

ACKNOWLEDGMENTS

Many people have contributed to the development of the IMP™ curriculum, including the hundreds of teachers and many thousands of students who used preliminary versions of the materials. Of course, there is no way to thank all of them individually, but the IMP directors want to give some special acknowledgments.

We want to give extraordinary thanks to these people who played unique roles in the development of the curriculum.

- **Bill Finzer** was one of the original directors of IMP and helped develop the concept of a problem-based unit.

- **Nitsa Movshovitz-Hadar** suggested the central problem for *Orchard Hideout* and wrote the first draft of that unit.

- **Matt Bremer** pilot-taught the entire curriculum, did the initial revision of every unit after its pilot testing, and did major work on subsequent revisions.

- **Mary Jo Cittadino** became a high school student once again during the piloting of the curriculum, which gave her a unique perspective on the curriculum.

- **Lori Green** left the classroom as a regular teacher after piloting Year 1 and became a traveling resource for IMP classroom teachers. She has compiled many of her classroom insights in the *Teaching Handbook for the Interactive Mathematics Program.*

- **Celia Stevenson** developed the charming and witty graphics that graced the prepublication versions of the IMP units.

In creating this program, we needed help in many areas other than writing curriculum and giving support to teachers.

The National Science Foundation (NSF) has been the primary sponsor of the Interactive Mathematics Program®. We want to thank NSF for its ongoing support, and we especially want to extend our personal thanks to Dr. Margaret Cozzens, Director of NSF's Division of Elementary, Secondary, and Informal Education, for her encouragement and her faith in our efforts.

We also want to acknowledge here the initial support for curriculum development from the California Postsecondary Education Commission and the San Francisco Foundation, and the major support for dissemination from the Noyce Foundation and the David and Lucile Packard Foundation.

Keeping all of our work going required the help of a first-rate office staff. This group of talented and hard-working individuals worked tirelessly on many tasks, such as sending out units, keeping the books balanced, helping us get our message out to the public, and handling communications with schools, teachers, and administrators. We greatly appreciate their dedication.

- Barbara Ford—Secretary
- Tony Gillies—Project Manager
- Marianne Smith—Communications Manager
- Linda Witnov—Outreach Coordinator

IMP National Advisory Board

We have been further supported in this work by our National Advisory Board—a group of very busy people who found time in their schedules to give us more than a piece of their minds every year. We thank them for their ideas and their forthrightness.

David Blackwell
Professor of Mathematics and
Statistics
University of California, Berkeley

Constance Clayton
Professor of Pediatrics
Chief, Division of Community
Health Care
Medical College of Pennsylvania

Tom Ferrio
Manager, Professional Calculators
Texas Instruments

Andrew M. Gleason
Hollis Professor of Mathematics
and Natural Philosophy
Department of Mathematics
Harvard University

Milton A. Gordon
President and Professor of
Mathematics
California State University,
Fullerton

Shirley Hill
Curator's Professor of Education
and Mathematics
School of Education
University of Missouri

Steven Leinwand
Mathematics Consultant
Connecticut Department of
Education

Art McArdle
Northern California Surveyors
Apprentice Committee

Diane Ravitch (1994 only)
Senior Research Scholar,
Brookings Institution

Roy Romer (1992-1994 only)
Governor
State of Colorado

Karen Sheingold
Research Director
Educational Testing Service

Theodore R. Sizer
Chairman
Coalition of Essential Schools

Gary D. Watts
Educational Consultant

We want to thank Dr. Norman Webb of the Wisconsin Center for Education Research for his leadership in our evaluation program, and our Evaluation Advisory Board, whose expertise was so valuable in that aspect of our work.

- David Clarke, University of Melbourne
- Robert Davis, Rutgers University
- George Hein, Lesley College
- Mark St. John, Inverness Research Associates

Finally, we want to thank Steve Rasmussen, President of Key Curriculum Press, Casey FitzSimons, Key's Project Editor for the IMP curriculum, and the many others at Key whose work turned our ideas and words into published form.

Dan Fendel   Diane Resek   Lynne Alper   Sherry Fraser

Students must be prepared for the world that they will inherit. Whether or not they choose to enter college immediately after high school, we must equip them to handle new problems with confidence and perseverance. Our ever-changing world requires that students grow into critically thinking adults who are prepared to absorb new ideas and who will become lifelong learners. The Interactive Mathematics Program (IMP) aids in this development.

IMP enhances students' understanding of mathematics by obliging them to present reasoned arguments. The group activities in IMP foster teamwork and the development of oral and written communication skills. These skills are honed by requiring students to write intelligible explanations about the processes that they followed to reach their conclusions.

As a parent of an IMP student, I have found that IMP enables students to experience mathematics in action and to recognize that mathematics is not simply an esoteric subject. On the other hand, IMP also offers students the opportunity to experience how beautiful and open-ended mathematics is.

As a professional mathematician, I believe that IMP teaches mathematics in the way that it should be taught. Mathematics does not arise naturally in nicely defined semester-long modules labeled Algebra I, Geometry, Algebra II, and Trigonometry/Precalculus. IMP effectively breaks down the artificial barriers created by such divisions.

I have found the Problems of the Week exceedingly interesting and intellectually stimulating—sufficiently so that I have shared several of them with members of my faculty. It is so refreshing to interact with my son around mathematics that is quite challenging to me also. He can appreciate my excitement and that mathematics can be fun.

As a parent and educator, I know the concerns that students, parents, school officials, and others have about colleges' expectations of entering students. What I value most, as do many of my colleagues at other top institutions, is that students have experienced good teaching in well-constructed courses that emphasize communication and creative thinking, and in which the learning that takes place is genuine and meaningful.

At Colorado School of Mines, a school of engineering and applied science, we require that our students develop strong communication skills and learn to work effectively as team members. To help our students enhance these skills further, we have established a writing center staffed by qualified professionals. In the beginning courses in calculus in our Department of Mathematical and Computer Sciences, we emphasize the working of real problems provided by the science and engineering disciplines. Students learn to think creatively and not be tied to one notation system. We also require our seniors to take turns at presenting reports on a research topic at weekly seminars. The other students submit reviews of their classmates' presentations and learn from the preparation of their assessments, in addition to providing valuable feedback to the presenter.

We expect that our students will not simply reflect their professors' thinking. Students have a responsibility to engage in independent thinking and to understand the power of thought as distinct from the power of authority. Students have a head start when they enter college courses with prior knowledge in solving complex problems that go beyond calculation and in coping with ambiguity.

The Interactive Mathematics Program helps prepare students for life, not just for college calculus. Because the Program emphasizes creative thinking, communication skills, and teamwork, it should serve our students well.

Graeme Fairweather

Graeme Fairweather
Professor and Head
Department of Mathematical and Computer Sciences
Colorado School of Mines
Golden, Colorado

Orchard Hideout

Meadows or Malls?

DAYS 1–2: Recreation Versus Development: A Complex Problem 155

Small World, Isn't It?

DAYS 3–5: Average Growth 288

DAYS 6–10: All in a Row 298

DAYS 11–16: Beyond Linearity 312

DAYS 17–23: A Model for Population Growth ...327

DAYS 24–29: The Best Base 344

DAYS 30–32: Back to the Data .356

Appendix: Supplemental Problems 364

Pennant Fever

DAYS 24–28: Pascal's Triangle 449

DAYS 29–31: The Baseball Finale 458

Appendix: Supplemental Problems 465

Glossary 485

Note to Students

This textbook represents the third year of a four-year program of mathematics learning and investigation. As in the first two years, the program is organized around interesting, complex problems, and the concepts you learn grow out of what you'll need to solve those problems.

If you studied IMP Year 1 or 2

If you studied IMP Year 1 or 2, then you know the excitement of problem-based mathematical study. The Year 3 program extends and expands the challenges that you worked with previously. For instance:

- In Year 1, you began developing a foundation for working with variables. In Year 2, you learned how to solve linear equations algebraically. In Year 3, the opening unit focuses on quadratic equations, using the analysis of the path of a fireworks rocket as the central problem.

- In Year 1, you used the normal distribution to help predict the period of a 30-foot pendulum. In Year 2, you learned about the chi-square statistic to understand statistical comparisons of populations. In Year 3, you'll learn about the binomial distribution and apply it to a variety of situations including a baseball pennant race.

You'll also use ideas from geometry to see how to make a "hideout" from an array of trees, you'll use matrix algebra to help a city decide how to allocate land resources, and you'll study rates of change and derivatives in order to make predictions about world population growth.

If you didn't study IMP Year 1 or 2

If this is your first experience with the Interactive Mathematics Program (IMP), you can rely on your classmates and your teacher to fill in what you've missed.

Meanwhile, here are some things you should know about the program, how it was developed, and how it is organized.

The Interactive Mathematics Program is the product of a collaboration of teachers, teacher-educators, and mathematicians who have been working together since 1989 to reform the way high school mathematics is taught. About one hundred thousand students and five hundred teachers used these materials before they were published. Their experiences, reactions, and ideas have been incorporated into this final version.

Our goal is to give you the mathematics you need in order to succeed in this changing world. We want to present mathematics to you in a manner that reflects how mathematics is used and that reflects the different ways people work and learn together. Through this perspective on mathematics, you will be prepared both for continued study of mathematics in college and for the world of work.

This book contains the various assignments that will be your work during Year 3 of the program. As you will see, these problems require ideas from many branches of mathematics, including algebra, geometry, probability, graphing, statistics, and trigonometry. Rather than present each of these areas separately, we have integrated them and presented them in meaningful contexts, so you will see how they relate to each other and to our world.

Each unit in this four-year program has a central problem or theme, and focuses on several major mathematical ideas. Within each unit, the material is organized for teaching purposes into "days," with a homework assignment for each day. (Your class may not follow this schedule exactly, especially if it doesn't meet every day.)

At the end of the main material for each unit, you will find a set of supplementary problems. These problems provide you with additional opportunities to work with ideas from the unit, either to strengthen your understanding of the core material or to explore new ideas related to the unit.

Although the IMP program is not organized into courses called "Algebra," "Geometry," and so on, you will be learning all the essential mathematical concepts that are part of those traditional courses. You will also be learning concepts from branches of mathematics—especially statistics and probability—that are not part of a traditional high school program.

To accomplish your goals, you will have to be an active learner, because the book does not teach directly. Your role as a mathematics student will be to experiment, to investigate, to ask questions, to make and test conjectures, and to reflect, and then to communicate your ideas and conclusions both orally and in writing. You will do some of your work in collaboration with fellow students, just as users of mathematics in the real world often work in teams. At other times, you will be working on your own.

We hope you will enjoy the challenge of this new way of learning mathematics and will see mathematics in a new light.

Dan Fendel   Diane Resek

Lynne Alper   Sherry Fraser

Fireworks

The World of Quadratics

David Miyamoto explains to Jared Maligro the meaning of the graph he generated on the graphing calculator for "A Corral Variation."

In the Year 2 unit *Solve It!* you saw that every linear equation in one variable can be solved using straightforward algebraic techniques. The next level of complexity after the linear equation is the quadratic equation. As you'll see, the central problem of this unit involves a quadratic function and quadratic equations.

In the opening days of this unit, you will begin your exploration of the world of quadratic functions and equations, focusing mainly on the graphs of quadratic functions.

Fireworks

The Jefferson High junior varsity soccer team has just won the championship. To celebrate this triumph, the school will be putting on a fireworks display, and the team members are helping with the planning.

The fireworks will use rockets launched from the top of a tower near the school. The top of the tower is 160 feet off the ground. The mechanism will launch the rockets so that they are initially rising at 92 feet per second.

The team members want the fireworks from each rocket to explode when the rocket is at the top of its trajectory. They need to know how long it will take for the rocket to reach the top, so that they can set the timing mechanism. Also, in order to inform spectators of the best place to stand to see the display, they need to know how high the rockets will go.

The rockets will be aimed toward an empty field and shot at an angle of 65 degrees above the horizontal. The team members want to know how far the rockets will land from the base of the tower so they can fence off the area in advance. (*Note:* The field where the rockets will land is at the same level as the base of the tower.)

Some Formulas

Antonio is on the soccer team. His sister Hilda is in Year 4 of IMP. She says she learned some physics and mathematics in the unit *High Dive* that would be helpful to Antonio's team.

Continued on next page

She says that there is a function $h(t)$ that will give the rocket's height off the ground in terms of the time t elapsed since launch. Specifically, if t is in seconds and $h(t)$ is in feet, then

$$h(t) = 160 + 92t - 16t^2$$

(You can probably see where the numbers 160 and 92 come from. The coefficient -16 in the term $-16t^2$ has to do with the force of gravity. You will learn more about this when you study *High Dive*.)

Hilda also says that the team can find the horizontal distance the rocket travels with this function:

$$d(t) = \frac{92t}{\tan 65°}$$

Again, t is the number of seconds since the rocket was launched, and $d(t)$ is the distance in feet. (You will also find out where this function comes from when you study *High Dive*.)

But that was all the information Hilda would give the soccer team, and none of the players have studied *High Dive* yet. See whether you can help the soccer team find the answers to its questions.

1. Draw a sketch of the situation.

2. Write a clear statement of the questions the soccer team wants answered.

3. Describe how you might use Hilda's functions to help answer the questions you stated in Question 2.

4. Using whatever methods you choose, try to get some answers (or partial answers) to the questions you stated in Question 2.

The Standard POW Write-up

The standard POW write-up for Year 3 includes the same five categories that you used in Year 2.

1. *Problem Statement:* State the problem clearly in your own words. Your problem statement should be clear enough that someone unfamiliar with the problem could understand what it is that you are being asked to do.

2. *Process:* Describe what you did in attempting to solve this problem, using your notes as a reminder. Include things that didn't work out or that seemed like a waste of time. Do this part of the write-up even if you didn't solve the problem.

   If you get assistance of any kind on the problem, you should indicate what the assistance was and how it helped you.

3. *Solution:* State your solution as clearly as you can. Explain how you know that your solution is correct and complete. (If you only obtained a partial solution, give that. If you were able to generalize the problem, include your more general results.)

   Your explanation should be written in a way that will be convincing to someone else—even someone who initially disagrees with your answer.

Continued on next page

4. *Evaluation:* Discuss your personal reaction to this problem. For example, you might comment on the following:

   • Did you consider it educationally worthwhile? What did you learn from it?

   • How would you change the problem to make it better?

   • Did you enjoy working on it?

   • Was it too hard or too easy?

5. *Self-assessment:* Assign yourself a grade for your work on this POW, and explain why you think you deserved that grade.

A Corral Variation

Dairyman Johnson raises cattle. There is a long, straight fence along the border between his property and that of his neighbor, rancher Gonzales.

Dairyman Johnson likes rectangles, and he also values efficiency. He realizes that the fence between his property and that of rancher Gonzales can serve as part of a fenced-in pen for some of his cattle.

Gonzales's land

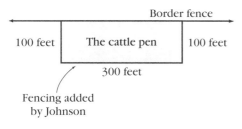

Border fence

100 feet | The cattle pen | 100 feet

300 feet

Fencing added by Johnson

Johnson's land

His plan is to use part of this existing fence along the border as one side of a rectangular pen and to build the other three sides using 500 feet of fencing he has purchased. For example, he might build the pen so it looks like the diagram at the left.

1. What is the area of the cattle pen shown in the diagram?

2. Choose three other possibilities for the dimensions of the rectangular pen, and find the area for each pen you create. Keep in mind that dairyman Johnson can use as much or as little of the existing fence as he likes and that he wants to use a total of 500 feet of fencing for the other three sides.

3. Suppose the pen extends x feet away from the existing fence along the border. (For example, in the diagram, x would be 100 feet.) Find an expression for the area in terms of x.

4. Try to determine the value of x that will maximize this area.

Growth of Rat Populations

Two rats, one male and one female, scampered on board a ship that was anchored at a local dock. The ship set sail across the ocean. When it anchored at a deserted island in late December, the two rats abandoned the ship to make their home on the island.

Under these ideal conditions, it might be interesting to estimate the number of offspring produced from this pair in one year. You should make these four assumptions.

• The number of young produced in every litter is six, and three of those six are females.

• The original female gives birth to six young on January 1 and produces another litter of six every 40 days thereafter as long as she lives.

• Each female born on the island will produce her first litter 120 days after her birth and then produce a new litter every 40 days thereafter.

• The rats are on an island with no natural enemies and plenty of food, so no rats will die in this first year.

What will be the total number of rats by the following January 1, including the original pair?

Continued on next page

Write-up

1. *Problem Statement*

2. *Process:* Include a discussion of how you came up with a way of organizing your information. Also, describe any approaches you tried that didn't work out.

3. *Solution:* Be sure to explain how you kept track of the results and how you arrived at your numerical answer.

4. *Evaluation*

5. *Self-assessment:* Include a statement as to how confident you are about the correctness of your numerical answer.

Adapted from *Mathematics Insight and Meaning,* Jan de Lange, Freudenthal Institute, Utrecht University, The Netherlands, 1987.

The Ups and Downs of Quadratics

Your task in this activity is to explore how the graph of a quadratic function is related to its coefficients. The specific questions here provide a framework for that exploration.

1. Explain how you can tell by looking at the coefficients of a quadratic function whether the vertex of the graph is a minimum or a maximum.

For Questions 2 through 4, begin by graphing the quadratic function defined by the equation $y = x^2 + 5x + 3$. Adjust the viewing window of your graphing calculator so you get a good view of the graph.

You will be trying to create new functions whose graphs vary from this one in specific ways. You should do this simply by changing the coefficients, *without changing the viewing window*. As you graph new functions, you should leave the graph of the original function on the screen for comparison.

2. Try to create a new function whose graph is your original graph moved up or down. That is, the graph of the new function should have exactly the same shape as the original one, but the new vertex should be higher or lower on the screen. Describe your efforts and the results you get. Be sure to record the function you find and sketch its graph.

Continued on next page

3. Try to create a new function whose graph is your original graph moved left or right. That is, the graph of the new function should have exactly the same shape as the original one, but the new vertex should be to the left or to the right on the screen. Describe your efforts and the results you get, and record the function and its graph.

4. Try to create a new function that has the same vertex as your original graph but whose graph is "wider" or "narrower." Describe your efforts and the results you get, and record the function and its graph.

Quadratics and Other Polynomials

You've looked at two problem situations so far in this unit, both of which involve expressions with the square of the variable.

- The *Fireworks* problem involves the expression $160 + 92t - 16t^2$.

- In *Homework 1: A Corral Variation,* the area for dairyman Johnson's pen can be described using the expression $x(500 - 2x)$, which also can be written as $500x - 2x^2$.

Quadratic Expressions and Functions

Both $160 + 92t - 16t^2$ and $x(500 - 2x)$ are examples of **quadratic expressions.**

If the variable is x, the **standard form** for a quadratic expression is $ax^2 + bx + c$, where a, b, and c are specific numbers. (Because such an expression has three terms, it is also called a **trinomial.**) For instance, the standard form for dairyman Johnson's area expression is $-2x^2 + 500x + 0$, so for this example, $a = -2$, $b = 500$, and $c = 0$. The *Fireworks* expression uses the variable t, and its standard form is $-16t^2 + 92t + 160$, so $a = -16$, $b = 92$, and $c = 160$.

The number a is called the **coefficient of the quadratic term.** This coefficient can't be zero, because otherwise the expression would be linear rather than quadratic.

The number b is called the **coefficient of the linear term,** and the number c is called the **constant term.** In the case of dairyman Johnson's area expression, the constant term is zero.

Continued on next page

A function defined by a quadratic expression is called a **quadratic function.** For instance, the function defined by the equation $y = 160 + 92t - 16t^2$ is a quadratic function. We informally refer to the coefficients from the quadratic expression as "the coefficients of the function."

We can associate a **quadratic equation** with each quadratic expression by setting the expression equal to zero. For example, for the expression $2x^2 + 5x - 7$, we have the associated quadratic equation $2x^2 + 5x - 7 = 0$.

Graphs of Quadratic Functions

You've seen that the graphs of quadratic functions all have roughly the same shape, which is called a **parabola.**

The graphs of quadratic functions fall into two categories—those that open upward and those that open downward. That is, they have either a minimum point or a maximum point. This point, whether a minimum or a maximum, is called the **vertex** of the graph.

Continued on next page

Interactive Mathematics Program

Polynomials

Any expression that is a sum of whole-number powers of the variable, each multiplied by a coefficient, is called a **polynomial,** and each item being added is called a **term.** (We normally do not explicitly write coefficients that are equal to 1. Also, polynomials can involve differences as well as sums, but by using negative coefficients, we can write every polynomial as a sum. A single term is also considered a polynomial.)

The highest power of the variable is called the **degree** of the polynomial. Thus, all linear expressions are polynomials of degree 1 and all quadratic expressions are polynomials of degree 2. A polynomial of degree 3 is called a **cubic** polynomial.

A number by itself (that is, just a constant term), is also considered a polynomial. If the number is not zero, the degree of the polynomial is 0. (The number 0 by itself, considered as a polynomial, is not assigned a degree.) Here are some examples.

Polynomial	Degree
$5t^2$	2
$8w - 2$	1
$5z^3 - z^2 + 9z + 7$	3
$x^6 + 4x^2$	6
23	0

It's sometimes helpful to include the "missing" terms— that is, the terms whose coefficients are zero. For example, you might write the polynomial $x^6 + 4x^2$ as $x^6 + 0x^5 + 0x^4 + 0x^3 + 4x^2 + 0x + 0$.

Rats in June

POW 1: Growth of Rat Populations asks you to find out how many rats there will be on January 1, one year after the original female has her first litter. This assignment gets you started on that task.

Figure out how many rats there are on June 1, part of the way through that year.

Product Equations

1. Write down at least five number pairs to solve the equation $vw = 50$. (Keep in mind that v and w do not have to be whole numbers and don't even have to be positive.)

2. Write down at least five number pairs to solve the equation $vw = 100$.

3. Write down at least five number pairs to solve the equation $vw = 0$.

4. Discuss your results. How does Question 3 compare to the first two examples? Why is it so different?

5. Write down at least five number pairs to solve the equation $(r - 2)(s + 1) = 100$.

6. Write down at least five number pairs to solve the equation $(r - 2)(s + 1) = 0$.

Factoring and Solving

Adrienne Hypolite awaits the results of Lisa Newton's calculations to see if Lisa's results agree with hers.

Zero is a special number, and one of its special properties leads to a technique for solving certain quadratic equations (and other polynomial equations as well).

As you explore factoring, you'll be using the distributive property quite a bit, with special attention to the case in which a quadratic expression can be written as the product of two identical factors.

Factored Intercepts

One of your tasks in the *Fireworks* problem is to figure out how long it will take for the rocket to land. Here are some other ways to ask the same question.

- How long does it take until the rocket returns to ground level?

- What are the roots of the function $h(t) = 160 + 92t - 16t^2$?

- What are the *t*-intercepts of the graph of the function $h(t) = 160 + 92t - 16t^2$?

- What are the solutions to the equation $160 + 92t - 16t^2 = 0$?

The equation $160 + 92t - 16t^2 = 0$ is an example of a quadratic equation.

In *Homework 3: Product Equations,* you saw that the only way for a *product* to be zero is for at least one of the factors to be zero. In this activity, you will look at how this fact about products can be used to solve quadratic equations.

1. a. Graph the function $f(x) = (x + 2)(x - 3)$ on a graphing calculator and estimate its *x*-intercepts.

    b. Substitute the *x*-values you found in part a into the function to see if they really give a result of zero. If they do not, think about how those values might be adjusted to get the exact *x*-intercepts. (Remember that your *x*-values were just estimates from the graph.)

2. Go through steps a and b from Question 1 for the function $g(x) = (x - 5)(x + 7)$.

Continued on next page

3. Go through steps a and b from Question 1 for the function $k(x) = (x + 9)(2x - 7)$.

4. Examine your results from Questions 1 through 3.

   a. Find a method for identifying the intercepts without graphing, directly from the expressions that define the functions.

   b. Use the zero property to explain your method.

5. Use your method from Question 4a to find the x-intercepts of the graphs of each of these functions without graphing. Then check your work by substitution.

   a. $F(x) = (x - 4)(x + 1)$

   b. $G(x) = (2x - 5)(x + 12)$

   c. $H(x) = x(x + 4)(8 - 3x)$

Make Your Own Intercepts

In *Factored Intercepts,* you looked at functions that were expressed as products and used that form to find the *x*-intercepts of the functions. This assignment goes in the other direction—you are told what the *x*-intercepts should be, and you need to find a function that has them.

1. Write an equation for a function whose graph has exactly two *x*-intercepts, one at $x = 4$ and the other at $x = 2$.

2. Write an equation for a function whose graph has exactly two *x*-intercepts, one at $x = -6$ and the other at $x = 3$.

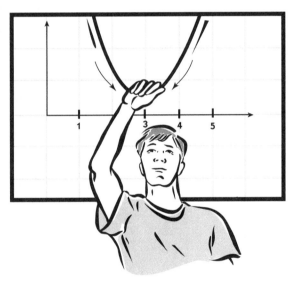

3. Write an equation for a function whose graph has exactly three *x*-intercepts, one at $x = -5$, another at $x = 1$, and the third at $x = 5$.

4. Do you think it's possible to create a function with *any* given set of *x*-intercepts? Explain your answer.

5. Do you think there is more than one function that fits the condition in Question 1? Can you find another such function? What about the conditions in Question 2 or Question 3?

Revisiting a Mystery

Do you remember the housing developer and the city planner from the Year 2 unit *Solve It?* As you may recall, the developer had submitted plans to the planner for some houses she wanted to build. But the planner thought the plans were boring because the lots were all square and all the same size.

After some discussion, the planner and the developer decided that the lots should include other types of rectangles. So the developer proceeded to change the lengths of some of the sides of the lots.

The developer wrote plans for the new lot sizes but put them in code, using the variable X to represent the length of a side of the original square lots. For example, if the original square lot was extended 4 meters in one direction and 3 meters in the other, the developer represented the new lot by the factored-form expression $(X + 4)(X + 3)$.

1. a. Draw a diagram illustrating the lot represented by the expression $(X + 4)(X + 3)$.

   b. Find an algebraic expression without parentheses for the area of this lot. That is, write $(X + 4)(X + 3)$ as a quadratic expression in standard form.

In *Solve It!* you helped the city planner decode some of the housing developer's expressions. Now it's time to do some more.

Continued on next page

2. Here is what the planner found written in the developer's plans one day.

   "Build a lot whose area is $X^2 + 4X + 2X + 8$."

   Help the planner by finding out how the developer planned to change the original square lot.

3. What do you suppose each of these entries means?

   a. "Build a lot whose area is $X^2 + 4X + 6X + 24$."

   b. "Build a lot whose area is $X^2 + 6X + 2X + 12$."

4. The entries got even more mysterious. Figure out for the planner what each of these entries means.

   a. "Build a lot whose area is $X^2 + 5X + 6$."

   b. "Build a lot whose area is $X^2 + 8X + 15$."

   c. "Build a lot whose area is $X^2 + 5X - 14$."

   d. "Build a lot whose area is $X^2 - 7X + 10$."

Factoring Begun

You've seen that finding the x-intercepts for the graph of a quadratic function can be simplified if the expression defining the function can be factored. For example, writing the expression $x^2 - x - 6$ as the product $(x + 2)(x - 3)$ makes it clear that the x-intercepts for the function $f(x) = x^2 - x - 6$ are at $(-2, 0)$ and at $(3, 0)$. But factoring a quadratic expression is not always an easy task. The first stage in learning how to factor quadratic expressions is getting a feel for what happens when you multiply linear expressions.

1. Write each of these products as a quadratic expression of the form $x^2 + bx + c$. That is, write each product in standard form.

   a. $(x + 3)(x + 5)$

   b. $(x - 4)(x + 7)$

   c. $(x - 6)(x - 2)$

2. Using what you learned in Question 1, try to write each of these quadratic expressions as a product of two linear expressions. That is, try to write each expression in factored form.

   a. $x^2 + 5x + 6$

   b. $x^2 + 2x - 15$

   c. $x^2 - 3x + 10$

   d. $x^2 - 9x + 8$

   e. $x^2 - 16$

   f. $x^2 - 10x + 6$

3. Find the x-intercepts for the functions defined by each of the expressions in Questions 1 and 2.

Who's Perfect?

Some quadratic expressions have a special type of factorization, in which the two factors are the same. For example, $x^2 - 6x + 9$ is equal to the product $(x - 3)(x - 3)$, which can also be written as $(x - 3)^2$. Expressions such as $x^2 - 6x + 9$, which can be written as the square of another expression, are called **squares** or **perfect squares.**

Your task in this assignment is to see which quadratic expressions are perfect squares. You should restrict yourself to quadratic expressions whose x^2-coefficient is 1. That is, you want to find a rule that tells you whether an expression of the form $x^2 + bx + c$ is a perfect square.

1. Multiply out each of these expressions, look at the trinomials you get, and examine how the coefficients of those trinomials are related to the expression you are squaring.

   a. $(x + 4)^2$

   b. $(x - 5)^2$

   c. $(x + 7)^2$

2. Generalize your work from Question 1. As needed, make up some more examples of your own and look for patterns. Then state a general rule that will tell you if a quadratic expression with x^2-coefficient equal to 1 is a perfect square.

More About Perfection

1. In *Who's Perfect?* you were asked to find a general rule that tells you when a quadratic expression with x^2-coefficient equal to 1 is a perfect square. Explain that rule using an area diagram.

2. In each of these expressions, find a number for the constant term c so that the expression will be a perfect square. (This is called **completing the square.**)

   a. $x^2 + 6x + c$

   b. $x^2 - 12x + c$

   c. $x^2 + 9x + c$

3. a. Make a table showing at least six number pairs that fit the equation $y = (x - 3)^2$.

   b. Plot those points and then connect your points with a smooth curve that you think represents the graph.

4. Repeat steps a and b of Question 3 for the equation $y = (x - 5)^2$.

5. Repeat steps a and b of Question 3 for the equation $y = (x + 7)^2$.

6. Generalize from the curves you got in Questions 3 through 5 to describe the graph of the function $y = (x - h)^2$. Your description should include the coordinates of the vertex for the graph.

The Algebra of the Vertex

Melody Koker stops to ask if there are any questions before continuing with her presentation.

You've seen that the vertex is a key element of the graph of a quadratic function. The vertex also plays an important part in solving real-world problems involving quadratic functions, because it shows the maximum or minimum value of the function.

In the final segment of this unit, you will examine exactly how you can use algebra to find the vertex of the graph of any quadratic function. You will then apply this approach to the central problem of the unit.

The Same but Different

1. a. Graph the quadratic function $f(x) = (x - 2)^2$ on a graphing calculator.

   b. Find the vertex for this graph.

   c. Explain how you can be certain that you have the exact vertex.

2. Go through the steps from Question 1 for each of these functions.

   a. $g(x) = (x + 4)^2$

   b. $h(x) = (x - 3)^2 + 2$

   c. $k(x) = (x + 5)^2 - 7$

   d. $r(x) = 3(x + 1)^2 + 16$

   e. $s(x) = -2(x - 4)^2 + 9$

3. Explain how you could find the vertices for functions like those in Questions 1 and 2 without graphing.

4. Give some other examples of quadratic functions whose vertices are easy to find. Make your examples as varied as you can.

5. a. Verify that the expression $(x - 3)^2 + 2$ (from Question 2b) can be written in standard form as $x^2 - 6x + 11$.

   b. Which expression is easier to use, $(x - 3)^2 + 2$ or $x^2 - 6x + 11$, in looking for the vertex of this function? Explain your answer.

6. How can you tell by looking at the algebraic expression for a quadratic function whether its vertex is a minimum or a maximum?

Make Your Own Vertices

In *The Same but Different,* you were given some quadratic functions and asked to find their vertices. In this assignment, you will reverse the process.

1. **a.** Find an algebraic expression for a quadratic function whose graph has its vertex at $(3, 4)$.

   b. Make a partial table of values for your function and use the table to sketch a graph of the function.

   c. Does your graph seem to confirm that $(3, 4)$ is the vertex for your function?

2. Repeat steps a through c from Question 1 for the point $(3, -4)$.

3. Repeat steps a through c from Question 1 for the point $(0, 0)$.

4. For each of these points, find a quadratic function whose graph has its vertex at the given point.

   a. $(-4, 2)$

   b. $(-4, -5)$

5. Generalize your work from Questions 1 through 4. In other words, consider a general point (h, k) and write an expression for a quadratic function whose vertex is at (h, k). Then justify your answer. That is, explain how you know that your function will have the desired vertex.

6. Find a quadratic function different from the one you used in Question 1 but whose graph also has its vertex at $(3, 4)$. (*Hint:* Look at Questions 2d and 2e in *The Same but Different.*)

Vertex Form Begun

In *Homework 5: Factoring Begun,* you prepared for factoring quadratic expressions by getting a feel for what happens when you multiply two linear expressions. This activity has a similar first step for learning how to put quadratic expressions into vertex form.

For now, you will consider only quadratic expressions in which the x^2-coefficient is equal to 1.

1. Multiply out each of these vertex form expressions to get an equivalent quadratic expression in standard form. In other words, write each of these as an expression of the form $x^2 + bx + c$.

    a. $(x + 5)^2 + 9$

    b. $(x - 3)^2 - 12$

    c. $(x + 4)^2 - 7$

    d. $(x - 1)^2 + 8$

2. Use what you learned from your work in Question 1 to try to write each of these quadratic expressions in vertex form. In other words, find equivalent expressions of the form $(x - h)^2 + k$.

    a. $x^2 - 6x + 4$

    b. $x^2 + 12x - 17$

    c. $x^2 - 8x + 5$

    d. $x^2 - 20x$

    e. $x^2 + 11x - 7$

How Much Can They Drink?

You may recall farmer Minh from the Year 2 unit *Do Bees Build It Best?* He had built a drinking trough for his animals that had a triangular cross-section, as shown here. Unfortunately, that trough eventually wore out, and he has decided to replace it with one having a rectangular cross-section.

He has a sheet of metal that is 40 inches wide and 80 inches long. His plan is to bend the sheet along two lines parallel to the 80-inch side, to make a U-shape that will form the bottom and the long sides of the trough. He'll use some other pieces of metal for the two ends.

For example, he might mark the sheet with two lines that are 5 inches from each 80-inch edge. These are the dashed lines shown below.

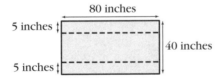

Then he would bend up the 5-inch-wide sections, to form a shape like the one shown below. Finally, he would attach pieces at the ends to complete the structure.

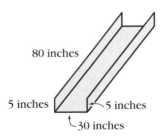

Continued on next page

The completed trough might look like the picture shown here. In this case, the trough would be 30 inches wide, 80 inches long, and 5 inches high.

Farmer Minh wants to maximize the volume of water that the trough will hold. Can you help him?

1. Find the volume of the trough with the rectangular cross-section as just described. That is, find out how much water this trough would hold if it were full.

2. Find the volumes for two other troughs farmer Minh could make this way, using dimensions other than 5 inches for the width of the sections being bent up.

3. Find a formula for the volume of the trough if the sections he bends up on the sides each have a width of x inches.

4. By guess-and-check, find the value of x that will make the volume a maximum.

5. Think about how you would write the formula from Question 3 in vertex form.

Corrals and Pens Again

1. In *Homework 1: A Corral Variation,* you found the expression $500x - 2x^2$ (or something equivalent) as the area of dairyman Johnson's pen. You probably used either guess-and-check or a graph to see that the area is biggest when $x = 125$ feet.

   a. Show that the vertex form expression $-2(x - 125)^2 + 31{,}250$ is equivalent to $500x - 2x^2$.

   b. Use the vertex form expression in part a to explain why a value for x of 125 gives the maximum area for dairyman Johnson's pen. Also, show how to use the vertex form expression to find that maximum area.

2. You saw in *Do Bees Build It Best?* that of all rectangles with a given perimeter, a square is the one with the biggest area. In this problem, you will use vertex form to prove this statement for a special case.

   a. Use x to represent the width of a rectangle with perimeter 200, and find an expression for the area in terms of x.

   b. Show that your expression in part a is equivalent to the vertex form expression $-(x - 50)^2 + 2500$.

   c. Use the vertex form expression in part b to explain why, of all rectangles with perimeter 200, a square has the maximum area, and to find that maximum area.

Fireworks Height Revisited

It's now time to return to the central problem of this unit, *Fireworks*. As you will recall, the Jefferson High junior varsity soccer team is helping to plan a fireworks display.

The display will use rockets launched from the top of a tower that is 160 feet off the ground. Each rocket will be rising initially at 92 feet per second.

The soccer team knows that the rocket's height off the ground (in feet) after t seconds can be found using the function $h(t) = 160 + 92t - 16t^2$. Use vertex form to find out *exactly* how long it will take for the rocket to reach its maximum height and what that maximum height is.

Quadratic Query

Your task in this assignment is to summarize what you've learned about quadratic expressions, functions, and equations, including ideas about the graphs of quadratic functions. This assignment will be a required part of your portfolio.

Explain the terms that you use and give examples of any algebraic techniques you think are important.

11 *Fireworks* Portfolio

Now that *Fireworks* is completed, it is time to put together your portfolio for the unit. Compiling this portfolio has two parts:

• Writing a cover letter summarizing the unit

• Choosing papers to include from your work in this unit

Cover Letter for *Fireworks*

Look back over *Fireworks* and describe the central problem of the unit and the main mathematical ideas. This description should give an overview of how the key ideas were developed and how they were used to solve the central problem.

As part of the compilation of your portfolio, you will select some activities that you think were important in developing the key ideas of this unit. Your cover letter should include an explanation of why you are selecting each particular item.

Selecting Papers from *Fireworks*

Your portfolio for *Fireworks* should contain these items:

• *Fireworks Height Revisited*

• *Homework 10: Quadratic Query*

• Other key activities

Include one or two other activities that you think were important in developing the key ideas of this unit.

• *POW 1: Growth of Rat Populations*

Supplemental Problems

Most of the supplemental problems for this unit continue the focus on quadratic functions and quadratic equations. Some have a broader algebraic focus. Here are some examples.

- *Check It Out!* presents a general issue about techniques for solving equations.

- *Factors of Research* gives you an opportunity to learn more about factoring.

- The results from *Vertex Forms Everywhere* and *Vertex Form and Intercepts Together* show how you can use the ideas of this unit to solve any quadratic equation.

- *Equilateral Efficiency* is a very challenging problem that applies ideas of this unit to prove a geometry principle used in the Year 2 unit *Do Bees Build It Best?*

Check It Out!

Matilda and her friend were reviewing ideas about how to solve equations. It seemed as if one basic principle involved doing the same thing to both sides of an equation.

Matilda was applying this idea to a problem her friend had made up when something strange happened. This was the problem she was working on.

$$\sqrt{2X - 3} = -5$$

She didn't want to have a square root in the problem, so she squared both sides of the equation to get

$$(\sqrt{2X - 3})^2 = (-5)^2$$

She simplified both sides of this equation, which gave her

$$2X - 3 = 25$$

and then she proceeded as usual:

$$2X - 3 + 3 = 25 + 3$$

$$2X = 28$$

$$\frac{2X}{2} = \frac{28}{2}$$

$$X = 14$$

The trouble began when she substituted her answer back into the original equation. Substituting 14 for X, she wanted to verify that $\sqrt{2 \cdot 14 - 3}$ was the same as -5. But when she simplified the expression $\sqrt{2 \cdot 14 - 3}$, she got $\sqrt{25}$, which is 5, not -5.

Continued on next page

In other words, $X = 14$ was not a solution to the original equation.

1. Why do you think that the solution did not check? What do you suppose Matilda did wrong?

2. An apparent solution that does not check is called an **extraneous solution.** Use Matilda's method to solve these equations, and see if you can find a rule for determining when there will be an extraneous solution.

    a. $\sqrt{3y - 2} = -7$

    b. $\sqrt{5w + 6} = 9$

    c. $\sqrt{4A + 1} + 12 = 1$

    d. $\sqrt{2c - 3} = 5$

Imagine a Solution

You've seen that solving quadratic equations is closely related to finding the x-intercepts of graphs of quadratic functions. Because some of these graphs don't have any x-intercepts, it makes sense that some quadratic equations won't have any solutions.

1. Explain why the equation $x^2 = -1$ has no solution, in two ways:

   • Directly in terms of the equation

   • Using the graph of the function defined by the expression $x^2 + 1$

But what if we made up a new number that would be the solution to this equation? This new number might help us find solutions to many other equations as well.

Several centuries ago, some mathematicians decided to see what would happen if they did this. The number they invented is now represented by the symbol i, so $i^2 = -1$ and $\sqrt{-1} = i$. This led to a whole new family of numbers, such as $2i$, $-i$, and so on. These are called **imaginary numbers.**

2. Write these numbers in terms of this new number i, and explain your reasoning.

   a. $\sqrt{-25}$

   b. $\sqrt{-100}$

Continued on next page

3. a. Investigate what happens when you raise i to
   different powers. For example, find the value of i^3,
   of i^4, of i^5, and so on.

   b. Use your results to find i^{3057} and explain your
   answer.

   c. Write a general rule for finding the value of i^n
   without doing lots of repetition.

More and More Mysterious

The housing developer from *Revisiting a Mystery* liked symmetry very much. However, because the city planner would not allow square lots, the developer was looking for a way to do something symmetrical with rectangular lots.

She decided it would be interesting to see what happened if she started with square lots and increased the width by some amount and decreased the length by the same amount. For example, if she increased the width by 4 meters and decreased the length by that same amount, the area could be represented as $(X + 4)(X - 4)$. The developer found that if she multiplied out expressions like this and wrote them in standard form, she got an interesting pattern.

Find the pattern that the developer found and describe it fully. Then justify the pattern using both algebra and a diagram.

Factors of Research

You've done some work with the factoring of quadratic expressions in this unit, and the activity *More and More Mysterious* looked at one special kind of quadratic expression. But there is more to the topic of factoring than you've seen in this unit.

The questions in this activity suggest some further areas of exploration, but you might come up with others on your own. You may find it helpful to look in a traditional algebra textbook for ideas, problems, and questions to consider.

1. In *Homework 5: Factoring Begun*, you considered only quadratic expressions in which the coefficient of x^2 was equal to 1. Are there ideas and techniques for factoring more general quadratic expressions?

2. What about the factoring of polynomials other than quadratics? Is it possible? Are there any standard techniques?

3. The situation in *More and More Mysterious* leads to a form of factoring called *difference of squares*. What about differences of cubes? of fourth powers?

Twin Primes

You know that a *prime number* is a whole number greater than 1 whose only whole number divisors are 1 and itself. But you may not be aware that there are also such things as **twin prime numbers.** These are pairs of prime numbers that are only two apart, such as 5 and 7, or 17 and 19, or 41 and 43.

There are many interesting things to notice about twin primes. This activity mostly concerns the following characteristic of twin primes.

> For any pair of twin primes *except* the combination 3 and 5, if you multiply the two twin primes together and add 1 to the product, you get a number that has these two properties.
>
> • It's a perfect square.
>
> • It's a multiple of 36.

For example, if you start with 11 and 13, you get $(11 \cdot 13) + 1$, which is 144. This result is equal to 12^2, so it's a perfect square, and it's equal to $4 \cdot 36$, so it's a multiple of 36.

Note: If you use the twin primes 3 and 5, you get $(3 \cdot 5) + 1$, which is 16. So even in this case, the result is a perfect square, but it isn't a multiple of 36.

1. Experiment with some other pairs of twin primes, as well as with pairs of numbers that are not twin primes, and try to get some insight into what is happening.

Continued on next page

2. *Prove* the two facts about the process of multiplying twin primes (except 3 and 5) and adding 1:

- The result is always a perfect square.

- The result is always a multiple of 36.

You will need to use a variable in your proof. Think about what number your variable should stand for.

Adapted with permission from *Mathematics Teacher,* © December, 1989, by The National Council of Teachers of Mathematics.

Number Research

As you have seen in the mathematics courses you have taken, there are names given to certain groups of numbers. For instance, the numbers $1, 2, 3, 4, 5, \ldots$ are sometimes referred to as the **counting numbers.** You have also worked with the set of **integers,** which are the numbers $\ldots -3, -2, -1, 0, 1, 2, 3, \ldots$. And in *Imagine a Solution,* you learned about another kind of number.

Your task here is to research names for different sets of numbers and learn about how those sets of numbers relate to one another. Then make a poster summarizing your findings.

Here are some names to get you started in your research.

• Whole numbers

• Rational numbers

• Imaginary numbers

• Complex numbers

• Transcendental numbers

Vertex Forms Everywhere

You've seen that putting a quadratic expression into vertex form, $a(x - h)^2 + k$, can be useful in understanding the graph of the corresponding quadratic function. Your task in this activity is to show that *every* quadratic expression can be put into vertex form.

Start with the standard form for the general quadratic expression, $ax^2 + bx + c$, and show how to transform this into an equivalent expression in vertex form. Although you may want to use numerical examples for ideas, your final result should be a vertex form in which h and k are replaced by expressions in terms of a, b, and c.

As a final step, give the coordinates of the vertex for the general quadratic expression, $ax^2 + bx + c$. (These coordinates will be expressed in terms of a, b, and c.)

Vertex Form and Intercepts Together

Vertex form is a useful tool for finding the vertex of the graph of a quadratic equation. You've seen that *x*-intercepts are another important feature of such graphs. This activity will help you see how to use vertex form to find these intercepts.

For the questions below, give *exact answers* (which may involve the square-root symbol) rather than decimal approximations, and explain your answers.

1. a. Solve the quadratic equation $x^2 - 10 = 0$. (*Reminder:* This equation has two solutions.)

   b. Find the *x*-intercepts of the function defined by the equation $y = x^2 - 10$.

   c. Explain why Questions 1a and 1b are really the same question.

2. a. Solve the quadratic equation $(x - 4)^2 - 10 = 0$. (*Hint:* Compare this to Question 1a.)

   b. Find the *x*-intercepts of the function defined by the equation $y = (x - 4)^2 - 10$.

   c. Solve the quadratic equation $x^2 - 8x + 6 = 0$.

   d. Explain why Questions 2a through 2c are really all the same question.

Continued on next page

3. a. Write the quadratic equation $x^2 + 6x - 5 = 0$ in a form that looks like the equation in Question 2a.

   b. Use your result from Question 3a to solve the equation $x^2 + 6x - 5 = 0$.

4. Now generalize to an arbitrary quadratic function in vertex form. That is, consider the function defined by the equation $y = a(x - h)^2 + k$. Find the x-intercepts for the graph of this function in terms of a, h, and k. In other words, solve the equation $a(x - h)^2 + k = 0$, getting an expression for x in terms of the other variables.

5. How does putting a quadratic function into vertex form show that the function has at most two roots?

Quadratic Symmetry

You've perhaps noticed that the graphs of quadratic functions are symmetrical and that the vertical line through the vertex forms a line of symmetry. In other words, for every point on the graph to the right of this line, there is a matching point an equal distance to the left of this line, with the same y-coordinate.

Your main task in this activity is to *prove* that fact.

1. Suppose you have a quadratic function defined by the equation $y = a(x - h)^2 + k$, so its vertex is the point (h, k).

   a. What is the equation of the vertical line through the vertex? (*Hint:* What do the points on this line have in common?)

   b. Suppose a point on the graph is t units to the right of the line of symmetry. What is its x-coordinate?

   c. Suppose a point on the graph is t units to the left of the line of symmetry. What is its x-coordinate?

   d. Show that the two x-values from parts a and b give the same y-value.

2. Explain how the results from Question 1 prove the symmetry of the graph.

Continued on next page

3. Suppose you know that the points $(3, 7)$ and $(10, 7)$ both lie on the graph of a particular quadratic function. What can you conclude about the vertex of this graph?

4. Generalize from Question 3. Suppose the points (u, w) and (v, w) lie on the graph of a quadratic function. What can you conclude about the vertex of this graph?

Equilateral Efficiency

You saw in the Year 2 unit *Do Bees Build It Best?* that of all rectangles with a given perimeter, the square is the one with the biggest area. It seems reasonable to expect that this result might generalize to other regular polygons.

In fact, it's true that for any given number of sides and fixed perimeter, the regular polygon with that number of sides has the largest area.

In this activity, you will explore why this is true for triangles. You will use Hero's formula, which gives the area of a triangle in terms of the lengths of its sides. Hero's formula says that if a triangle has sides of lengths *a*, *b*, and *c*, then its area is given by the equation

$$A = \sqrt{s(s - a)(s - b)(s - c)}$$

where $s = \frac{a+b+c}{2}$. (The number represented by *s* is called the **semiperimeter** of the triangle, because it is equal to half the perimeter.)

1. a. Use Hero's formula to calculate the area of an equilateral triangle with a perimeter of 300 feet. That is, substitute a value of 100 for *a*, *b*, and *c*, and 150 for *s*, into the equation.

   b. Explain some other method for finding the area of this triangle, and show that the two methods give the same answer.

Continued on next page

2. Use Hero's formula to find the areas of other triangles with a perimeter of 300 feet. That is, try different combinations of values of a, b, and c whose sum is 300, and use Hero's formula to find the area in each case. Look for patterns or general principles that describe your results.

The rest of this activity involves proving that the equilateral triangle is the most "efficient."

3. Continue with the case of a triangle whose perimeter is 300 feet.

   a. Suppose a is equal to 80. Use Hero's formula to find an expression for the area in terms of just b. (*Hint:* In this case, $b + c$ must be equal to 220. Get an expression for c in terms of b and then express the area in terms of just b. Remember that s is still equal to 150 because the perimeter is still 300.)

Continued on next page

b. Prove that your area expression in terms of b (from Question 3a) has its maximum when $b = 110$.

Hint: This area expression should be the square root of some quadratic expression. All you need to show is that this quadratic expression is a maximum when $b = 110$. You can do this using ideas from the supplemental problem *Quadratic Symmetry* (especially Question 4), by first showing that values of 70 and 150 for b give the same area.

c. Repeat the approach in Questions 3a and 3b using some other values for a. Then generalize your results. That is, if you know a, how should you choose b and c (in terms of a) in order to maximize the area?

d. Use the result from Question 3c to develop an expression that gives the maximum possible area for a given value of a.

e. Find the value of a that maximizes your expression in Question 4d. *Note:* Do not expect to be able to prove algebraically that your answer is the maximum. That requires calculus.

f. Explain what your answer from Question 3e has to do with "equilateral efficiency."

4. What does your work in Question 3 tell you about triangles of arbitrary perimeter? Explain.

What About One?

Most digital watches show the hour, the minute, and the second in a format like that below. Your question in this problem is

What fraction of the time is at least one of the digits a 1?

To begin with, you should assume that the watch is using 12-hour mode. For example, two hours after noon is shown as 2:00, not as 14:00.

When you answer the question for this situation, consider some or all of these variations.

• What if you use a 24-hour mode?

• What if you include a date on the watch (using a format such as 10-17 for October 17).

• What if the watch shows only the hour and the minute?

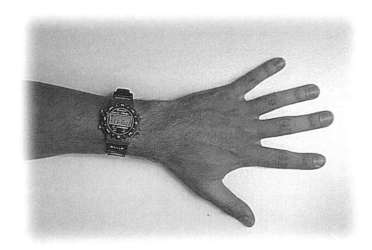

Orchard Hideout

Orchards and Mini-Orchards

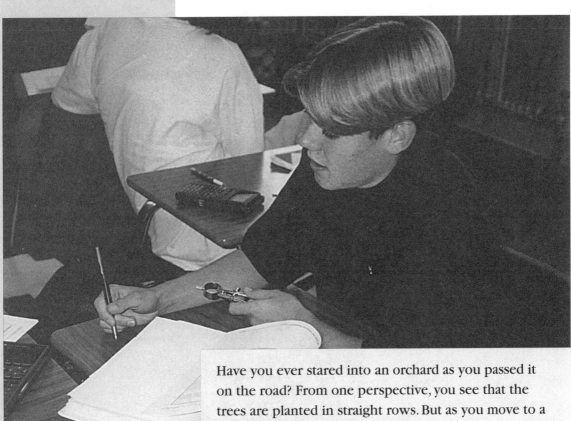

Ryan Miller is developing the mathematical definition for a circle.

Have you ever stared into an orchard as you passed it on the road? From one perspective, you see that the trees are planted in straight rows. But as you move to a different spot, all you see is a mass of trees.

The main characters of this unit, Madie and Clyde, have planted an orchard. They want to know how long it will take before they can no longer see from the center of the orchard to the outside world.

You begin this unit with a look at their overall problem, and then you'll examine some simpler cases. The opening days also include some assignments related to the first POW of the unit.

Orchard Hideout

Madie and Clyde wanted some peace and quiet. Most of all, they wanted privacy. So they left the city and bought a piece of land out in the countryside.

The lot they bought was in the shape of a circle. They decided to plant an orchard on this lot in nice neat rows.

Here's how they set up their orchard.

First, they planted their first row along an east-west line through the center of the circle. The trees were equally spaced, except that they left out the tree that would have been located at the exact center of the circle. There were 50 trees to the east of the center and 50 to the west. The trees at the ends of this east-west row were exactly on the boundary of their property.

Then they planted a north-south line of trees through the center, using the same spacing as before and omitting the

Continued on next page

tree at the center. Again, there were 50 trees to the north of the center and 50 to the south. And, again, the trees at the ends of this north-south row were exactly on the boundary of their property.

They used each of the trees in their north-south row as the center of an east-west row, filling in the orchard with rows of trees. They always used the same distance between trees in every row.

Madie and Clyde realized that if the trees kept growing, the tree trunks would eventually become so big that it would become impossible to see out from the center of the orchard. The center of the orchard would then be like a hideout.

Here is the main question of this unit.

> *How soon after they plant the orchard will the center of the lot become a true "orchard hideout"?*

1. Study the problem. What does this situation look like? Make a model, perhaps using a smaller orchard as an example.

2. Make a list of questions you need to ask in order to understand this problem better. Try to answer some of your questions.

Adapted from "The Orchard Problem," pp. 43–53, in *Mathematical Gems I,* by Ross Honsberger, published by the Mathematical Association of America, 1973.

A Geometric Summary

As you can see, the central problem of this unit involves circles, straight lines, and all sorts of distances. In order to solve the problem, you will be using many ideas from geometry (including trigonometry).

Here is a summary of basic definitions and essential principles from geometry that were included in Years 1 and 2 of the Interactive Mathematics Program. Over the course of the unit, you will develop other key ideas.

I. Polygon Angle Sums

The "angle sum property" for triangles states:

In any triangle, the sum of the measures of the angles is exactly 180°.

(One proof of this principle is based on properties of parallel lines, discussed in part V.)

In general, the sum of the measures of the angles of a polygon depends only on how many sides the polygon has. This sum is always a multiple of 180°.

II. Similarity

Two polygons are considered similar if they have the same shape (though not necessarily the same size). Here is the formal definition.

> **Definition** Two polygons are defined as **similar** if their corresponding angles are equal and their corresponding sides are proportional in length.

This cloth from East Africa shows many differently-shaped triangles. Every triangle has an angle sum of 180°, no matter what its shape.

Continued on next page

Here are two basic principles for proving similarity of triangles.

If the corresponding angles of two triangles are equal, then the triangles must be similar.

If the corresponding sides of two triangles are proportional in length, then the triangles must be similar.

The angle sum property for triangles leads to a simpler version of the "corresponding angles" principle.

If two angles of one triangle are equal to two angles of another triangle, then the triangles must be similar.

III. Congruence

Congruence is a special case of similarity. Two polygons are considered congruent if they have the same shape and the same size. This means that they are similar and that the ratio of corresponding sides is 1. Here is the formal definition.

Definition Two polygons are defined as **congruent** if their corresponding angles are equal and their corresponding sides are equal in length.

Here are two principles for proving congruence. The first applies to all polygons, and the second is specifically for triangles.

If two polygons are similar and some pair of corresponding sides are equal in length, then the polygons must be congruent.

If two sides and the angle they form in one triangle are equal to the corresponding parts of another triangle, then the triangles must be congruent.

Continued on next page

IV. Right Triangles

A right triangle is a triangle in which one of the angles is a right angle. The sides of a right triangle have special names.

Definition In a right triangle, the sides forming the right angle are the **legs** and the side opposite the right angle is the **hypotenuse.**

The relationship between the lengths of the sides of a right triangle is summed up in the Pythagorean theorem.

In any right triangle, the sum of the squares of the lengths of the legs is equal to the square of the length of the hypotenuse.

Wooden poles along the hypotenuses provide extra support for this complex roof structure in Gansu Province, China.

The trigonometric functions describe ratios within a right triangle. Here are the basic definitions.

Definition If $\triangle ABC$ is a right triangle with a right angle at C, the trigonometric functions **sine, cosine,** and **tangent** for $\angle A$ are defined by these ratios:

$$\sin A = \frac{BC}{AB}$$

$$\cos A = \frac{AC}{AB}$$

$$\tan A = \frac{BC}{AC}$$

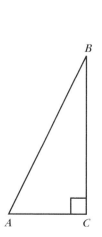

Each trigonometric function has an **inverse function** that is used to determine an angle if the value of the trigonometric function is known. For example, if x is a number between 0 and 1, the inverse sine of x (written $\sin^{-1} x$) is the angle between $0°$ and $90°$ whose sine is x.

Continued on next page

Interactive Mathematics Program

V. Parallel Lines

Certain parts of a diagram like the one shown here have special names.

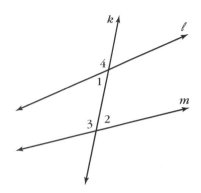

> **Definition** If two lines ℓ and m are crossed by a third line k, the line k is called a **transversal.** A pair of angles like angles 1 and 2 are called **alternate interior angles.** A pair of angles like angles 3 and 4 are called **corresponding angles.**

Whether two lines crossed by a transversal are parallel is related to whether certain angles formed are equal.

For instance, in the diagram at the right, if lines R and S are parallel, then any pair of alternate interior angles (such as x and y) must be equal and any pair of corresponding angles (such as u and v) must be equal. Also, if any such pair of angles are known to be equal, then R and S must be parallel.

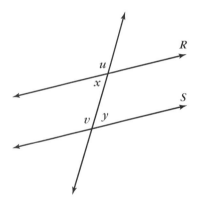

This Guatemalan weaver uses wooden sticks as transversals to cross the parallel threads of her yarn.

Continued on next page

Therefore, we have these principles.

If two parallel lines are crossed by a transversal, then any pair of alternate interior angles must be equal.

If two parallel lines are crossed by a transversal, then any pair of corresponding angles must be equal.

If a pair of alternate interior angles formed by a transversal across two lines are equal, then the two lines must be parallel.

If a pair of corresponding angles formed by a transversal across two lines are equal, then the two lines must be parallel.

VI. Perimeter, Area, Volume, and Surface Area

Here are several basic definitions regarding perimeter, area, volume, and surface area.

Definition The **perimeter** of a polygon is the sum of the lengths of its sides.

Definition The **area** of a plane figure is the number of square units it contains.

Definition The **volume** of a solid figure is the number of cubic units it contains.

Definition A **right prism** is a three-dimensional figure formed by moving a polygon through space, in a direction perpendicular to the plane it lies in. The initial and final positions of the polygon form its **bases.** The other faces form the **lateral surface** of the prism.

Continued on next page

The figures shown here are examples of prisms.

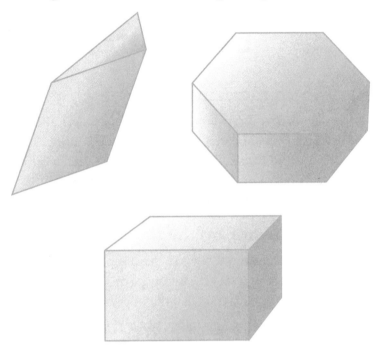

These principles describe basic formulas for finding area, volume, and surface area.

> *The area of a rectangle is equal to the product of its length and its width.*
>
> *The area of a triangle is equal to half the product of its base and the corresponding altitude.*
>
> *The volume of a rectangular solid is equal to the product of its length, width, and height.*
>
> *The volume of a right prism is equal to the product of its height and the area of its base.*
>
> *The lateral surface area of a right prism is equal to the product of its height and the perimeter of its base.*

Geometry and a Mini-Orchard

Part I: Summarizing Geometry

Read *A Geometric Summary,* which includes ideas about geometry and trigonometry that you will need during this unit. As you read through it, think about what each principle or definition means, and create diagrams for yourself to clarify the ideas.

Part II: A Mini-Orchard

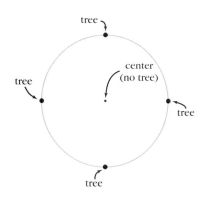

Imagine that Madie and Clyde's orchard is planted on a lot whose radius is 1 unit. At an early stage, this orchard might be represented by a diagram like the one shown here.

Suppose you are standing in the center of this orchard. If you look due east or north or west or south, your line of sight will be blocked by a tree. But if you look in a different direction, you will be able to see out of the orchard through the gap between trees. As the trees start to grow, the gap between trees will narrow.

Now imagine that you remain at the center of the orchard, waiting patiently as the trees grow.

1. In what direction should you look to be able to see out of the orchard for as long a time as possible? That is, what line of sight will be the last to get blocked by the growing trees? (If there is more than one answer, be as general as possible.)

2. What is the minimum radius required for each tree trunk in order to make the center of the orchard into a true "orchard hideout"? In other words, how big must the trees become so that it is impossible for you to see out of the orchard from the center?

Equally Wet

1. Two delicate flowers were planted in a garden. The gardener, Leslie, has a sprinkler that sprays water around in a circle. The closer a flower is to the sprinkler, the more water it gets.

   To be sure that her flowers each get the same amount of water, Leslie needs to place the sprinkler where it will be the same distance from each of the flowers.

   What are her choices about where to put the sprinkler? Describe all the possibilities. (*Reminder:* The flowers are already in place, and Leslie needs to adjust the position of the sprinkler relative to the flowers.)

Continued on next page

2. Now suppose Leslie plants three flowers and wants to know if it will still be possible to place the sprinkler the same distance from all three.

   a. Determine which arrangements of the flowers (if any) will make this possible and which (if any) will make it impossible. (As in Question 1, Leslie will be looking for a place to put the sprinkler after the flowers have already been planted.)

   b. For those arrangements for which it will be possible, describe how Leslie can find the correct location (or locations) for the sprinkler.

3. What about four flowers? Five flowers? Generalize as much as you can.

Your POW is to explain as fully as possible, for various cases, where Leslie can put the sprinkler in order to give the flowers the same amount of water. *Homework 2: Only Two Flowers* gets you started with the first question of the POW.

Write-up

1. *Problem Statement:* State the problem in mathematical language without reference to the context. That is, describe the problem in geometric terms without talking about flowers or sprinklers.

2. *Process*

3. *Solution*

4. *Evaluation*

5. *Self-assessment*

Adapted from "Simple Math," a series of mathematics video-dramas of the Israeli Instructional Television, with academic advisor Nitsa Movshovitz-Hadar and produced by Tamar Reiner.

Only Two Flowers

Your assignment is to answer the first question from
POW 2: Equally Wet. That is, if two flowers are planted,
what are the possible places to put a sprinkler so that it
will be exactly the same distance from each flower?

Be sure that your answer includes all possible solutions,
and give your answer in two ways.

• With a diagram showing all the solutions

• With a description in words of the set of solutions

A Perpendicularity Proof

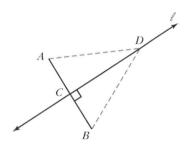

Is *every point* on the perpendicular bisector of a line segment equidistant from the two endpoints of the segment?

Your task in this activity is to write a proof of that principle, based on the diagram shown here. In this diagram, *A* and *B* could be any two points. *C* is the midpoint of the line segment connecting *A* and *B*, *ℓ* is the line through *C* that is perpendicular to $\overline{AB}$, and *D* is some point on *ℓ*.

Prove, based on this information, that *D* is equidistant from *A* and *B*. In other words, prove that the lengths *AD* and *BD* are equal.

From Two Flowers to Three

In *Homework 2: Only Two Flowers,* you determined where to place the sprinkler if Leslie had only two flowers to water. From that assignment and the discussion of it, you should now have a simple description of the full set of options she would have for the location of the sprinkler for the case of two flowers.

Now consider a specific case using three flowers. Suppose the flowers are placed in a coordinate system at the points $(4, 2), (14, 2)$, and $(4, 8)$. Where can Leslie place the sprinkler so that it will be equidistant from all three points? Give a careful explanation of why the point you choose works.

More Mini-Orchards

Madie and Clyde want to know how big the radius of the trunk of each tree needs to be for the orchard to become a hideout. They call this the "hideout tree radius."

Of course, this value depends on the radius of the orchard itself. In *Homework 1: Geometry and a Mini-Orchard,* you examined the case of an orchard whose radius is 1 unit. But the orchard on a lot whose radius is 1 unit is pretty dull. Madie and Clyde are glad their lot is bigger than that.

What if their orchard were *just a little bit bigger?*

1. Sketch a mini-orchard for a lot with radius 2. Then answer these questions.

   a. How many trees are there in this mini-orchard?

   b. Approximately how big must the radius of each tree trunk become to make this orchard into a true hideout? In other words, approximately what is the hideout tree radius for an orchard of radius 2?

2. Sketch a mini-orchard for a lot with radius 3. Then answer these questions.

   a. How many trees are there in this mini-orchard?

   b. Approximately what is the hideout tree radius for an orchard of radius 3?

3. (Challenge) Find the *exact* value for the hideout tree radius for the orchards of radius 2 and 3.

In, On, or Out?

It's convenient to use coordinates to describe situations like Madie and Clyde's orchard. They plant a tree at any lattice point within the orchard, except that there is no tree at $(0, 0)$. (A **lattice point** is a point whose coordinates are both integers.)

In using this system to describe the orchard, it's helpful to have a way to decide whether a given point is within the orchard. This is fairly easy for points on the axes, but for other points, it can be more difficult.

For this assignment, suppose the orchard has a radius of 10 (instead of 50). The center of the orchard is still at $(0, 0)$.

Consider each of the points listed here. Decide whether the point is *inside* the boundary of the orchard, *outside* the boundary, or *exactly on* the boundary, and explain how you decided. You may want to use a diagram in thinking about this problem.

1. $(11, 0)$
2. $(10, 0)$
3. $(10, 1)$
4. $(9, 3)$
5. $(9, 4)$

6. $(9, 5)$
7. $(9, 6)$
8. $(8, 5)$
9. $(8, 6)$
10. $(8, 7)$

11. $(7, 6)$
12. $(7, 7)$
13. $(7, 8)$

Coordinates and Distance

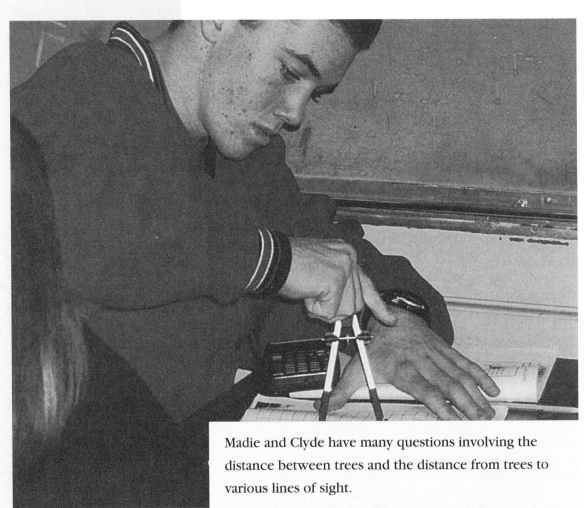

Sean O'Hara uses the coordinate system to model a mini-orchard.

Madie and Clyde have many questions involving the distance between trees and the distance from trees to various lines of sight.

By introducing coordinates into the orchard, you've made it possible to use the Pythagorean theorem to great advantage. Over the next few days of the unit, you'll see some important formulas involving coordinates and distance.

Other Trees

1. Madie and Clyde have another circular plot of land, smaller than the first, and have decided to plant an orchard on this plot, too. They have set up coordinates as before, with the center of the orchard at $(0, 0)$, and will plant trees at all points with integer coordinates that lie within the orchard except $(0, 0)$.

   This orchard is of such a size that the tree at $(5, 12)$ is on the boundary. What are the coordinates of the other trees that must also be on the boundary? Explain your answer.

2. Generalize Question 1 for a lot of any size. Suppose a circular orchard of any size is set up as usual with trees on the lattice points. If the point (a, b) is on its boundary, what other trees must also be on the boundary? Make your answer as complete as possible. (*Hint:* You may want to examine other examples like that in Question 1.)

Sprinkler in the Orchard

Madie and Clyde were working in the scorching sun when they realized that their little seedlings needed water. So they hauled out their sprinkler and placed it in the center of their orchard.

1. Suppose the sprinkler waters a circular area with a radius of 14 units. (Assume that the trees do not block the water from one another.) State whether the trees at each of these locations will be watered, and explain your answers.

   a. $(-6, -13)$ c. $(-12, -8)$

   b. $(-9, 10)$

2. Obviously, Madie and Clyde cannot reach all their trees when they put this sprinkler in the center of the orchard. After watering the trees near the center, they move the sprinkler to $(28, -19)$ to do some more watering. (For other reasons, they had temporarily uprooted the tree at that location.) They also adjust the sprinkler so the water now covers a circle of radius 18 units. Which of these trees will it reach?

   a. $(16, -7)$ c. $(20, -35)$

   b. $(38, -34)$

3. Assume that the sprinkler continues to operate so that it reaches all trees within 18 units. In what places would you place the sprinkler so that you could water the entire orchard in as few waterings as possible?

   You should start this problem from scratch, ignoring the waterings from $(0, 0)$ and from $(28, -19)$ that were discussed in Questions 1 and 2.

The Distance Formula

There is a well-known formula in mathematics, the **distance formula,** that is closely related to the Pythagorean theorem. This assignment will help you develop that formula.

The distance formula is used to help you determine the distance between two points in the coordinate plane, say, (x_1, y_1) and (x_2, y_2). The formula gives you the distance between the two points in terms of the coordinates x_1, x_2, y_1, and y_2.

1. a. Find the distance between the points $(5, 3)$ and $(7, 6)$.

    b. Describe in detail what you did to find your answer.

2. a. Find the distance between the points $(2, 5)$ and $(6, 3)$.

    b. Describe in detail what you did to find your answer.

3. Suppose (x_1, y_1) and (x_2, y_2) are the coordinates of two points. Generalize what you did in Questions 1 and 2 to create a formula or set of instructions that gives the distance between the two points.

4. Does your generalization still work if any of the coordinates x_1, x_2, y_1, or y_2 are negative numbers? Explain with examples.

How Does Your Orchard Grow?

Madie and Clyde were trying to figure out how big the radius of the tree trunks had to become for their orchard to become a hideout. But they realized that once they figured this out, they still wouldn't know how long it would take for the trees to grow to that size.

They went back to the nursery where they had bought the trees. The people at the nursery couldn't say when the orchard would become a hideout, but they were able to tell Madie and Clyde how fast the cross-sectional area of each tree trunk would increase.

When they got home, Madie and Clyde realized that they also didn't know the current cross-sectional area of their trees. They went out to measure, but, of course, they couldn't simply cut a cross section in the trunk and measure the area, because that would kill the tree. Instead, they measured the circumference of the trunk.

Your Task

Imagine that you are Madie or Clyde and that you know two things.

- The amount of increase each year of the cross-sectional area of your trees

- The current circumference of your trees

Assume that you also know the hideout tree radius. That is, you know how big the radius of each tree trunk needs to be for the orchard to become a hideout.

Develop a plan for how to use this information to figure out *how long it will take* until your orchard becomes a hideout. Identify any geometric questions you would need to answer to use your plan.

A Snack in the Middle

Already some of Madie and Clyde's trees need pruning. Every afternoon they choose two trees that seem to need it the most, and each of them works on one of those two trees.

Pruning makes Madie and Clyde hungry, so they decide to set up a snack table between the two trees they are working on. They know they will both want to eat at various times during the afternoon, so they agree to set up the table at the midpoint of the segment connecting the two trees.

1. Suppose Madie is working on the tree at $(24, 6)$ and Clyde is working on the tree at $(30, 14)$. What are the coordinates of the point where they should set up the snack table? Prove that your choice is really equidistant from $(24, 6)$ and $(30, 14)$.

2. If they are working on the trees at $(-3, 4)$ and $(5, 12)$, where should they set up the table? Prove that your choice is really equidistant from $(-3, 4)$ and $(5, 12)$.

3. If they are working on the trees at $(6, 2)$ and $(11, -4)$, where should they set up the table? Prove that your choice is really equidistant from $(6, 2)$ and $(11, -4)$.

4. To save everyone work, make up a general formula for Madie and Clyde. Suppose the trees they are pruning are at (x_1, y_1) and (x_2, y_2). Find a formula for the midpoint between these two trees in terms of $x_1, y_1, x_2,$ and y_2.

Equidistant Points and Lines

Tommy Smith has much to include in his cover letter for the unit.

POW 2: Equally Wet involves the set of points equidistant from two or more given points. You're about to see some other problems that also involve equal distances.

As you explore these problems, including your next POW, think about how these ideas might help Madie and Clyde with their orchard problem.

Proving with Distance—Part I

1. This diagram shows a quadrilateral with vertices $(5, 20)$, $(9, 23)$, $(12, 19)$, and $(8, 16)$.

   Prove that this figure is a square. (*Reminder:* A *rhombus* is a quadrilateral with four equal sides. A square is a rhombus that has four right angles.) Don't simply show that the figure in the diagram is a rhombus.

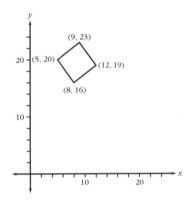

2. Choose a set of four points in the coordinate plane that form a quadrilateral. (This can be *any* quadrilateral—it does not have to be a square. For simplicity, you may want to choose points in the first quadrant.)

   a. Plot the points carefully and connect them to form a quadrilateral.

   b. Connect the midpoints of the sides of your quadrilateral to form a smaller quadrilateral.

3. Repeat the two parts of Question 2 starting with a different set of four points.

4. Examine each of the smaller quadrilaterals you created.

   a. What general conjecture might you make about the lengths of the sides when you create a smaller quadrilateral this way?

   b. Find the coordinates of the midpoints in each of Questions 2 and 3, and verify your conjecture from Question 4a for each case using the distance formula.

Down the Garden Path

Leslie (the gardener in *POW 2: Equally Wet*) has decided to plant only two flowers. She has placed them in her two favorite spots in the garden.

Now she has another problem. She wants to make a straight-line path through her garden, with one flower on each side of the path.

Leslie has decided that the two flowers should be the same distance from the path. That way, people walking along the path will see them both equally well (although they may pass by the two flowers at different points along the path).

1. How can Leslie design a path that is equidistant from each flower? Write down simple, step-by-step instructions for her.

2. Is your path the only one possible? Describe all possible straight-line paths that are equidistant from each flower.

Perpendicular and Vertical

1. A **tangent to a circle** is a line that intersects the circle in exactly one point.

   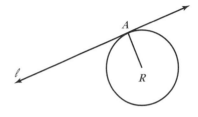

   The diagram at the right shows a circle with center R and a line ℓ that is tangent to the circle at point A. In other words, A is on both the circle and the line, and it is the only point on both.

   a. Explain how you can be sure that A is the point on ℓ that is closest to R. In other words, show that the segment from R to A is the shortest path from R to line ℓ.

   b. Based on Question 1a, what can you conclude about the relationship between $\overline{RA}$ and line ℓ?

2. When two lines intersect, such as lines ℓ and m in the diagram at the right, they form four separate angles, which are labeled here as 1, 2, 3, and 4.

   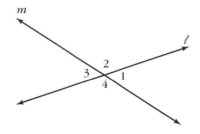

   a. Suppose $\angle 1 = 20°$. Find the other three angles.

   Pairs of "opposite" angles, such as the pair $\angle 1$ and $\angle 3$ or the pair $\angle 2$ and $\angle 4$, are called **vertical angles.**

   b. Prove in general that vertical angles are equal. That is, show that $\angle 1 = \angle 3$ and $\angle 2 = \angle 4$. (You should not use the value 20° for $\angle 1$, but you can use the reasoning by which you found the other angles in Question 2a.)

3

On Patrol

Two main highways cross each other as they go through a certain county. The highway patrol wants to set up a station that will be the same distance from the two highways.

Reminder: The distance from a point, such as the station, to a line, such as a highway, is defined as the *shortest* possible distance from the point to the line. You have *proved* that this shortest path is perpendicular to the line.

1. What are the choices about where to put the station? (Assume that the two highways are straight.)

2. A neighboring county has three main highways. (Assume that all three highways are straight.)

   a. Do all the highways have to cross one another? What are the possibilities for how they might cross? Draw some diagrams to illustrate the general categories.

   b. Is it possible to place the station the same distance from all three highways? How does the answer to this question depend on how the three highways intersect? Consider all possible arrangements of the highways and the possible locations of the station for each arrangement.

3. What about four highways? What about five? How can you generalize the result?

Continued on next page

Write-up

1. *Problem Statement:* State the problem in mathematical language without reference to the context. That is, describe the problem in geometric terms without talking about patrol stations or highways.

2. *Process*

3. *Solution*

4. *Evaluation*

5. *Self-assessment*

Adapted from "Simple Math," a series of mathematics video-dramas of the Israeli Instructional Television, with academic advisor Nitsa Movshovitz-Hadar and produced by Tamar Reiner.

Proving with Distance—Part II

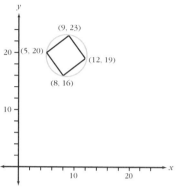

You showed in *Homework 8: Proving with Distance—Part I* that the points $(5, 20), (9, 23), (12, 19),$ and $(8, 16)$ are the vertices of a square. The first diagram shows this square, as well as a circle that passes through the vertices of the square. We say that such a circle is **circumscribed about** the square (or that the square is **inscribed in** the circle).

1. Find the center and radius for this circumscribed circle and prove that your answers are correct.

There is also a circle that passes through the *midpoints* of this square, as shown in the second diagram, and the sides of the square are all tangent to that circle. We say that such a circle is **inscribed in** the square (or that the square is **circumscribed about** the circle).

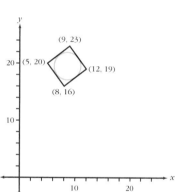

2. Find the center and radius for this inscribed circle and prove that your answers are correct.

3. Is there a circumscribed circle for every quadrilateral? Justify your answer.

All About Circles

Amber Shira and Summer Kienitz use compasses and straightedges to compare circles to their circumscribed squares.

As you saw in *How Does Your Orchard Grow?*, Madie and Clyde need to understand how the circumference, area, and radius of a circle are related to one another.

Your next task is to use polygons to help them understand the relationships. What do circles have to do with polygons? You'll see that the answer is as easy as pie (sort of).

Squaring the Circle

Madie and Clyde need to know how the area and circumference of a circle are related to its radius. You will help them by completing a series of activities comparing the circle to various circumscribed regular polygons. In this activity, you will compare the circle to the circumscribed square.

To draw such a figure, it's easiest to start by drawing a square on a sheet of grid paper. Then draw a circle inside the square so that it just touches the sides of the square. (In other words, the circle is inscribed in the square.)

The questions here involve area, circumference, and perimeter. You should find the numbers requested by making measurement estimates, rather than by using formulas.

1. a. Estimate the area of the circle. That is, estimate the number of grid squares it contains.

   b. Estimate the area of the square.

Continued on next page

c. Find the ratio of your answers. That is, find the numerical value of the fraction

$$\frac{\text{area of the circle}}{\text{area of the circumscribed square}}$$

2. a. Estimate the circumference of the circle. (You may want to use string to estimate this length.)

   b. Estimate the perimeter of the square.

   c. Find the ratio of your answers. That is, find the numerical value of the fraction

$$\frac{\text{circumference of the circle}}{\text{perimeter of the circumscribed square}}$$

3. Now repeat Questions 1 and 2 for a larger circle and square. How do the ratios for the new circle-and-square pair compare to the ratios for the first pair?

4. Do you think the ratio you found in Question 1c will be the same no matter what circle you start with? Write a careful explanation for your answer.

5. Do you think the ratio you found in Question 2c will be the same no matter what circle you start with? Write a careful explanation for your answer.

Historical Note: For centuries, mathematicians struggled with the problem of trying to use certain formal "construction" methods to draw a square whose area is the same as that of a given circle. The German mathematician Ferdinand von Lindemann showed in 1875 that this is impossible. The title of this activity is a playful reference to that famous problem.

Using the
Squared Circle

In *Squaring the Circle*, you compared circles to their circumscribed squares and found ratios involving area, circumference, and perimeter.

1. Give the estimates agreed on in class for each of these ratios.

   a.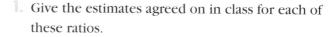

   b.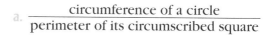

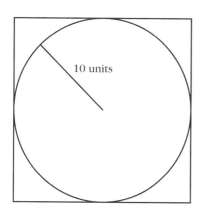

2. Consider the circle and circumscribed square shown here, in which the circle has a radius of 10 units.

   a. Find the length of a side of the square. *Hint:* Draw a different radius for the same circle.

   b. Find the exact perimeter of the square.

   c. Combine your ratio in Question 1a with your answer to Question 2b to get an estimate of the circumference of the circle.

3. a. Examine the process you went through to answer Question 2c. Write a clear explanation of how to use the ratio in Question 1a to give an estimate of the circumference of a circle from its radius.

   b. Use your explanation in Question 3a to write a formula (based on your ratio) that gives an estimate of the circumference of a circle in terms of its radius.

4. **a.** Find the exact area of the square in Question 2.

   b. Use your answer from Question 4a and your estimate of the ratio in Question 1b to estimate the area of the circle.

5. **a.** Examine the process you went through to answer Question 4. Write a clear explanation of how to use the ratio in Question 1b to find the area of a circle from its radius.

   b. Use your explanation in Question 5a to write a formula (based on your ratio) that gives the area of a circle in terms of its radius.

Hexagoning the Circle

You got approximate formulas for the circumference and area of a circle of radius r by comparing the circle to its circumscribed square.

In this activity, you will find formulas for the perimeter and area of the *regular hexagon* circumscribed about that circle. These values should provide fairly good estimates for the circumference and area of the circle.

1. Begin with a circle of radius 10. Find the perimeter and area of the regular hexagon circumscribed about this circle.

2. Generalize your work in Question 1 to a circle of radius r. Retrace your steps from Question 1 to create formulas for the perimeter and area of the circumscribed regular hexagon in terms of r.

Octagoning the Circle

In *Hexagoning the Circle,* you found formulas for the perimeter and area of a regular hexagon that is circumscribed about a circle of radius r.

In this assignment, your task is to develop similar formulas for the circumscribed regular octagon (eight-sided polygon).

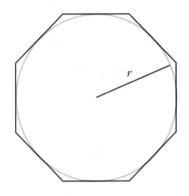

1. Begin with a circle of radius 10. Find the perimeter and area of the regular octagon circumscribed about this circle.

2. Generalize your work in Question 1 to a circle of radius r. Retrace your steps from Question 1 to create formulas for the perimeter and area of the circumscribed regular octagon in terms of r.

Polygoning the Circle

The circumference C and the area A of a circle of radius r can be found from formulas of the form

$$C = k_c r \text{ and } A = k_a r^2$$

where k_c and k_a are specific numbers called **constants of proportionality** (or *proportionality constants*).

There are similar formulas for regular polygons circumscribed about the circle. You have already developed such formulas for the square, the regular hexagon, and the regular octagon. Comparing the circle to these circumscribed polygons can give estimates of the values of k_c and k_a. The more sides the polygon has, the better the estimate.

Pick a number of sides (other than 4, 6, or 8), and develop formulas for the perimeter and area of the regular polygon with that many sides circumscribed about a circle of radius r.

Another Kind of Bisector

In your work on *POW 2: Equally Wet*, you came across the idea of a perpendicular bisector, which is a particular line that splits a line segment into two equal parts. But line segments aren't the only geometric figures that have bisectors.

An **angle bisector** is a ray that splits an angle into two equal parts. For example, in the diagram at the right, if $\angle RST = 50°$ and angles *RSU* and *UST* each equal 25°, then ray $\overrightarrow{SU}$ is the bisector of $\angle RST$.

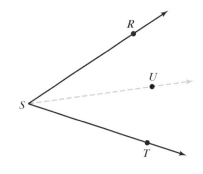

Suppose two lines ℓ and *m* intersect at point *A*, as shown in the diagram below. In this diagram, *B* and *D* are two points on ℓ, and *C* and *E* are two points on *m*. The intersecting lines ℓ and *m* form four angles at *A*, namely, $\angle BAC$, $\angle CAD$, $\angle DAE$, and $\angle EAB$.

1. The diagram shows that $\angle BAC = 70°$. Find the size of each of the other three angles.

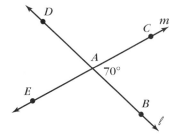

Continued on next page

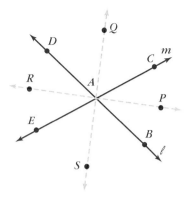

2. In the diagram at the left, the dashed rays represent the four angle bisectors. That is, $\overrightarrow{AP}$ bisects $\angle BAC$, $\overrightarrow{AQ}$ bisects $\angle CAD$, $\overrightarrow{AR}$ bisects $\angle DAE$, and $\overrightarrow{AS}$ bisects $\angle EAB$.

   a. Prove that the two angle bisectors $\overrightarrow{AP}$ and $\overrightarrow{AR}$ are part of the same line. That is, show that points *P, A,* and *R* are collinear. (*Hint:* Use the fact that $\angle BAC = 70°$ to show that $\angle PAR = 180°$.)

   b. Prove that the angle bisectors $\overrightarrow{AQ}$ and $\overrightarrow{AS}$ are part of the same line.

   c. Prove that the line containing $\overrightarrow{AP}$ and $\overrightarrow{AR}$ is perpendicular to the line containing $\overrightarrow{AQ}$ and $\overrightarrow{AS}$.

3. Your work in Question 2 was based on the fact that $\angle BAC = 70°$. Now represent $\angle BAC$ as *x* and prove parts a, b, and c of Question 2 in general. *Hint:* Express other angles in terms of *x*.

Proving Triples

The set of numbers 3, 4, and 5 is called a **Pythagorean triple,** because $3^2 + 4^2 = 5^2$. This numerical relationship means that a triangle whose sides have lengths 3, 4, and 5 will be a right triangle.

More generally, a Pythagorean triple is defined as any trio of positive whole numbers a, b, and c that satisfy the equation $a^2 + b^2 = c^2$.

The numbers 4, 5, and 7 do *not* form a Pythagorean triple because $4^2 + 5^2$ does not equal 7^2, and a triangle whose sides have these lengths will not be a right triangle.

1. Show that 5, 12, and 13 form a Pythagorean triple.

2. Suppose you multiply each member of a Pythagorean triple by the same positive number. For instance, you multiply 3, 4, and 5 each by 6 to get 18, 24, and 30.

    a. Determine whether 18, 24, and 30 form a Pythagorean triple.

    b. Will the process of multiplying each member of a Pythagorean triple by the same number always give you another Pythagorean triple? Give at least two more examples that support your conclusion.

3. Prove the conclusion you reached in Question 2b. (*Hint:* There are at least two possible approaches. One involves similar triangles, and the other uses the distributive property.)

A Marching Strip

Do you remember our economical king from *Eight Bags of Gold* and *Twelve Bags of Gold* (in the Year 1 unit *The Pit and the Pendulum*)?

Well, he's back, and he has another weighty problem.

The king is planning a new rectangular courtyard in the palace, which will be laid out using square tiles. He has chosen some very pretty, but very inexpensive, tiles. However, his advisor has informed him that some of the tiles will have to be a more expensive type.

You see, visiting dignitaries will always walk along a certain diagonal, from one corner of the courtyard to the opposite corner, so the tiles along the diagonal will get lots of wear and tear. Therefore, those tiles must be more durable (and hence more expensive). That is, every tile that contains a segment of the diagonal must be an extra-strength, expensive tile. (If a tile touches the diagonal only at a corner, it can be a regular tile.)

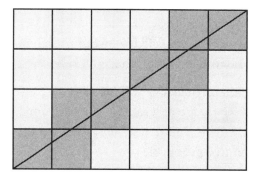

For example, the diagram above shows what the situation would look like if the king made a 4-by-6 courtyard. In this case, eight tiles (shaded darker than the rest) include some portion of the diagonal, and so these would need to be the more expensive kind.

Continued on next page

1. The king wants to know how many of these special tiles he needs to order. At the moment, he is planning to have a 63-by-90 courtyard. That is, he will have 63 rows of tiles with 90 tiles in each row.

   If he stays with this plan, how many special tiles will he need?

2. The king keeps changing his mind about the dimensions of the courtyard, so it would be especially helpful if you could find a general formula for him.

   Suppose the courtyard has r rows with c tiles in each row. How many special tiles will the king need? (The example illustrated in the diagram, which required eight special tiles, was the case $r = 4$ and $c = 6$.)

Write-up

1. *Problem Statement*

2. *Process*

3. *Solution*

4. *Evaluation*

5. *Self-assessment*

Adapted with permission from the *Mathematics Teacher,* © May, 1991, by the National Council of Teachers of Mathematics.

15

Orchard Growth Revisited

In *How Does Your Orchard Grow?,* you were asked to describe a plan for solving the central unit problem based on certain information. That activity led to a search for formulas for the area and circumference of a circle in terms of its radius.

Now you have those formulas, and you can carry out the plan if you are given the necessary information about the trees. Here are two key facts about the trees in Madie and Clyde's orchard.

• The cross-sectional area of a tree trunk increases by 1.5 square inches per year.

• Right now, the tree trunks each have a circumference of 2.5 inches.

Although you don't yet know the hideout tree radius, you can begin to solve the unit problem. Your task in this assignment is to answer this question.

> *How long will it take for the trees to grow to a radius of 1 foot?*

Historical Note: The first use of the symbol π for the circumference-to-diameter ratio was in 1706, by the English writer William Jones (1675–1749), and the symbol came into general use in this sense when the Swiss mathematician Leonhard Euler (1707–1783) adopted it in 1737.

Cable Complications

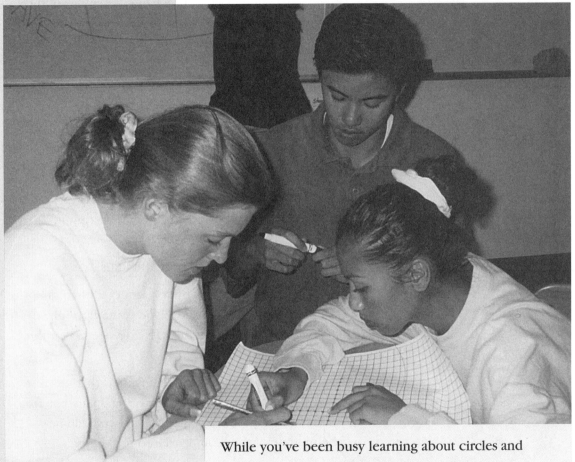

Kacie Rolie, Reggie Reyes, and Priscilla Pasion work together to determine where the last line of sight is.

While you've been busy learning about circles and coordinate formulas, Madie and Clyde have been dealing with another problem. There is an electrical cable that might get in the way of their planting.

While you solve this new problem, think about how it might be related to a key part of the main unit problem—finding the hideout tree radius for the orchard of radius 50.

Cable Ready

When Madie and Clyde bought their orchard, a straight electrical cable ran along the ground from the center of the orchard, at $(0, 0)$ in their coordinate system, to the point they called $(30, 20)$.

They thought they might get started on their planting while they waited for the electrical company to move the cable safely underground, but they had to be sure not to plant any trees right on the cable.

1. a. Could they have planted a complete mini-orchard of radius 1 at the center of their lot without planting right on the cable?

   b. What about a mini-orchard of radius 2?

   c. What is the radius of the biggest complete mini-orchard that Madie and Clyde could have planted without planting on the cable? (Assume that the tree trunks were very thin.)

2. Suppose that Madie and Clyde planted that "biggest possible" complete mini-orchard from Question 1c. How big would the tree trunks have to become before one of them bumped into the cable?

Your group should prepare a poster that summarizes your work on Question 2 for presentation to the class.

Going Around in Circles

1. At one time, Madie and Clyde had planned to plant a lawn instead of an orchard.

   Suppose the unit distance in their coordinate system is 10 feet. [For instance, this would be the distance from $(0,0)$ to $(1,0)$.]

   If a box of grass seed will cover 300 square feet of ground, how many boxes would Madie and Clyde have needed for their entire orchard? (*Reminder:* The radius of their orchard is 50 units, which you are assuming in this problem represents 500 feet.)

2. A circular track has a diameter of 200 meters. How far is it around the track?

3. The distance around a circular pond is 100 feet. Will a 30-foot board be long enough to use as a bridge across the pond at the center?

4. A contractor has just finished laying down some beautiful tiles on the floor of a circular room. Then he remembers that he was supposed to hang a banner in the room announcing the grand opening. The banner will reach across the room at its widest point, and the contractor needs to know this distance immediately so he can order the banner. Unfortunately, he can't walk across the newly laid tile. Fortunately, he remembers that the floor needed 2830 square feet of tile.

   How long should the banner be?

Daphne's Dance Floor

Daphne has a dream. She owns a farm and would like to put a huge dance floor in one of her meadows. Many families live in the area, but they have no place to go dancing. She thinks that with a big-name band (like the Rocking Pebbles), she'll be able to attract a full house.

She wants to make her dance floor circular, 100 feet across, which means a radius of 50 feet. She needs to order wood for the floor and for the railing to go around it, so she needs to find the area and circumference for a circle with a radius of 50 feet.

She doesn't know any formulas, but she has plenty of common sense. So, with her trusty compass, she makes a circle that has a radius of exactly 1 foot. Then she carefully wraps a string around her circle to measure the circumference.

Continued on next page

1. What is the circumference of a circle with a radius of 1 foot?

Because the radius of her dance floor will be exactly 50 times as big as the radius of the circle she drew, Daphne figures that the circumference of the dance floor will also be 50 times as big as that of her circle. She plans to use this value to calculate how much railing to order.

2. a. Multiply your answer to Question 1 by 50 to get Daphne's estimate of the circumference of the dance floor.

   b. Use the formula for circumference to get the actual circumference of a circle with a radius of 50 feet.

   c. Compare your answers to Questions 2a and 2b and explain whether Daphne's method works.

Next Daphne carefully cuts out some 1-inch squares and finds out how many of them it takes, including fractions, to fill in her small circle.

3. What is the area, in square inches, of a circle with a radius of 1 foot?

As her last step, Daphne multiplies this number by 50 and figures that this tells her how many square inches of wood flooring she will need to build her dance floor.

4. a. Multiply your answer to Question 3 by 50 to get Daphne's estimate.

   b. Use the formula for area to get the actual area, in square inches, of a circle with a radius of 50 feet.

   c. Explain where Daphne's plan went wrong and what she should have done instead.

Defining Circles

Earlier in this unit, you found that the equation $x^2 + y^2 = r^2$ describes the circle of radius r with center at the origin $(0, 0)$. That is, points whose coordinates fit the equation are on the circle, and points that do not fit the equation are not on the circle.

In this assignment, you will generalize this formula to circles whose center does not have to be at the origin.

The first two questions should help you get started thinking about distances and coordinates.

1. Suppose the tree in the orchard at $(6, 2)$ has been replaced by a sprinkler, and the water reaches all points within 5 units of the sprinkler. Which trees get wet?

2. Suppose a blade of grass is growing in the open space in the orchard, at the point with coordinates $(7.9, 6.1)$. Will this blade of grass get wet from the sprinkler in Question 1? How do you know?

3. Now suppose a blade of grass is growing in the open space in the orchard, at the point with coordinates (x, y).

   a. How can you tell if this blade of grass will get wet from the sprinkler in Question 1?

   b. Write an equation for the points on the boundary of the region watered by the sprinkler.

4. Suppose the sprinkler is at (a, b) and that it reaches all points within r units. Write an equation for the circle that forms the boundary of the region that the sprinkler waters.

The Standard Equation of the Circle

The Equation of a Circle

According to the distance formula, the distance from (x, y) to (a, b) is given by the expression

$$\sqrt{(x - a)^2 + (y - b)^2}$$

This formula can be used to write the equation of a circle, because a circle is the set of points that are some fixed distance from a given point.

The equation $\sqrt{(x - a)^2 + (y - b)^2} = r$ says, in algebraic form, that the point (x, y) is r units from (a, b), so the graph of this equation is the circle with center at (a, b) and radius r.

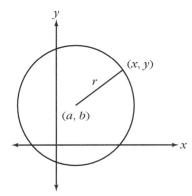

For convenience, we usually square both sides of this equation to avoid the square-root symbol. The standard form for the equation of this circle is

$$(x - a)^2 + (y - b)^2 = r^2$$

Continued on next page

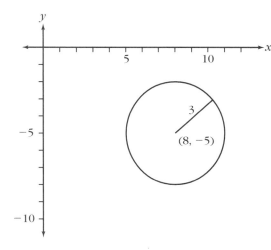

For example, the equation

$$(x - 8)^2 + (y + 5)^2 = 9$$

represents the circle with center $(8, -5)$ and radius 3, as shown here.

Transforming the Equation

Multiplying out the terms of

$$(x - 8)^2 + (y + 5)^2 = 9$$

and simplifying the result gives the equivalent equation

$$x^2 - 16x + y^2 + 10y + 80 = 0$$

More generally, the equation of a circle is always equivalent to an equation of the form

$$x^2 + cx + y^2 + dy + e = 0$$

where the coefficients $c, d,$ and e depend on the particular center and radius of the circle.

Reversing the Process

Often this process can be done in reverse, going from an equation of the form

$$x^2 + cx + y^2 + dy + e = 0$$

to an equation that has the standard form

$$(x - a)^2 + (y - b)^2 = r^2$$

Transforming the equation in this way (when possible) allows you to identify the center and radius of the graph simply by looking at the equation.

The key technique is called **completing the square.** For example, the expression $x^2 - 16x$ suggests the perfect square $(x - 8)^2$, because expanding $(x - 8)^2$ gives $x^2 - 16x + 64$.

Completing the Square and Getting a Circle

Examine each of these equations. If possible, find an equivalent equation in the form $(x - a)^2 + (y - b)^2 = r^2$ and identify the center and radius of the circle that the equation represents. If this is not possible, explain why not.

1. $x^2 - 8x + y^2 - 6y - 11 = 0$

2. $x^2 - 10x + y^2 + 12y + 28 = 0$

3. $x^2 + 3x + y^2 - 4y - 7 = 0$

4. $x^2 + 6x + y^2 + 2y + 13 = 0$

Lines of Sight

Julie Thorpe and Rosie Buckman use physical models to find the volume and lateral surface area of a cylinder.

In what direction should Madie and Clyde look to see out of their orchard for the longest time possible? And how long will it take until their orchard becomes a hideout?

You're closing in on the solution to the unit problem (and the trees may be closing in on you!). You will need to combine many ideas from the unit in order to answer Madie and Clyde's question.

The Other Gap

Using symmetry can make it much easier to locate the "last" line of sight, because some gaps between trees are like other gaps.

For instance, for the orchard of radius 3, all the gaps represented by the four shaded areas shown in this diagram are equivalent to the one in the first quadrant.

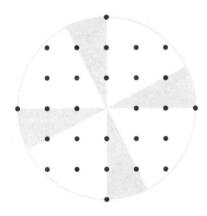

In fact, by symmetry, every gap is equivalent to one of the two gaps shown in the next diagram. The darkly shaded area represents the gap between the trees at point A and point B. The lightly shaded area represents the gap between the trees at point B and point C. [A is at $(1, 1)$, B is at $(2, 1)$, and C is at $(1, 0)$.]

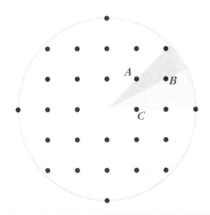

Continued on next page

Within each of these two gaps, there is one optimal line of sight, that is, a line of sight that stays unblocked as long as possible. Each is the optimal line in its gap because it goes through the midpoint of the segment connecting the two trees that "bound" that gap. These optimal lines of sight are shown in the next diagram.

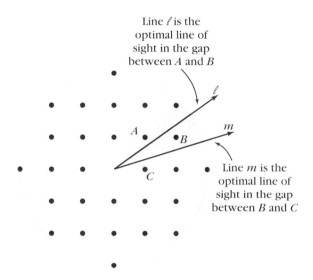

Line ℓ is the optimal line of sight in the gap between *A* and *B*

Line *m* is the optimal line of sight in the gap between *B* and *C*

Line ℓ is in the gap between *A* and *B*. It goes through the midpoint of $\overline{AB}$, which is $\left(1\frac{1}{2}, 1\right)$. This line of sight follows the same path as the cable in *Cable Ready,* and you know from *Cable Ready* that this line of sight becomes blocked when the tree trunks reach a radius of about 0.28 units.

The focus of this activity is on line *m*, which is the optimal line of sight in the gap between *B* and *C*. Line *m* goes through the midpoint of $\overline{BC}$, which is $\left(1\frac{1}{2}, \frac{1}{2}\right)$. Your task in this activity is to answer this question.

> *How big must the tree trunks become in order to block this line of sight?*

Cylindrical Soda

A soft drink company sells its soda in cylindrical cans that are 12 centimeters tall and have a radius of 3 centimeters. The selling price for a can of soda this size is 80¢.

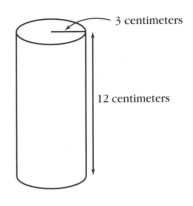

3 centimeters

12 centimeters

1. Find the volume of this container (in cubic centimeters). *Hint:* Think about how the volume of a box is related to the area of its base, and apply similar reasoning for the cylinder.

The Lateral Surface Department of the company is responsible for purchasing metal for the curved surface of the cylindrical cans. (In other words, they buy the metal for all of the can except for the top and bottom.)

2. How much metal should this department order per can (in square centimeters)? Assume that there is no waste. (*Hint:* Think about how the lateral surface area of a box is related to the perimeter of its base, and apply similar reasoning for the cylinder.)

3. Suppose the manufacturer decides to make a new container, called "the tall one." This can will be twice as tall as the standard size, but the top and bottom will remain, as before, circles with radius 3 centimeters.

   a. If the manufacturer keeps the cost per ounce of soda the same, what should be the selling price for "the tall one"?

   b. How will the metal needed for the lateral surface area of "the tall one" compare to the metal needed for the standard container?

Continued on next page

4. Now suppose the manufacturer decides to make another new container, called "the wide one." This container will be three times as wide as the standard size. That is, the radius of the base will be 9 centimeters instead of 3 centimeters. The height of this new container will be the standard 12 centimeters.

a. If the manufacturer keeps the cost per ounce of soda the same, what should be the selling price for "the wide one"?

b. How will the metal needed for the lateral surface area of "the wide one" compare to the metal needed for the standard container?

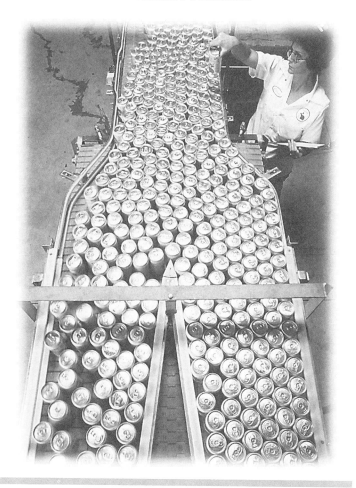

Lines of Sight for Radius Six

Line *m,* shown in the diagram at the right, is one of the last lines of sight to be blocked for the orchard of radius 3. This line goes through the gap between the tree at $B = (2, 1)$ and the tree at $C = (1, 0)$, and passes through the midpoint between these two trees, which is at $\left(1\frac{1}{2}, \frac{1}{2}\right)$. By symmetry, there are other lines of sight that are just as good as *m,* but no line of sight is better than *m.*

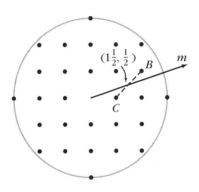

What are the last lines of sight for other orchards?

The diagram below shows the first quadrant portion of the orchard of radius 6. The center of the orchard is marked by a small dot, and the trees are represented by shaded circles.

Examine different lines of sight from the center out of this orchard, and try to determine which of them will remain unblocked the longest.

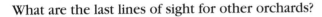

Orchard Time for Radius Three

You know that for the orchard of radius 3, the line of sight *m* shown below is one of the last to be blocked. The perpendicular distance from the tree at $(1, 0)$ to this line is $\frac{1}{\sqrt{10}}$ units, which is approximately 0.32 units.

Recall these facts about Madie and Clyde's orchard (from *Homework 15: Orchard Growth Revisited*).

• The cross-sectional area of a tree trunk increases by 1.5 square inches per year.

• Right now, the tree trunks each have a circumference of 2.5 inches.

Here is one additional piece of information about the orchard.

• The unit distance [for instance, the distance from $(0, 0)$ to $(1, 0)$] is 10 feet.

Your task in this assignment is to answer this question:

> *How long will it take for this line of sight to be blocked?*

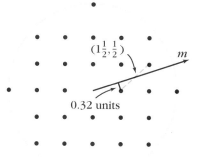

Hiding in the Orchard

As you probably recall, Madie and Clyde planted their orchard on a circular lot of radius 50 units. They wondered how long it would take until they could no longer see out of the orchard from the center of the lot.

You now have the information you need to solve their problem.

- The cross-sectional area of a tree trunk increases by 1.5 square inches per year.

- Right now, the tree trunks each have a circumference of 2.5 inches.

- The unit distance [for instance, the distance from $(0, 0)$ to $(1, 0)$] is 10 feet.

- The last line of sight is the line that goes from the origin through the point $\left(25, \frac{1}{2}\right)$.

Your task is to put all of this information together to answer this question.

> *How soon after they planted the orchard would the center of the lot become a true "orchard hideout"?*

22

Big Earth, Little Earth

Suppose you were able to wrap a very long piece of string tightly around the equator of the earth. And suppose that at the same time, your friend were to wrap a piece of string tightly around the equator of a classroom globe. (Of course, your friend's string would be much shorter.)

For simplicity, assume that the earth is a perfect sphere with a radius of 4000 miles and that the globe is a perfect sphere with a radius of 6 inches. Remember that 1 mile is equal to 5280 feet.

1. Find the length of each piece of string.

Now suppose you each replaced your string with a piece that was 1 foot longer. Of course, your strings would no longer fit tightly around their equators. But if the radius of the earth got a little bit bigger, your string would be tight again. Similarly, if the radius of the globe grew a little bit, your friend's string would be tight again.

2. How much bigger would each radius have to get? Which radius would have to grow more—that of the earth or that of the globe—in order for the string to fit tightly? Justify your answer.

Beginning Portfolios

Part I: A Coordinate Summary

Many of the ideas in this unit involved the coordinate system. For example, you developed a formula for finding the distance between two points in the coordinate plane in terms of their coordinates.

Write a summary of the main ideas about coordinates that you learned or used in this unit. Include important formulas and equations and their explanations as well as examples of how coordinates played a role in solving the unit problem. Also indicate which activities played an important role in your understanding of these ideas.

Part II: Me, Myself, and Pi

Perhaps you had heard something about the number π before starting this unit, or perhaps not. In either case, your work in this unit with circles and circumscribed polygons should give you further insight into this important number.

Write an essay on what you thought about π before this unit and what you think now. Include any misconceptions you had that you have now corrected. Also indicate which activities played an important role in your understanding of π.

24

Orchard Hideout Portfolio

Now that *Orchard Hideout* is completed, it is time to put together your portfolio for the unit. Compiling this portfolio has three parts.

- Writing a cover letter in which you summarize the unit

- Choosing papers to include from your work in this unit

- Discussing your personal mathematical growth in this unit, especially with regard to the relationship between geometry and algebra

Cover Letter for *Orchard Hideout*

Look back over *Orchard Hideout* and describe the central problem of the unit and the main mathematical ideas. This description should give an overview of how the key ideas of area and circumference of circles and distances between points or between points and lines were developed, and how these ideas were used to solve the central problem.

In compiling your portfolio, you will select some activities that you think were important in developing the key ideas of this unit. Your cover letter should include an explanation of why you selected the particular items.

Continued on next page

Selecting Papers from Orchard Hideout

Your portfolio for *Orchard Hideout* should contain these items.

• *Hiding in the Orchard*

• A Problem of the Week

  Select any one of the three POWs you completed in this unit (*Equally Wet, On Patrol,* or *A Marching Strip*).

• *Homework 23: Beginning Portfolios*

  Include the write-up you did for this assignment as well as the activities you discussed in the assignment.

• Other key activities

  Identify two concepts that you think were important in this unit other than those discussed in *Homework 23: Beginning Portfolios.* For each concept, choose one or two activities that helped your understanding improve, and explain how the activity helped.

Personal Growth

Your cover letter for *Orchard Hideout* describes how the mathematical ideas develop in the unit. As part of your portfolio, write about your own personal development during this unit. You may want to address this question.

> *How did the unit improve your understanding of the relationship between algebra and geometry?*

You should include here any other thoughts about your experiences with this unit that you want to share with a reader of your portfolio.

Supplemental Problems

The supplemental problems in *Orchard Hideout* expand the themes from geometry that pervade the unit. Here are some examples.

- *The Perpendicular Bisector Converse* and *Why Do They Always Meet?* follow up on ideas from *POW 2: Equally Wet.*

- *Inscribed Angles* and *Angles In and Out* are among several problems involving angles and angle measurement.

- *Right in the Center* and *Hypotenuse Median* are related problems involving the use of coordinates.

Right and Isosceles

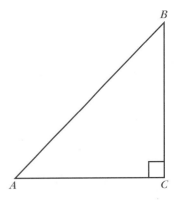

Right triangles are special, and so are isosceles triangles. Some triangles have the special property of fitting into both categories.

Triangle ABC has a right angle at C and sides $\overline{AC}$ and $\overline{BC}$ have the same length.

1. What is the size of $\angle A$? Justify your answer.

2. Find the *exact* values of sin A, cos A, and tan A, based on geometric principles. Do not rely on a calculator for your answers.

The Perpendicular Bisector Converse

In *POW 2: Equally Wet,* you were asked where a sprinkler could be placed so that it watered two flowers equally. In mathematical terms, this means finding the set of points that are equidistant from two given points. You saw that this set forms the perpendicular bisector of the segment connecting the two points.

One part of this result from the POW involves proving this "If ..., then ..." statement, which you did in the activity *A Perpendicularity Proof.*

> *If D is on the perpendicular bisector of the segment connecting points A and B, then the distances AD and BD are equal.*

In this statement, the hypothesis is "*D* is on the perpendicular bisector of the segment connecting points *A* and *B*" and the conclusion is "the distances *AD* and *BD* are equal."

When the hypothesis and conclusion of an "If ..., then ..." statement are interchanged, the result is called the **converse** of the original statement. For some true "If ..., then ..." statements, the converse is true, but for others, the converse is false.

Continued on next page

Your Task

Your task in this activity is to prove that the converse of the statement you proved earlier is also true. That is, prove this statement.

> *If the distances AD and BD are equal, then D is on the perpendicular bisector of the segment connecting points A and B.*

Hint: Start with a diagram like the one at the right, and assume that the hypothesis is true. That is, assume $AD = BD$.

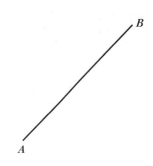

Then draw a perpendicular segment from D to $\overline{AB}$, as in the diagram below.

You need to show that C, the foot of the perpendicular, is the midpoint of $\overline{AB}$. In other words, show that $AC = BC$. The key is finding a way to use the hypothesis that AD and BD are equal.

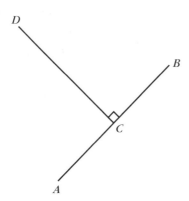

PROBLEM

Counting Trees

If Madie and Clyde planted their orchard on a lot of radius 1, it would include only the four trees on the axes. All four of those trees lie on the boundary of the orchard.

If they expanded to a lot of radius 2, their orchard would include 12 trees. Again, there would be exactly four trees on the boundary.

1. Sketch the orchard of radius 3 and find out how many trees it has on its boundary.

2. Sketch the orchard of radius 5 and find out how many trees it has on its boundary.

3. Is it possible for an orchard to have a tree on its boundary whose coordinates are equal? (Assume that the radius of the lot is a positive integer.)

4. Use your examples and your answer to Question 3 to develop a general statement about the number of trees on the boundary of an orchard. You may find your work on *Homework 5: Other Trees* useful.

Perpendicular Bisectors by Algebra

The perpendicular bisector of a line segment is the set of points that are equidistant from the endpoints of the segment. The coordinate system provides a way to think about perpendicular bisectors algebraically.

1. Start with the two points $(4, 3)$ and $(8, 5)$ and a general point (x, y).

    a. Write an expression for the distance from (x, y) to $(4, 3)$.

    b. Write an expression for the distance from (x, y) to $(8, 5)$.

    c. Form an equation by setting the two expressions equal to each other.

The equation you get in Question 1c says, in effect, "(x, y) is equidistant from $(4, 3)$ and $(8, 5)$," so this should be the equation of the perpendicular bisector of the segment connecting those two points.

2. Simplify the equation from Question 1c as much as possible. (You should be able to simplify it so that it becomes a linear equation.)

Continued on next page

3. a. Find the coordinates of the midpoint of the segment connecting $(4, 3)$ and $(8, 5)$.

 b. Verify that the coordinates you found in Question 3a fit the equation from Question 2.

 c. Explain why the coordinates of the midpoint *should* fit the equation.

4. Plot the points $(4, 3)$ and $(8, 5)$ and draw the segment connecting them. Then graph your equation from Question 2. Does the result fit your expectations? Explain.

5. Suppose (a, b) and (c, d) are any two points. Use the steps in Questions 1 and 2 to write the equation of the set of points equidistant from these two points. That is, find a linear equation for the perpendicular bisector of the segment connecting (a, b) and (c, d).

Midpoint Proof

In *Homework 7: A Snack in the Middle,* you were asked to find the midpoint of the segment connecting $(24, 6)$ and $(30, 14)$. The answer is $(27, 10)$, and part of your task in the homework was to prove that $(27, 10)$ is equidistant from the two endpoints of the segment.

Unfortunately, this doesn't prove that $(27, 10)$ is the midpoint, because *any* point on the perpendicular bisector of the segment will be equidistant from the two endpoints.

1. Find at least two other points that are equidistant from $(24, 6)$ and $(30, 14)$.

2. Explain how you know that $(27, 10)$ is actually on the line segment connecting $(24, 6)$ and $(30, 14)$. (*Hint:* Find a linear equation whose graph includes those two points, and show that $(27, 10)$ also fits the equation.)

3. How would you prove in general that the midpoint formula actually gives the midpoint?

Why Do They Always Meet?

Start with any triangle. Draw the perpendicular bisector of one of its sides. Then draw the perpendicular bisector of a different side.

Because these two perpendicular bisectors aren't parallel, they must meet at some point.

1. Prove that the third perpendicular bisector must go through this same point. In other words, show that all three perpendicular bisectors meet in a single point. (*Hint:* Use the principle that the perpendicular bisector of a line segment consists of all points equidistant from the endpoints of the segment.)

2. Explain how the result from Question 1 shows that every triangle has a circumscribed circle.

3. Explain how this idea applies to the three-flower case of *POW 2: Equally Wet.* (*Hint:* Picture the flowers as the vertices of the triangle.)

4. If you didn't answer the sprinkler problem for four flowers or more in your POW, work on it some more, using the ideas from Questions 1 through 3.

Inscribed Angles

In examining the three-flower case of *POW 2: Equally Wet,* you may have realized that any triangle can be inscribed in a circle. You can find the center of this circle by looking for the place where the perpendicular bisectors of the sides all meet, because that point is equidistant from all three vertices.

(The supplemental problem *Why Do They Always Meet?* asks you to *prove* that the three perpendicular bisectors all meet in one point.)

This activity looks at the special case in which the center of the circle is actually on one of the sides of the triangle.

In the diagram below, $\triangle ABC$ is inscribed in a circle whose center, point D, is on side $\overline{AB}$. Because $\overline{AB}$ is a diameter of the circle, we say that $\angle ACB$ is **inscribed in a semicircle.** The diagram also shows the radius from D to C and uses the small letters $u, v, w, x, y,$ and z to represent the sizes of the angles indicated. For example, u is the size of $\angle ADC$.

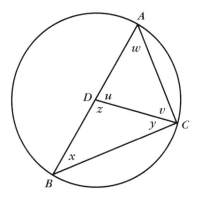

Continued on next page

Your task is to prove this statement.

> *An angle inscribed in a semicircle must be a right angle.*

You can use these steps to construct a proof.

1. Explain why $x = y$ and $v = w$. (*Hint:* Use the fact that $\overline{DA}$, $\overline{DB}$, and $\overline{DC}$ are all radii of the circle.)

2. Explain why $x + y + z = 180°$ and $u + v + w = 180°$.

3. Explain why $u + z = 180°$.

4. Combine the equations from Questions 1 through 3 to prove that $v + y = 90°$. In other words, prove that $\angle ACB$ is a right angle.

More Inscribed Angles

In the supplemental problem *Inscribed Angles*, you were asked to prove that an angle inscribed in a semicircle must be a right angle. This is actually a special case of a more general principle. To state this general principle, we need to introduce some terminology.

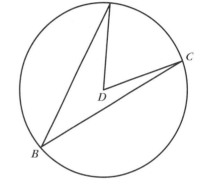

If an angle *ABC* is situated with points *A, B,* and *C* on a circle, as in the diagram at the right, we say that the angle is **inscribed in the circle.** The angle formed by the radii from the center *D* to points *A* and *C,* which is ∠*ADC,* is called the **corresponding central angle.**

Here is the general principle.

> *An angle inscribed in a circle is half the size of the corresponding central angle.*

Before proving the general principle, you need to consider first the case in which $\overline{AB}$ is actually a diameter of the circle, as shown below. (This diagram is part of the diagram from the activity *Inscribed Angles.*)

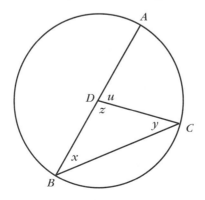

Continued on next page

1. Prove in this case that ∠*ABC* is half the size of ∠*ADC*. (*Hint:* Look at the relevant parts of Questions 1 through 3 of *Inscribed Angles*.)

2. Apply the special case from Question 1 to prove the general case. (*Hint:* In the diagram below, show that ∠*ABE* is half the size of ∠*ADE* and that ∠*CBE* is half the size of ∠*CDE*.)

3. Explain why the result from *Inscribed Angles* is a special case of this principle.

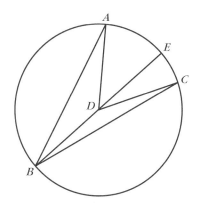

Angles In and Out

If you worked on either of the supplemental problems *Inscribed Angles* or *More Inscribed Angles,* you saw a diagram like the first one at the right.

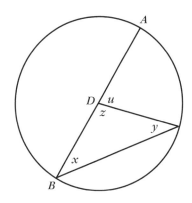

You may have realized in the course of your work that $u = x + y$. In fact, this is a special case of a more general principle that has nothing to do with circles or inscribed angles.

Consider the second diagram, in which $\triangle PQR$ is an arbitrary triangle and point S is a point on the extension of side $\overline{PQ}$. The letters a, b, c, and d represent the sizes of the angles indicated.

You may recall that an angle such as $\angle SQR$ is called an **exterior angle** for $\triangle PQR$. Angle PQR is called the **adjacent interior angle** for this exterior angle, and angles QPR and QRP are called the **nonadjacent interior angles.**

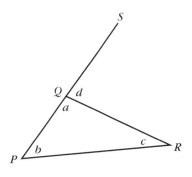

Your task in this activity is to prove this statement.

> *In any triangle, each exterior angle is equal to the sum of the two nonadjacent interior angles.*

In other words, you must prove that $d = b + c$.
(*Hint:* Find two different angle sums that are each 180°.)

Midpoint Quadrilaterals

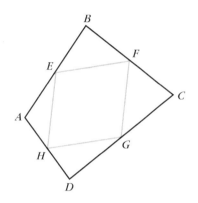

In Question 2 of *Homework 8: Proving with Distance— Part I*, you picked four points in the coordinate plane and connected them to form a quadrilateral.

You then found the midpoints of the sides of that quadrilateral and connected them to form a new quadrilateral, which we will refer to as the **midpoint quadrilateral**.

Your final diagram should have looked something like the pair of quadrilaterals shown here.

It turns out, as you may have conjectured, that the midpoint quadrilateral is always a parallelogram, no matter what quadrilateral you start with. Your task in this activity is to prove this. (In *Homework 8: Proving with Distance—Part I*, you were asked to prove that the opposite sides of the specific quadrilateral had equal lengths.)

Before beginning, you need to recall that a *parallelogram* is defined as a quadrilateral whose opposite sides are parallel.

An Outline Using Triangles

This activity provides a three-part outline for you to use in constructing a proof. Parts I and II really involve only triangles.

Continued on next page

The diagram at the right is formed from part of the original diagram, by drawing the diagonal $\overline{AC}$ of the original quadrilateral. So $\triangle ABC$ could be any triangle, and E and F are the midpoints of sides $\overline{AB}$ and $\overline{BC}$.

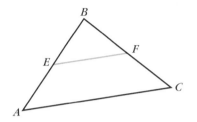

In $\triangle ABC$, we will refer to $\overline{AC}$ as the **base** and to $\overline{EF}$ as the **midline** (because it connects two midpoints).

In Parts I and II, you will prove two statements about this diagram.

• The length EF is half the length AC.

• $\overline{EF}$ is parallel to $\overline{AC}$.

You may want to think ahead about how you would use the second of these statements to prove that $EFGH$ is a parallelogram. (That's Part III.) Keep in mind that these statements apply to *any* triangle.

Part I: The Length of the Midline Is Half the Length of the Base

The proof of this statement suggested in Questions 1 and 2 uses coordinates. (The study of geometry using coordinates is called **analytic geometry**.)

To make things completely general, suppose that point A is (r, s), B is (t, u), and C is (v, w).

1. Find expressions for the lengths EF and AC in terms of these coordinates.

2. Use your expressions from Question 1 to prove that EF is half of AC.

Continued on next page

Part II: The Midline Is Parallel to the Base

The proof of this statement suggested in Questions 3 and 4 uses similarity but does not involve coordinates. (The more general study of geometry, without coordinates, is sometimes called **synthetic geometry.**)

3. Prove that $\triangle EBF$ is similar to $\triangle ABC$. (*Hint:* Use the result from Question 2 to show that corresponding sides of these two triangles are proportional.)

4. Prove $\overline{EF}$ that is parallel to $\overline{AC}$. (*Hint:* First, use the result from Question 3 to show that $\angle BEF = \angle BAC$. Then use ideas about transversals and their corresponding angles.)

Part III: *EFGH* Is a Parallelogram

5. Prove that quadrilateral *EFGH* is a parallelogram. [*Hint:* Use the fact that for *any* triangle, the midline is parallel to the base (and use the definition of a parallelogram).]

Equidistant Lines

As part of your discussion of the activity *Down the Garden Path,* you proved this statement.

> *If a line goes through the midpoint of $\overline{AB}$, then it is equidistant from points A and B.*

Your task is to prove the converse of this statement, which is obtained by interchanging the hypothesis and the conclusion. In other words, prove this statement:

> *If a line is equidistant from points A and B, then it goes through the midpoint of $\overline{AB}$.*

You can use the diagram below to set up the problem. In this diagram, you are given two points *A* and *B* and a line *ℓ*. Point *C* is the point where *ℓ* meets $\overline{AB}$.

The hypothesis says to assume that *ℓ* is equidistant from *A* and *B*, which means that the perpendicular distances *AD* and *BE* are equal.

You need to prove that *C* is the midpoint of *AB*.

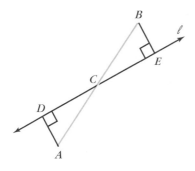

Right in the Center

1. Consider the triangle whose vertices are $(4, 1)$, $(12, 7)$, and $(24, -9)$.

   a. Prove that this is a right triangle.

   b. Find the midpoint of the hypotenuse of this triangle.

   c. Show that the midpoint of the hypotenuse is equidistant from all three vertices.

2. Use the results from Question 1 to find the center and radius for a circle that goes through all three vertices of the triangle.

3. Find the equation for the circle in Question 2 and verify that the coordinates of the points $(4, 1)$, $(12, 7)$, and $(24, -9)$ all fit the equation. (*Note:* This part of the activity requires ideas from *Homework 18: Defining Circles*.)

Thirty-Sixty-Ninety

The supplemental problem *Right and Isosceles* focused on one special type of triangle. The focus of this problem is on the equilateral triangle.

Triangle *ABC* in this diagram is equilateral, and $\overline{AD}$ is the altitude from *A* to $\overline{BC}$.

1. Find the angles in right triangle *ABD*.

2. Use the diagram to find the *exact* values of sin 30°, cos 30°, tan 30°, sin 60°, cos 60°, and tan 60°. Do not rely on a calculator for your answers.

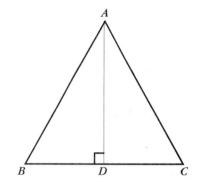

More About Triples

As you have seen, a *Pythagorean triple* is any trio of positive whole numbers *a, b,* and *c* that satisfy the equation $a^2 + b^2 = c^2$. The triple 3, 4, and 5 and the triple 5, 12, and 13 are two of the most familiar examples.

Your task in this activity is to learn more about such triples. Here are two questions to get you started, but don't be limited by them. (The study of problems like these is part of a branch of mathematics called *number theory.* You may want to consult a book on number theory for ideas.)

1. Is it possible to have a Pythagorean triple *a, b,* and *c* in which *a* and *b* are equal? Justify your answer.

A *primitive* Pythagorean triple is one in which *a, b,* and *c* have no common whole-number factor (other than 1).

2. Assume that *a, b,* and *c* form a primitive Pythagorean triple, with $a^2 + b^2 = c^2$.

   a. Prove that *a* and *b* cannot both be even numbers.

   b. Prove that *a* and *b* cannot both be odd numbers. (This is harder than part a.)

   c. Prove that *c* must be an odd number.

Darts

To pass the time while their trees are growing, Madie and Clyde hung a dart board on one of their trees. The dart board looks like the one shown here, in which the radii of the circles are in the ratio of $1:2:3$.

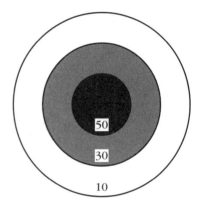

As the diagram shows, a dart that lands in the white ring around the outside earns 10 points; a dart in the shaded ring earns 30 points; and a dart that hits the black circle in the center earns 50 points.

Assume that Madie and Clyde always hit the dart board and that they have an equal chance of landing at any point on the board. What is the expected value for their score per dart? (*Reminder:* You can find the expected value by taking an average over a large number of trials.)

Adapted with permission from the *Mathematics Teacher,* © December, 1990, by the National Council of Teachers of Mathematics.

PROBLEM

The Inscribed Circle

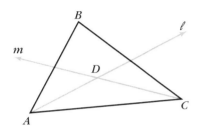

You saw in *POW 3: On Patrol* that a point on an angle bisector is equidistant from the two lines that form that angle.

This fact and its converse can be used to prove that every triangle has an inscribed circle. (This is similar to the result from Question 2 of the supplemental problem *Why Do They Always Meet?*)

Consider $\triangle ABC$, shown here, and suppose that rays ℓ and m are the bisectors of angles BAC and BCA. Let D be the point where these two rays meet.

1. Prove that the ray from B through D bisects $\angle ABC$. *Hint:* Use the general principle about angle bisectors from *POW 3: On Patrol*.

2. Explain how the result in Question 1 proves that every triangle has an inscribed circle. (An inscribed circle is a circle to which the sides of the triangle are all tangent.)

Medians and Altitudes

If you worked on the supplemental problem *Why Do They Always Meet?*, you saw why the perpendicular bisectors of the sides of a triangle all meet in a single point. That point is called the **circumcenter** of the triangle, because it is the center of the circumscribed circle.

The diagram at the right shows a triangle, its perpendicular bisectors, and the circumscribed circle.

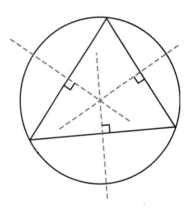

A similar principle holds for angle bisectors, namely, the three angle bisectors of a triangle also all meet in a single point. That point is called the **incenter** of the triangle, because it is the center of the inscribed circle. (This principle was established in the supplemental problem *The Inscribed Circle*.)

This activity involves two other, similar principles. (Unfortunately, the proofs of these two principles are much more difficult, so this is a very challenging activity.)

Part I: Medians

In any triangle, the line segment connecting a vertex to the midpoint of the opposite side is called a **median.** For example, in $\triangle RST$, point W is the midpoint of $\overline{RS}$, so $\overline{TW}$ is a median.

Prove that in any triangle, the three medians meet in a single point.

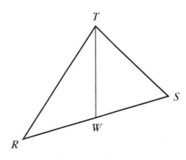

Continued on next page

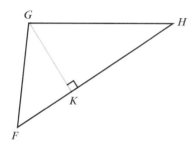

Part II: Altitudes

In any triangle, the line segment from a vertex perpendicular to the line containing the opposite side is called an **altitude.** For example, in $\triangle FGH$, $\overline{GK}$ is perpendicular to $\overline{FH}$, so $\overline{GK}$ is an altitude.

Prove that in any triangle, the three altitudes meet in a single point.

Hypotenuse Median

In the supplemental problem *Right in the Center,* you were asked to show that the midpoint of the hypotenuse of a certain right triangle was equidistant from all three vertices.

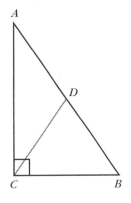

As you may have guessed, this was not a coincidence, and your task in this problem is to prove the general principle.

In any triangle, the line segment connecting a vertex to the midpoint of the opposite side is called a median, so we can refer to $\overline{CD}$ in the accompanying diagram as the **median to the hypotenuse.** (Here, $\triangle ABC$ is a right triangle and D is the midpoint of $\overline{AB}$.)

The goal of this activity is to prove this principle.

> *The length of the median to the hypotenuse is exactly half the length of the hypotenuse.*

We will refer to this principle as the **median-to-the-hypotenuse property.**

Here are outlines for two different ways to prove this principle. Try to prove it both ways.

1. First, prove that the two diagonals of any rectangle are the same length and bisect each other. Then draw in the full rectangle around $\triangle ABC$, and use the fact about the diagonals of a rectangle to prove the median-to-the-hypotenuse property.

2. Place the triangle in the coordinate system with C at the origin and A and B on the coordinate axes. Assign coordinates to the points A and B in a way that makes $\triangle ABC$ a general right triangle. Then find the coordinates of D and use the result to prove the median-to-the-hypotenuse property.

Not Quite a Circle

You've seen that $x^2 + y^2 = r^2$ is the equation of a circle with center $(0, 0)$ and radius r. In other words, a point with coordinates (x, y) is on this circle if and only if the coordinates fit the equation.

Your task in this activity is to experiment with certain variations on this equation to determine what shapes they define.

Specifically, think of the equation as $1 \cdot x^2 + 1 \cdot y^2 = r^2$, and look at what happens to the graph of the equation if numbers other than 1 are used as coefficients for x^2 and y^2. That is, consider equations such as these.

- $9x^2 + 16y^2 = 144$

- $25x^2 + 16y^2 = 400$

- $4x^2 + 4y^2 = 25$

Restrict yourself to coefficients and constant terms that are perfect squares, as in these examples. This will allow you to write these numbers as squares of other numbers. For example, the equation $9x^2 + 16y^2 = 144$ can be written as $3^2 \cdot x^2 + 4^2 \cdot y^2 = 12^2$.

Investigate specific examples and report on what you have learned about the graphs of equations of the form $a^2x^2 + b^2y^2 = c^2$.

Knitting

As the years went on, Madie and Clyde decided to start a family. They would spend their afternoons sitting out among the trees, knitting booties and doing geometry problems.

They figured that a ball of yarn with about a 3-inch diameter would be needed for each bootie.

1. If Madie had a ball with a 1-foot diameter, how many booties would it yield?

2. How many booties would they get from a ball with a 2-foot diameter? How does this compare to your answer to Question 1?

Adapted with permission from the *Mathematics Teacher,* © December, 1990, by the National Council of Teachers of Mathematics.

Meadows or Malls?

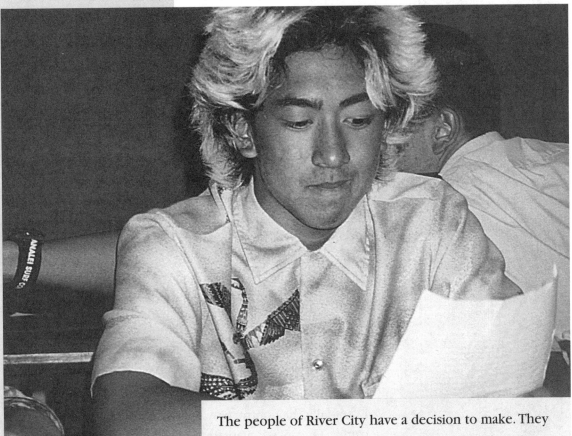

Recreation Versus Development: A Complex Problem

DAYS 1-2

Rex Moribe thinks about how to represent the constraints algebraically.

The people of River City have a decision to make. They must decide how much land to use for recreation, how much to use for development, and exactly which land to use for each purpose.

To help them make their decision, you will apply many ideas about algebra, geometry, and the relationship between the two. The first stage is simply to make some sense of this very complicated situation.

Meadows or Malls?

Who would have thought that so much good fortune could cause so much trouble? Well, this time it surely did in River City. Actually, there were three separate pieces of good fortune.

First, when Mr. Goodfellow died, he left his 300-acre farm to the city. His will had no stipulations, so the city could do whatever it wished with the property.

Then the U.S. Army closed its 100-acre base on the edge of town, and the federal government gave the land to the people of River City to use in any way they chose.

Finally, there were 150 acres of land that had been leased to a mining company 99 years ago. Now, the lease was up. Because the company had not found enough minerals there to make a profit for many years, it did not wish to renew the lease. So that land was also available to the city with no restrictions on its use.

Altogether, that made 550 acres of land that the city could use in any way it decided. The problem was that a city isn't exactly an "it." A city contains many people who don't always agree. And the people in River City definitely did not agree on how to use the 550 acres.

Eventually, the controversy centered on two opposing camps. One group wanted to use as much of the land as possible for *development*—that is, for stores, businesses, and housing. The other group wanted to use as much of the land as possible for *recreation*—that is, for park land, hiking trails, a wildlife preserve, and picnic areas.

Continued on next page

The business community won an initial victory by getting the city council to agree that at least 300 acres would go for development. The business community also thought that the more attractive sites—the army base and mining land—should go for development, while any recreation land could come from Mr. Goodfellow's farm property. But the environmental and sporting interests felt that some of the more attractive land should go for recreation.

The two groups finally came up with a two-part compromise.

• At most 200 acres of the army base and mining land could go for recreation.

• The amount of army base land used for recreation and the amount of farmland used for development together had to total exactly 100 acres.

Everyone realized that the city would have to improve any land used for development, putting in sewers, streets, power lines, and so on. The city would also have to spend some money on any land used for recreation.

The city manager made a chart like the one shown here listing, for each parcel, how much each type of land use would cost the city. Everyone agreed that they wanted to keep the costs to River City to a minimum.

Parcel	Improvement costs per acre for recreation	Improvement costs per acre for development
Mr. Goodfellow's farm	$50	$500
Army base	$200	$2,000
Mining land	$100	$1,000

Continued on next page

So the matter was turned over to the city manager. She had to decide how to split the land use between development and recreation so as to minimize the cost to the city of the necessary improvements while at the same time ensuring that at least 300 acres went for development and that the two-part compromise was followed.

Now, she had tackled some complicated problems in her time, but this seemed a bit much for her to handle. So she turned the matter over to a consulting firm of city planners.

Your Task

Your group will function as that consulting firm, working on this problem over the course of the unit. Your task for now is to find out as much as you can about the problem. By the end of the unit, you will identify the best solution.

1. Find one way to allocate the land and satisfy the constraints. Find the cost to the city for this solution even though you may recognize that it is not the least costly allocation.

2. What approaches to solving this problem might you have tried if you had more time? What approaches did you try that didn't seem to work?

Meadows, Malls, and Variables

1. Use the variables defined below to write a set of constraints that express the *Meadows or Malls?* problem.

   - G_R is the number of acres of Mr. Goodfellow's land to be used for recreation.

   - A_R is the number of acres of army land to be used for recreation.

   - M_R is the number of acres of mining land to be used for recreation.

   - G_D is the number of acres of Mr. Goodfellow's land to be used for development.

   - A_D is the number of acres of army land to be used for development.

   - M_D is the number of acres of mining land to be used for development.

Continued on next page

2. Use the variables from Question 1 to write an algebraic expression for the city's cost based on how the land is allocated.

3. Check whether each of these allocations satisfies the constraints you defined in Question 1. If it does, find the cost to the city. If it does not, show which constraint or constraints it violates.

a. $G_R = 250$
$A_R = 50$
$M_R = 150$
$G_D = 50$
$A_D = 50$
$M_D = 0$

b. $G_R = 200$
$A_R = 0$
$M_R = 0$
$G_D = 100$
$A_D = 100$
$M_D = 150$

That's Entertainment!

An entertainer has an ordinary deck of playing cards. He gives them to his subject, turns his back, and has her shuffle the deck thoroughly.

Keeping his back to her so he can't see what she's doing, he then tells her to make some piles according to these instructions.

1. First, she turns over the top card of the deck.

   If this is a picture card (jack, queen, or king), she puts it back somewhere in the middle of the deck and picks the new top card of the deck. She keeps going until she gets a card that is not a picture card. That is, she continues until she gets an ace, 2, 3, 4, 5, 6, 7, 8, 9, or 10, and places that card face up on the table.

2. Beginning with the number on that card, she starts counting to herself until she gets to 12. (Aces are treated as 1.) With each count, she takes one card from the top of the deck and places it face up on top of the pile she is creating. When she reaches 12, she turns the pile over so that the card she started with is face down on top.

   For example, if she initially turns up an 8, she places a card on top of the 8 and silently counts "9." Then she places a card on top of the pile and silently counts "10," then another card on top and counts "11," and finally, another card on top and counts "12." At that point, she turns over the pile, with the 8 face down on top. In this example, the pile would have five cards altogether.

Continued on next page

---

3. Once the pile is complete, she repeats instructions 1 and 2, working with the remaining cards. She keeps creating new piles until she runs out of cards.

If she runs out of cards while trying to complete a pile, she picks up all the cards in that incomplete pile.

The woman follows the instructions. When she is done, the entertainer turns around and asks her to give him the cards from her final, incomplete pile.

He sees that she has given him five cards, but he does not look to see which cards they are. He also sees that she has made six complete piles.

He then tells her to take the top card from each pile and add the numerical values of these cards together, without showing him the cards or telling him the sum.

She does this, and he then tells her the sum she got.

Your Task

Your task in this POW is to figure out what the sum was and how the entertainer figured it out.

Write-up

1. *Problem Statement*

2. *Process*

3. *Solution*

4. *Evaluation*

5. *Self-assessment*

Adapted from *MATHEMATICS: Problem Solving Through Recreational Mathematics,* by Averbach and Chein, Copyright © 1980 by W.H. Freeman and Company. Used with permission.

Heavy Flying

Linda Sue is a stunt pilot, but she has found that she can't make a living only doing stunts. So she has bought a transport plane from Philip. He agrees to help her set up her business.

Philip has two customers he no longer has time to serve and suggests that Linda Sue work for them delivering their merchandise. One is Charley's Chicken Feed and the other is Careful Calculators.

Continued on next page

Charley's Chicken Feed packages its product in containers that weigh 40 pounds and are 2 cubic feet in volume. Philip has been charging $2.20 a container.

Careful Calculators packages its materials in cartons that weigh 50 pounds and are 3 cubic feet in volume. Philip has been charging $3.00 a carton.

Philip has told Linda Sue that the plane can hold a maximum of 2000 cubic feet of materials and that the maximum weight it can carry is 37,000 pounds.

Charley's Chicken Feed and Careful Calculators have both told Linda Sue that they can give her as much business as she can handle. Of course, she wants to maximize the money she gets per flight so she can spend more time on stunt flying.

Your Task

Here is your task for now. (You'll finish the problem in class.)

1. Come up with several loads for Linda Sue that fit the constraints and figure out how much she will earn for each. (Assume that she charges the same rates that Philip did.)

2. Use variables and algebra to describe the constraints on what Linda Sue can carry.

A Strategy for Linear Programming

As preparation for solving the linear programming problem with six variables, Vanessa Niebla and Miguel Tinetti review the work they did in the Year 2 unit "Cookies."

River City's problem is somewhat like the problem that the Woos had in the Year 2 unit *Cookies*. Both are examples of **linear programming** problems, but *Meadows or Malls?* is more complicated because it involves six variables instead of only two.

Before tackling this six-variable problem, you will be reviewing what you know about two-variable linear programming. The goal is to develop a strategy that you might be able to adapt to the more general situation.

Programming and Algebra Reflections

Part I: Programming Reflections

In the Year 2 unit *Cookies,* you learned how to solve two-variable linear programming problems. You've now used ideas and methods from that unit to solve *Heavy Flying*.

To solve *Meadows or Malls?,* which has six variables, you need to generalize those methods. Answer these two questions to summarize what you know about two-variable problems as preparation for creating a generalization that works for more variables.

1. What type of information are you given in a two-variable linear programming problem, and what are you trying to do?

2. In as general terms as possible, what do you do to solve a linear programming problem in two variables?

Part II: Algebra Reflections

Solve each of these pairs of linear equations in two variables algebraically, and explain each step of the process.

3. $4x + y = 13$
$2x + y = 7$

4. $3x - 2y = 5$
$x + 3y = 9$

Ideas for Solving Systems

Many types of problems involve finding the common solution to a pair of linear equations, which is the same as finding the coordinates for the point where the graphs of the two equations intersect. Often, you can estimate the coordinates of this point by sketching the two graphs, but it's helpful to know some algebraic methods that will give you the exact solution.

No single method works best for every system of equations, but here are two common approaches. For simplicity, the examples have integer solutions, but the methods will work on any system that has a unique solution.

The "Setting y's Equal" Method

In this method, you solve both equations to get expressions for one variable in terms of the other. Then you set those expressions equal to each other. For instance, consider this pair of equations.

$$4x - y = 8$$

$$3x + y = 13$$

Adding y and subtracting 8 from both sides of the first equation, we get $4x - 8 = y$.

Subtracting $3x$ from both sides of the second equation, we get $y = 13 - 3x$.

At the point where the two lines meet, both of these equations hold true; that is, y is equal to both $4x - 8$ and $13 - 3x$, so $4x - 8 = 13 - 3x$.

Continued on next page

Solving, we get $x = 3$.

Substituting 3 for x in either $4x - 8$ or $13 - 3x$, we get $y = 4$.

You can check that $x = 3$, $y = 4$ is a solution for both of the original equations.

The Substitution Method

The idea in this method is to use one of the equations to express one of the variables in terms of the other and then to substitute that expression into the other equation. For instance, consider this pair of equations.

$$3x + 4y = 18$$

$$2x + y = 7$$

It's easiest to begin with the second equation because the coefficient of y is 1.

Subtracting $2x$ from both sides you get the equivalent equation $y = 7 - 2x$.

At the point where the graphs of the two original equations intersect, the coordinates must satisfy this new equation. Therefore, you can substitute $7 - 2x$ for y in the first equation. In other words, x must satisfy the equation

$$3x + 4(7 - 2x) = 18$$

Solving this equation gives $x = 2$.

Once you know $x = 2$ at the point of intersection, you can substitute 2 for x in the equation $y = 7 - 2x$ to get $y = 3$.

As before, you can check your solution by substituting the values for x and y in the original equations.

Programming Puzzles

1. A Nonroutine Routine

Skateboarder Lance Stunning is about to enter a free-style competition and is busy preparing his routine. His two key moves are the pool drop-in and the rail slide. Lance has to decide how many of each move he should include in the routine to maximize his score.

Lance figures he has the stamina to make at most 25 of these moves in his performance. He also knows that his performance can be at most three minutes long.

Each pool drop-in takes four seconds to perform, and each rail slide takes nine seconds. Lance also knows that if he includes more than 20 of either move, the judges will get bored, and he will get a poor score.

Version a: Suppose the judges give each pool drop-in 5 points and each rail slide 10 points. What combination of moves will give Lance the best possible score?

Version b: Suppose the judges give each pool drop-in 7 points and each rail slide 5 points. What combination of moves will give Lance the best possible score?

Version c: Suppose the judges give each pool drop-in 3 points and each rail slide 8 points. What combination of moves will give Lance the best possible score?

Continued on next page

2. Planning the Prom

Pam and Remy are organizing the junior prom. They plan to sell two types of tickets—individual tickets and couples tickets. The ballroom where the prom will be held holds a maximum of 400 people.

Pam is pretty opinionated. She believes the prom will be more successful when more people go as couples. So that at least half the people at the prom will be in couples, Pam and Remy decide that the number of individual tickets they sell should be at most twice the number of couples tickets.

Remy ordered door prizes to be handed out at the prom (one prize for each ticket, even if it's a couples ticket). Unfortunately, the supplier delivered only 225 prizes, and it's too late to get more, so they can sell a total of at most 225 tickets.

Version a: Suppose individual tickets sell for $22 and couples tickets sell for $30. How many of each type of ticket should they sell to maximize the money they take in?

Version b: Suppose individual tickets sell for $15 and couples tickets sell for $35. How many of each type of ticket should they sell to maximize the money they take in?

Version c: Suppose individual tickets sell for $30 and couples tickets sell for $20. How many of each type of ticket should they sell to maximize the money they take in?

Continued on next page

Interactive Mathematics Program

3. Working Two Jobs

Raj works as a health aide both at a hospital and at a neighborhood clinic. Because he is also going to school part-time, Raj can work no more than 20 hours per week.

Raj likes working at the clinic better than the hospital, so he always wants to work at least as many hours there as at the hospital. However, he wants to keep his job at the hospital in hopes of getting a better position there eventually. In order to keep the hospital job, he must work there at least four hours a week.

Version a: Suppose Raj gets $20 per hour working at the hospital and $15 at the clinic. How many hours should Raj work at each job to maximize his earnings?

Version b: Suppose Raj gets $17 per hour working at the hospital and $19 at the clinic. How many hours should Raj work at each job to maximize his earnings?

Version c: Suppose Raj gets $18 per hour working at the hospital and $16 at the clinic. How many hours should Raj work at each job to maximize his earnings?

Donovan Meets the Beatles

Aji and Sunshine want to make a tape of old songs from the 1960s and, as a public service, donate it to their school library to be broadcast during school picnics. Sunshine's parents were big fans of the 60's singer Donovan, and they named her after his song "Sunshine Superman." Aji's folks were devotees of the Beatles, and Aji and Sunshine have agreed that their tape will consist entirely of songs by Donovan and the Beatles.

Because Sunshine is named after a Donovan song, she wants to include at least as many Donovan songs on the tape as Beatles songs. Aji agrees, and in return, Sunshine agrees to include at least five Beatles songs.

To provide enough variety to make the tape interesting, they also decide that they should include at least 20 songs altogether.

Suppose Aji and Sunshine have to pay $11 in royalties for the rights to each Beatles song they use and $7 for each Donovan song. How many of each type song should they put on their tape in order to minimize their royalty costs?

Finding Corners Without the Graph

When a profit function is linear and the feasible region is a polygon, the profit function will always achieve its maximum at a corner point of the feasible region. But for problems involving three variables, drawing the feasible region can be difficult. (And it's impossible for more than three variables!)

So it's helpful to be able to locate the corner points without actually drawing the region. As preparation for more complex cases, consider the two-variable feasible region defined by these linear inequalities.

$$x + 2y \leq 8$$

$$2x + y \leq 13$$

$$y \leq 3$$

$$x \geq 0$$

$$y \geq 0$$

1. Each of these inequalities has a corresponding linear equation, whose graph is a straight line, and each corner point of the feasible region is the intersection of two of these lines. How many combinations of these equations are there, taking them two at a time?

2. For each of your combinations in Question 1, find the intersection point for the pair of lines. (If there is no intersection point, explain why not.)

3. Which of the intersection points from Question 2 are actually corner points of the feasible region defined by the inequalities? Explain how you know.

What Wood Would Woody Want?

Do you remember Woody from the *Shadows* unit? You may recall that he was very interested in trees, especially in measuring trees. Well, he has decided to develop his hobby into a trade and is opening a carpentry shop that makes tables and chairs.

The wood Woody buys is sold in terms of a unit called a *board foot,* which is based on boards with a standard thickness of 1 inch and a standard width of 1 foot. For example, a board that is 9 feet long, 1 inch thick, and 1 foot wide represents 9 board feet of lumber.

Woody has found that each chair requires 3 board feet of lumber and 2 hours of labor. Each table requires 7 board feet of lumber and 8 hours of labor. The profit he makes on each chair is $15, and the profit on each table is $45.

This week, Woody has 420 board feet of lumber and 400 hours of labor time available. (He doesn't do all of the work himself.) He wants to know how many chairs and how many tables he should make in order to maximize his profits.

Solve this problem using the general strategy for working on linear programming problems without drawing a feasible region. Use *C* for the number of chairs Woody makes and *T* for the number of tables. Explain your work carefully. (If you discover places where the strategy is unclear or doesn't seem to work correctly, make a note of them.)

Adapted with permission from the *Mathematics Teacher,* © May, 1991, by the National Council of Teachers of Mathematics.

Widening Woody's Woodwork

Consider a variation on the situation of Woody and his chairs and tables from *What Wood Would Woody Want?* Assume as before that each chair requires 3 board feet of lumber and 2 hours of labor and that each table requires 7 board feet of lumber and 8 hours of labor.

Now suppose Woody has expanded his operations so that he has 630 board feet of lumber and 560 hours of labor time available. Suppose also that Woody has changed his prices so that his profit on each chair is now $18 and his profit on each table is now $42.

Based on this new situation, how many chairs and how many tables should Woody make in order to maximize his profits?

More Equations

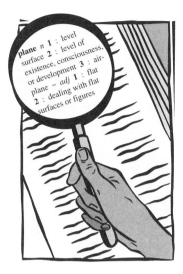

Part I: Pairs of Equations

In working on linear programming problems, you often need to solve pairs of linear equations. Use the substitution method or another algebraic method to try to solve each pair of equations, and show your work.

1. $5x + 3y = 7$ and $y = x - 3$
2. $3x + 2y = 11$ and $x + y = 4$
3. $5x - 3y = 5$ and $10x + 6y = 20$
4. $2x - 3y = 2$ and $4x - 6y = 9$
5. $2x + 4y = 12$ and $6x + 12y = 36$

Part II: Look It Up

The set of points in the xy-coordinate system is often referred to as the *coordinate plane,* and you will see that planes play an important role in this unit.

The word *plane* has a specific meaning in geometry, but it has other meanings in different contexts. Look up this word in the dictionary and find as many meanings as possible, including the geometric definition.

Equations, Points, Lines, and Planes

Oscar Monroy uses a model of the feasible region in three-dimensional space to identify coordinates while his teacher, Kevin Drinkard, looks on.

You have solved two-variable linear programming problems by looking at the intersections of lines using the *xy*-coordinate system. You will eventually get back to River City and its land-use problem. But first, you need to move to another level of complexity for graphs.

In the next portion of this unit, you will develop a coordinate system for three variables and see what the graph of a linear equation is in this new setting.

You will also look at how lines and planes intersect in order to generalize what you know about how lines intersect in the plane.

Being Determined

1. Do two lines *uniquely determine* a point? In other words, if ℓ_1 and ℓ_2 are lines in a plane, is there always one, and only one, point that lies on both of them?

   Explain your answer. In particular, if there are exceptions, state what they are and what happens in the exceptional cases. (*Reminder:* In mathematics, the word *line* always refers to a *straight* line, which does not have to be vertical or horizontal.)

2. Do two points *uniquely determine* a line? In other words, if P and Q are points, is there always one, and only one, line that goes through both P and Q?

   Explain your answer. In particular, if there are exceptions, state what they are and what happens in the exceptional cases.

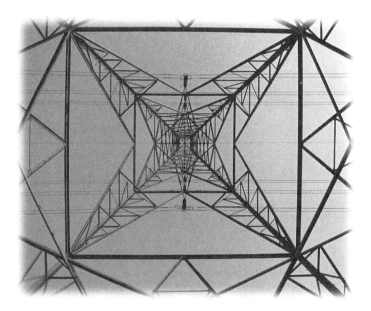

How Much After How Long?

1. The performing arts department put on its spring show both Friday and Saturday nights. The price of a ticket was the same both nights, and the cost of putting on the show was also the same both nights.

   The department made a profit of $400 on Friday when 100 people bought tickets and a profit of $500 on Saturday when 120 people bought tickets.

   a. How much did one ticket cost, and what was the cost of putting on the show each time?

   b. Let t represent the number of people who buy tickets and let p represent the amount of profit the performing arts department would make from selling that many tickets. Think of p as a function of t and find a rule for this function, expressing p in terms of t.

Continued on next page

2. Joey had already saved some money, but he decided to get a job and add his earnings to his savings so he could buy a car. After working 10 hours, he had a total of $210. After working 120 hours, he had $870.

   a. How much money did Joey make per hour, and how much money did he already have before he started working?

   b. Let h represent the number of hours Joey has worked and let m represent the amount of money he has accumulated altogether after h hours. Think of m as a function of h and find a rule for this function, expressing m in terms of h.

3. In Question 1, you had two combinations of ticket sales and profit.

   • Selling 100 tickets produced a $400 profit.

   • Selling 120 tickets produced a $500 profit.

   a. What were the two combinations in Question 2?

   b. In each question, having two combinations was enough information to allow you to find a rule that described the situation. What does this have to do with the activity *Being Determined*?

4. A line passes through the points $(2, 15)$ and $(7, 45)$. Find an equation for the line and explain how you got your answer.

The Points and the Equations

As you know, if P and Q are two distinct points in the plane, then there is a unique line that goes through them both. If the points are given as coordinate pairs in the xy-plane, then you may want to look for an equation whose graph is that line through the points.

1. For each of the pairs of points listed, find a linear equation whose graph will go through the two points. (Use x to represent the first coordinate and y to represent the second coordinate.)

   a. $(4, 9)$ and $(6, 13)$

   b. $(5, 13)$ and $(3, 7)$

   c. $(8, 8)$ and $(20, 14)$

   d. $(-2, 5)$ and $(1, -4)$

2. For each of the pairs of points in Questions 1a and 1b, create a word problem that would require the solver to find the equation. You can use Questions 1 and 2 of *Homework 8: How Much After How Long?* as sources of ideas for situations, or you can create your own situations.

The Three-Variable Coordinate System

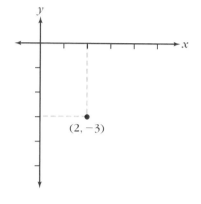

The familiar *xy*-coordinate system is used to represent pairs of numbers by points in the plane. For example, the diagram at the left shows how we might represent the combination of values $x = 2$ and $y = -3$.

A similar system can be used to represent *triples* of numbers. One common way to do this is to picture the *x*-axis and *y*-axis as "lying flat" and the *z*-axis as "coming out" perpendicular to that plane.

It's difficult to represent this system in two dimensions, but the diagram at the left below suggests one way to do this.

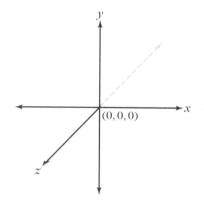

We consider the positive direction of the *z*-axis to be coming out of the page. The dashed line represents the negative portion of the *z*–axis.

As in the two-variable system, the point where the three axes meet is called the **origin** and represents the values $x = 0$, $y = 0$, and $z = 0$. We write this point simply as $(0, 0, 0)$.

In general, a triple of values is represented by going the appropriate distances in the appropriate directions from the origin.

Continued on next page

For instance, the point $(2, -3, 4)$ is found, as shown in the diagram at the right, by going two units to the right of the origin, 3 units down, and 4 units "toward you." This point represents the values $x = 2$, $y = -3$, and $z = 4$.

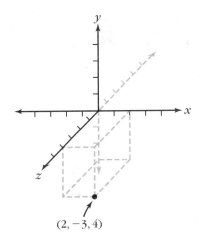

$(2, -3, 4)$

The collection of all points in this system is called the **three-dimensional coordinate system** and is often referred to simply as **3-space.** Because the world we live in is three-dimensional, this system is very useful in describing real-world phenomena, such as the position of an object in space.

Each pair of axes defines a plane, and these are known as the **coordinate planes.**

In the diagram at the right, the light green plane is called the *xy*-**plane,** the white plane is called the *xz*-**plane,** and the dark green plane is called the *yz*-**plane.**

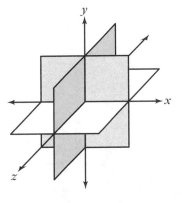

These planes divide 3-space into eight separate regions, known as **octants.** (The octants are analogous to the quadrants of the two-variable coordinate system.)

Although there is no standard numbering for all of the octants, the set of points whose coordinates are all positive is called the **first octant.**

10

What Do They Have in Common?

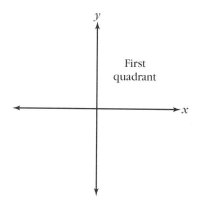

First quadrant

In the two-variable coordinate system (shown at the left), the points in the first quadrant share the fact that they have positive *x*-coordinates and positive *y*-coordinates.

Similarly, there are sets in the three-dimensional coordinate system whose points all have one or more characteristics in common.

Questions 1 through 8 describe various sets in geometric terms. For each of these sets, do two things.

• Give the coordinates for five specific points in the set.

• State what characteristic or characteristics the points in the set have in common, in terms of their coordinates.

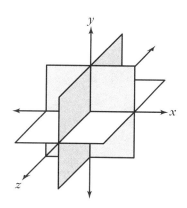

Use the accompanying diagram as a model of how the coordinate axes and coordinate planes are set up. The descriptions of the sets are based on the orientation of axes shown in this diagram.

1. The set of points in the *yz*-plane

2. The set of points in the *xz*-plane

3. The set of points on the *x*-axis

4. The set of points on the *z*-axis

5. The set of points above the *xz*-plane

6. The set of points behind the *xy*-plane

7. The set of points 1 unit to the left of the *yz*-plane

8. The set of points in the first octant

Trying Out Triples

You have been looking at the graphs of some special linear equations in three variables—namely, examples in which not all three variables appeared.

Tomorrow, you will be graphing the equation $x + y + \frac{1}{2}z = 4$, which is a linear equation that involves all three variables. As preparation, answer Questions 1 through 3 concerning the equation $x + y + \frac{1}{2}z = 4$.

1. Find a dozen or so different triples that are solutions to this equation.

2. Organize your solutions in some way that you think might be helpful in finding the graph of this equation.

3. Describe what you think this graph will look like, or make a sketch or model.

More Cookies

Do you remember Abby and Bing Woo? They were the owners of the bakery shop in the main problem from the Year 2 unit *Cookies*.

The Woos still make plain and iced cookies as they did in that problem. But now, by popular demand, they're also selling chocolate chip cookies.

Here's a reminder of the ingredients needed for the original plain and iced cookies.

- One dozen of the plain cookies requires 1 pound of cookie dough (and no icing).

- One dozen of the iced cookies requires 0.7 pounds of cookie dough and 0.4 pounds of icing.

Now you also need the information about the ingredients for the chocolate chip cookies.

- One dozen of the chocolate chip cookies requires 0.9 pounds of cookie dough and 0.15 pounds of chocolate chips (and no icing).

The Woos are limited by the amount of ingredients they have on hand.

- 120 pounds of cookie dough

- 32 pounds of icing

- 18 pounds of chocolate chips

In the past, the Woos were also limited by the amount of work time they had available. They now have other family members to help, so work time is no longer a limitation on how many cookies they can make. They have also bought more ovens, so oven space is no longer a limitation either.

Continued on next page

The Woos sell the plain cookies for $6.00 a dozen, and it costs them $4.50 a dozen to make those cookies. The iced cookies sell for $7.00 a dozen and cost $5.00 a dozen to make. The chocolate chip cookies sell for $10.00 a dozen and cost $7.75 a dozen to make.

As in the original situation, the Woos want to know how many dozens of each kind of cookie to make in order to maximize their profit.

Eventually, you will need to answer the Woos' question. For now, do this.

1. Write a set of constraints that express the situation just described using these variables.

   - P for the number of dozens of plain cookies

   - I for the number of dozens of iced cookies

   - C for the number of dozens of chocolate chip cookies

2. Find four different combinations of cookies that the Woos can make and find the total profit for each combination.

Just the Plane Facts

You've seen that two lines in a plane "usually" uniquely determine a point. That is, except for the special cases of parallel lines or two lines that are identical, two given lines will intersect in one and only one point.

Your task in this activity is to examine other cases of "determining." In each case, do two things.

- Describe the different ways in which the given objects can intersect.

- Explain your answers with diagrams, three-dimensional models, or other appropriate devices.

1. A line and a plane

2. Two planes

3. Three planes

4. Two lines (*Note:* Your work in Question 1 of *Being Determined* concerned lines that were *in the same plane.* Now think about the more general situation, in which the lines may or may not be in the same plane.)

5. Four planes

6. Any other combinations you'd like to investigate

Solving with Systems

You may be able to find the answers to these problems without using algebra. However, to help develop your algebraic skills for work with more difficult problems, you should define variables, write a system of equations, and use substitution to solve the systems for each problem.

1. Ming is a competitive surfer. (You may recall meeting Ming in the Year 2 unit *Is There Really a Difference?*)

   The two moves she used in her most recent competition are called an "off-the-lip" move and a "cutback." The particular wave she caught allowed her to do a total of six moves, and the judges awarded 6 points for each off-the-lip move and 8 points for each cutback. Ming got a total of 40 points.

   How many moves did she make of each type?

2. You may recall from *Programming Puzzles* that Pam and Remy were selling two types of tickets for the prom—individual tickets and couples tickets.

   Suppose they sold individual tickets for $10 and couples tickets for $18. Suppose further that they collected $1,500 from the sale of these tickets and that 160 people attended the event.

   How many tickets of each type were sold? (*Caution:* Don't forget that a couples ticket represents two people.)

Fitting a Line

Although a given line contains many points, a given *pair* of distinct lines determines a *unique* point, except when the lines are parallel. Similarly, although many lines go through a given point, a *pair* of distinct points always determines a *unique* line.

In *Being Determined,* you looked at these ideas from a geometric point of view. This assignment involves the *algebra* of finding the equation for a line that goes through two specific points.

Some Lines Through (1, 2)

First consider only the point $(1, 2)$. You can see that this point lies on the graph of the linear equation $y = 5x - 3$ by substituting 1 for x and 2 for y. Informally, we say that the line $y = 5x - 3$ "goes through" the point $(1, 2)$.

1. Show that the line $y = -5x + 7$ also goes through $(1, 2)$.

2. Find equations for two other lines that go through $(1, 2)$.

The Family of Lines Through (1, 2)

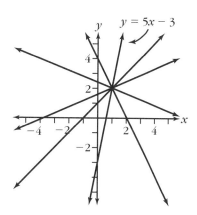

As the accompanying diagram suggests, there are infinitely many functions of the form $y = ax + b$ whose graphs go through $(1, 2)$. But exactly which linear functions are they? What values of a and b give lines through this point?

For instance, for the function $y = 5x - 3$, we have $a = 5$ and $b = -3$, so these values for a and b give a line through $(1, 2)$.

Continued on next page

3. a. Find the values of a and b for the equation $y = -5x + 7$.

   b. Find the values of a and b for each of the equations you found for Question 2.

   c. Look for a relationship between a and b that holds for all the lines that go through the point $(1, 2)$. Express this relationship as a linear equation involving a and b.

   Suggestion: If you are having trouble finding a relationship, find the equations for some more lines that go through $(1, 2)$, and compile a table of values for a and b. Then look for a pattern in your table.

The Family of Lines Through (–1, –6)

Now consider a second point, $(-1, -6)$. Again, as the diagram here suggests, there are infinitely many linear functions whose graphs go through that point.

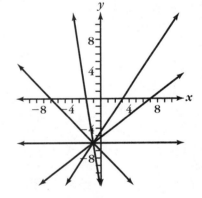

4. a. Find three examples of equations of the form $y = ax + b$ that go through this point.

   b. Find a linear equation involving a and b that must hold for any line $y = ax + b$ that goes through the point $(-1, -6)$. You might use a method like that suggested in Question 3c.

A Line Through Both Points

Now suppose you want a line $y = ax + b$ that goes through both points.

5. Find values for a and b so that the line $y = ax + b$ goes through both $(1, 2)$ and $(-1, -6)$.
   (*Hint:* Solve the pair of linear equations you got for Questions 3c and 4b.)

More Cookies

Renee Rice uses a three-dimensional model to present how planes and lines intersect.

In *Homework 12: More Cookies,* you were introduced to a linear programming problem in three variables involving the Woos and their bakery. In that assignment, you simply wrote the constraints and found some possible cookie combinations that the Woos could make.

Now you're ready to solve the problem, incorporating what you've learned about planes, linear equations in three variables, and the general strategy for solving linear programming problems.

SubDivvy

SubDivvy is a number game for two players. Here are the rules.

1. A starting number greater than 1—let's call it N—is chosen cooperatively by the two players.

2. Player 1 chooses a positive divisor of N that is different from N (that is, a number that divides "evenly" into N, so that the remainder is zero), and subtracts that divisor from N. The result of that subtraction is given to Player 2.

3. Player 2 works with the result of the subtraction just as Player 1 worked with N—by choosing a positive divisor of that number different from the number itself, and subtracting the chosen divisor from it. The result of the subtraction is given to Player 1.

4. Play continues, with players taking turns choosing divisors and subtracting, until the result reaches the number 1. The player who produces the result of 1 is the winner.

Here is a sample game, with explanations.

68	The number 68 is selected as the starting number N.
$-\,4$	Player 1 chooses 4, which is a divisor of 68, and subtracts.
64	The result of the subtraction is 64, which is given to Player 2.
$-\,16$	Player 2 chooses 16, which is a divisor of 64, and subtracts.
48	The result of the subtraction is 48, which is given to Player 1.

Continued on next page

-24 Player 1 chooses 24, which is a divisor of 48, and subtracts.

24 The result of the subtraction is 24.

-8 Player 2 chooses 8, which is a divisor of 24, and subtracts.

16 The result of the subtraction is 16.

-8 Player 1 chooses 8, which is a divisor of 16, and subtracts.

8 The result of the subtraction is 8.

-4 Player 2 chooses 4, which is a divisor of 8, and subtracts.

4 The result of the subtraction is 4.

-2 Player 1 chooses 2, which is a divisor of 4, and subtracts.

2 The result of the subtraction is 2.

-1 Player 2 chooses 1, which is a divisor of 2, and subtracts.

1 The result of the subtraction is 1, so the game ends, and Player 2 is the winner.

Your POW is to explore this game.

One important task is to explore the issue of who wins. Find whether there are certain starting numbers where the first player has a winning strategy—that is, a complete strategy by which the first player can win no matter what the second player does on any turn. Are there starting numbers where the second player has a winning strategy? Are there starting numbers where no player has a winning strategy? Which starting numbers are which?

Continued on next page

There are other questions to consider besides the issue of who wins. For instance, for different starting numbers, what can you say about the shortest game possible? The longest game possible? What generalizations can you make?

What are some other questions you can think of to investigate about this game?

Write-up

1. *Process*

2. *Solution*

3. *Evaluation*

4. *Self-assessment*

Adapted from *Foundations of Higher Mathematics: Exploration and Proof* (pages 6 & 7), by Daniel Fendel and Diane Resek. © 1990 Addison-Wesley Publishing Company Inc. Used by permission of Addison-Wesley Longman Inc.

The "More Cookies" Region and Strategy

In *Homework 12: More Cookies,* you were introduced to a more complex version of the original problem from the *Cookies* unit. We will refer to the situation in that assignment as "the *More Cookies* problem."

1. You have already developed a set of constraints for the *More Cookies* problem and seen that they are linear inequalities in three variables. You also have learned about setting up a coordinate system for equations involving three variables. In particular, you now know that the graph of a linear equation in three variables is a plane.

   Using that knowledge, give a general description of what the feasible region for the *More Cookies* problem should look like. (*Challenge:* Sketch or build a model of this region.)

2. Earlier in this unit, you developed a general strategy for solving two-variable linear programming problems. One element of that strategy was to identify corner points of the feasible region by finding the intersections of pairs of linear equations corresponding to the constraints.

   Explain how that part of the strategy could be adapted to work for linear programming problems involving three variables. (*Hint:* Think about what you learned in *Just the Plane Facts* about how planes intersect.)

Finishing Off the Cookies

Before leaving class, your group should develop a general plan for solving the *More Cookies* problem, that is, for finding the number of dozens of each type of cookie that will maximize the Woos' profit.

Your group should also decide on an assignment for each group member so that the group can quickly solve the *More Cookies* problem together tomorrow.

You may decide that each person should do a different piece of the problem for homework, or you may have several people doing the same thing as a check. It's up to you.

Your written work on this assignment has three parts.

1. State your group's general plan.

2. State your individual homework assignment as part of that plan.

3. Describe what you did and what conclusions you reached for your part of the plan.

Equations, Equations, Equations

Completing a three-variable linear programming problem will aid Randy Stevens, Emily Gubser, Kyle Abraham, and April Long in solving the more complex River City land-use problem.

You've seen that solving a linear programming problem involves solving systems of linear equations.

In the *More Cookies* problem, you had only three variables, and only one of the equations used more than one variable. Therefore, to solve the River City land-use problem, you're going to need to learn much more about solving such systems of equations. That's your task in the next portion of the unit.

Easy Does It!

In solving the *More Cookies* problem, you needed to find the common solution to some systems of three linear equations in three variables.

Those systems of equations were mostly simple ones, but real-life problems aren't always so straightforward. So here's a chance to learn something more about solving such systems. (In these problems, you should assume that there is no sales tax involved in the purchases.)

1. Consider this question.

   Will bought 4 packages of batteries and 1 package of blank tapes for $20.00. Tania bought 5 packages of batteries and 1 package of blank tapes for $23.00. How much does a package of batteries cost?

   You can probably answer this question without using equations, given that Will and Tania made almost the same purchases. But write down a pair of equations anyway, and explain how your intuitive reasoning about the problem could be expressed in terms of the equations.

Continued on next page

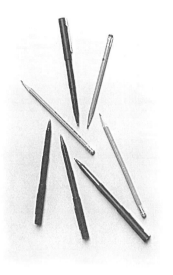

2. Here is a similar question.

Jennie bought 4 pens and 3 pencils for $3.75. Tanisha bought 4 pens and 6 pencils for $4.50. How much does a pencil cost and how much does a pen cost?

Again, you can probably answer this question without using equations, but write down a pair of equations anyway, and explain how your intuitive reasoning about the problem could be expressed in terms of the equations.

3. This problem is not quite as easy as Question 2, but the same sort of approach works fairly well.

Sanji bought 5 pears and 3 apples for $1.75. Ursula bought 10 pears and 7 apples for $3.80. How much does an apple cost?

Again, write down a pair of equations that express the situation, and explain how your intuitive reasoning about the problem could be expressed in terms of the equations.

Get Rid of Those Variables!

Read the situation described here and then move on to the questions. The situation probably sounds similar to the problems in *Homework 17: Easy Does It!*, but be sure to follow the instructions carefully after you read the initial information.

> *Erin bought 3 gallons of juice and*
> *7 pounds of carrots and spent $4.80.*
> *Jinho bought 5 gallons of juice and*
> *6 pounds of carrots and spent $6.30.*

1. Represent the information in the situation as a pair of linear equations.

2. a. Generate a list of at least ten more combinations of purchases whose cost is easy to figure out from the combinations you are given in this problem. (But don't figure out the price of a gallon of juice or a pound of carrots yet.)

   b. Represent each of the combinations from your list, with its cost, using an equation.

3. After you have created the list of equations in Question 2b, find a pair of equations in your list that makes it easy to see what the price of a gallon of juice or a pound of carrots is. Explain how to find these prices from your pair of equations.

   (If you don't find such a pair, create some more combinations, until getting the individual prices is as simple as it was on *Homework 17: Easy Does It!*)

Eliminating More Variables

Whenever you have a system of linear equations, you can create new ones by adding or subtracting two of those equations or by multiplying an equation by a constant. If the coefficients match up appropriately, then adding or subtracting equations makes one of the variables "disappear," giving an equation with one less variable.

This technique for solving systems of linear equations is called the **elimination method** (or **Gaussian elimination**).

Solve each of these pairs of equations using the elimination method. Be sure to show your work clearly.

1. $2a + 3b = 8$

   $4a + 9b = 22$

2. $4r + 3s = 18$

   $r + 2s = 7$

3. $2w + 3z = 10$

   $5w + 7z = 17$

4. $3p + 4q = 10$

   $5p - 4q = 6$

5. $-2c + 5d = 9$

   $3c + 2d = 15$

6. $2f - 6g = -16$

   $3f + 5g = 25$

Gardener's Dilemma

Part I: Leslie Returns

Leslie the landscape architect, whom you encountered
in *Orchard Hideout,* is back to ask for your help with
another problem.

There has been a drought, so Leslie would like to be able
to tell her clients how much water they will need for
their gardens.

She has divided the plants she uses into three general
categories—lawns, flowers, and shrubs. Her goal is
to determine how much water per square foot each
category requires.

Continued on next page

She looked up the water usage records for three families she worked for in the last drought. She knows that the amounts of water these families used at that time for each type of plant were adequate without being wasteful, so she'd like to reconstruct those amounts.

The table below shows the weekly water usage of these three families. Assume that the amount of water used per square foot of lawn, flowers, and shrubs is the same for each family.

	Number of square feet of lawn	Number of square feet of flowers	Number of square feet of shrubs	Number of gallons of water used
Family 1	900	120	40	1865
Family 2	0	160	800	180
Family 3	120	80	240	310

Define variables and write a system of equations that could be used to find the amount of water needed for a square foot of each category of plant. (You do not need to solve this system of equations.)

Part II: Elimination

Solve each of these systems using the elimination method.

1. $6c + 5d = 2$

   $2c + 7d = 22$

2. $5u + 9v = 13$

   $4u - 5v = 47$

3. $4x - 9y = -95$

   $18x + 20y = 480$

4. $-5r + 2s = -7$

   $3r - 4s = 3$

Elimination in Three Variables

Leslie's task in *Homework 19: Gardener's Dilemma* can be expressed by means of a system of three linear equations in three variables.

The elimination method you have used for two-variable systems can also be applied to three-variable systems, although the extra variable makes things a bit more complicated.

Because the coefficients in Leslie's equations are fairly large, that system isn't the best one for learning the method. Here are some simpler systems involving three linear equations and three variables. Solve each of them using the elimination method.

1. $4x + 2y + z = 9$

   $2x - y - z = 2$

   $x + 2y + 3z = 9$

2. $3u + v + w = 9$

   $u + v - w = 5$

   $u + 2v + w = 4$

3. $5r - s + 3t = -10$

   $-2r + 2s + t = 11$

   $r + s + t = 2$

More Equation Elimination

In this assignment, you will continue your work with the elimination method, trying to use that approach to solve each of these systems of linear equations in three variables.

1. $3a + 2b + 3c = 2$

   $2a + 5b - c = -3$

   $3b = -6$

2. $3u - v + 3w = 3$

   $2u - 4v + 5w = -10$

   $u + v + w = 1$

3. $x + y + z = 3$

   $x - y = 5$

   $y - z = -7$

4. $2d - e + f = 5$

   $d + 2e + f = 3$

   $3d + e + 2f = 8$

Equations and More Variables in Linear Programming

Sammie Liu works to refine her strategy for solving linear programming problems.

What do you do if one of your linear programming constraints is an equation instead of an inequality? What do you do if you have too many variables to make a graph?

In the next section of this unit, you will focus on two new linear programming problems, *Ming's New Maneuver* and *Eastside Westside Story*. The first addresses the issue of constraint equations, and the second extends all of the ideas about linear programming to four variables.

Ming's New Maneuver

Ming has finally perfected the tube ride and wants to use it along with her off-the-lip moves and cutbacks in her next competition.

The waves at this new beach are well suited for this move, but Ming cannot do the same move over and over, because she still needs to plan her ride to maximize her points.

In this competition, Ming must make exactly 20 moves. Also, because the sponsor of the event is a lipstick company, she is required to do at least three off-the-lip moves.

Ming decides that she should use at most 24 seconds for her tube rides and cutbacks. She also figures that the cutbacks will take 1 second each and that the tube rides will take 2 seconds each.

Here is the scoring system the judges have announced.

• Off-the-lip moves: 1 point each

• Cutbacks: 4 points each

• Tube rides: 5 points each

1. Set up a system of constraints for this problem, using L for the number of off-the-lip moves, C for the number of cutbacks, and T for the number of tube rides.

2. Determine how many of each type of move Ming should perform to maximize her point total.

Let Me Count the Ways

In solving the *More Cookies* problem, you needed to consider all combinations of constraints taken three at a time. (You may have realized that some of the resulting systems had no solution, so you could eliminate them immediately.)

This assignment illustrates some other situations in which you might want to make complete lists.

1. Paula goes into her favorite pizza place where there's a special price if she orders exactly two toppings on the pizza. (The two toppings have to be different.)

   The store has these eight toppings to choose from.

   - Anchovies
   - Mushrooms
   - Olives
   - Peppers
   - Onions
   - Sausage
   - Zucchini
   - Pineapple

   Make a complete list for Paula of all the combinations she has to choose from for her two-topping pizza. (You may recall a similar problem from the Year 1 unit *The Game of Pig*.)

   Note: It doesn't matter in what order the two choices are listed. For instance, you should consider "anchovies and mushrooms" to be the same choice as "mushrooms and anchovies."

Continued on next page

2. A certain school goes from seventh through twelfth grade. A Student Advisory Group has been elected that consists of six students, one from each grade level.

   a. Suppose the Student Advisory Group needs to pick a three-person committee to help plan the homecoming dance. Make a complete list of all the possible combinations that might be used in creating this committee.

   b. Suppose that before creating the committee, the group decides that the student representing the twelfth grade should definitely be on the committee (because this would be that class's last homecoming dance). What are all the possible committees now?

3. Pete works afternoons at the local grocery store. He's been there for a while, and he has enough seniority that he gets to choose which four afternoons he will work each week. (The store is open seven days a week.)

   Make a complete list of all his possible choices.

Three Variables, Continued

You know that the graph of a linear equation in three variables is a plane in 3-space. You also know that the intersection of three planes can be

• nothing

• a single point

• infinitely many points (either a line or a plane)

Each of these problems gives a system of three linear equations, so the graphs of the three equations are three planes. For each system, state which of the three types of intersection the graphs have, and justify your answer. If the intersection is a single point, find that point.

1. $a - b + 2c = 2$

   $2a + 2b - c = -3$

   $3a + b + c = 4$

2. $r + s + t = 2$

   $2r + 2s + 2t = 4$

   $3r + 3s + 3t = 6$

3. $u - v + w = 2$

   $u + v + w = 6$

   $u + v + 2w = 9$

4. $2x = 6$

   $3y + z = -7$

   $6x + 6y + 2z = 4$

Grind It Out

Solving systems of linear equations is an important part of various kinds of problems, including linear programming problems.

As the number of variables grows, the systems often become more difficult to solve. The central unit problem, *Meadows or Malls?,* involves six variables. This assignment gets you a bit closer to that level of complexity.

1. Solve this system of four linear equations in four variables.

$$2x + y - 3z + w = 6$$

$$x + y + 2z + w = -1$$

$$y - z + w = 0$$

$$x + z - w = 5$$

2. You know that two distinct lines "usually" intersect in a single point, so a system of two linear equations in two variables "usually" has a unique solution. Similarly, as you saw in *Just the Plane Facts,* three planes in 3-space will "usually" have a unique point of intersection, so a system of three linear equations in three variables "usually" has a unique solution. For more than three variables, it's no longer possible to draw diagrams or build models to see what's happening geometrically. Nevertheless, a system of *n* linear equations in *n* variables "usually" has a unique solution.

   Give the best explanation you can for why a system of four linear equations in four variables should "usually" have a unique solution.

Crack the Code

People have devised many kinds of secret codes to have private communications with each other, so that no one else can understand their messages.

Letter Substitution Codes

Many messages involve words. One of the most popular ways to encode a message of words is to substitute a different letter for each letter of the alphabet.

If the person who gets your message knows your system for replacing letters, it is easy to figure out your code. But even if that person does not know your system, it may not be too difficult to figure out your message, because of certain special letter combinations or the frequency with which certain letters occur.

A Letter-Number Code

This POW concerns codes for arithmetic problems rather than for word messages. To use such a code, you start with an arithmetic problem such as

$$\begin{array}{r} 35 \\ + 35 \\ \hline 70 \end{array}$$

To create a coded version of the problem, you replace each number with a letter, always using the same letter for a particular number. For example, you might replace 3 with A, 5 with D, 7 with O, and 0 with H. If you do this, the addition problem becomes

$$\begin{array}{r} AD \\ + AD \\ \hline OH \end{array}$$

(In using such a code, you need to be careful to distinguish between the number "0" and the letter "O.")

Continued on next page

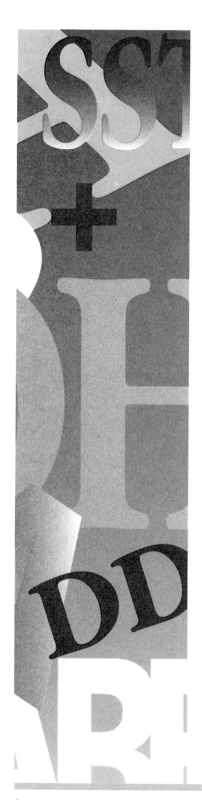

Figuring Out the Code

It's easy to make up such a code, and it's just as easy to figure out what the coded problem represents if you know the replacement system.

What's more interesting is trying to figure out the code merely by looking at the coded problem. That is, you are shown only the problem written with letters, and you have to figure out what the original arithmetic problem was.

The Rules

Problems like these usually follow certain rules.

- If a letter is used more than once in the same problem, it stands for the same number each time it is used.

- Different letters in the same problem always stand for different single-digit numbers.

- A letter standing for 0 never starts a number with more than one digit. For example, the final arithmetic problem can't have a number like "05" (but it can use "507" or "80" or even simply "0").

For some letter problems, it is very easy to reconstruct the original arithmetic problem; for others, it is not too hard; and for still others, it is quite difficult. Sometimes there is no possible answer, and sometimes there are many possible answers.

The Problems

See whether you can crack the codes for these problems based on the rules just listed. If you think there is only one right answer, prove it. If you think there are several

Continued on next page

possibilities, give them all and prove that there are no others. You will need to keep careful track of how you arrive at your answers.

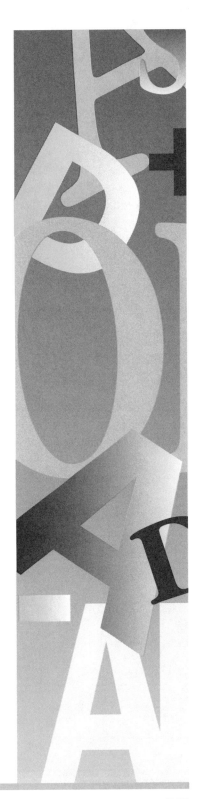

1. A B B
   −   A
   ———
      D D

2.   S S
   +   E E
   ———
      S S T

3.   A B
   +   B C
   ———
      A D E

4. *Note:* This one is *definitely* harder than the previous ones.

       S E N D
   + M O R E
   —————
   M O N E Y

5. Make up an example of your own that has a unique solution, and prove that the solution is unique.

Write-up

1. *Process and Solution:* Do a separate write-up for each of Questions 1 through 5, combining the *process* and *solution* components for each problem. Here, you must *prove* that your solutions are the only ones possible. You may find that explaining the process you went through to decipher the code will be part (or perhaps all) of your proof.

2. *Evaluation*

Constraints Without a Context

This system of linear constraints in three variables defines a feasible region.

 a. $x + 2y + z \leq 120$

 b. $3x + 2z \leq 12$

 c. $y + z = 8$

 d. $x \leq 10$

 e. $y \leq 7$

 f. $x \geq 0$

 g. $y \geq 0$

 h. $z \geq 0$

1. Create a list of systems of equations that you could solve so that the solutions to those systems would include all the corner points for this feasible region. (*Note:* If you can see that a particular system does not have a solution, you can omit it from your list, but you must explain how you know that it has no solution.)

2. Explain how you would use your list from Question 1 to determine what the *actual* corner points are for the feasible region.

Eastside Westside Story

For the longest time, River City had only one high school, known simply as River High, which was located on the west side of the river. But as the city grew on both sides of the river, the school became overcrowded.

Finally, the community decided to build a new school, on the east side of the river, which they called New High.

In order to promote the idea that both schools serve the entire city, the school board has mandated that at least half of the students attending New High should come from the west side of the river. (Of course, at least some students from the east side of the river will continue to attend River High.)

The school district has always provided buses to bring students to River High. Now the district needs to provide two sets of buses, and is anxious to minimize busing costs.

Here are some facts about the situation.

- There are 300 high school students living on the east side of the river and 250 living on the west side.

- New High can handle up to 350 students, and River High can handle up to 225.

- The average cost per day of busing students is

    √ $1.20 for each east-side student going to New High

    √ $2.00 for each east-side student going to River High

    √ $3.00 for each west-side student going to New High

    √ $1.50 for each west-side student going to River High

Continued on next page

The problem facing the River City school board (and you) is to find out how many students to send to each school so that the busing costs are minimized.

1. Write the constraints—that is, the equations and inequalities—that describe the problem, using these variables.

   - N_e is the number of New High students who live on the east side of the river.

   - R_e is the number of River High students who live on the east side of the river.

   - N_w is the number of New High students who live on the west side of the river.

   - R_w is the number of River High students who live on the west side of the river.

2. Write the "cost of busing" expression (using the variables from Question 1).

3. List the combinations of constraints you will need to examine.

4. Solve the various combinations of equations that you think you must look at.

5. Based on your solutions, write up your recommendation for the school board.

Fitting More Lines

In *Homework 14: Fitting a Line,* your task was to find a function of the form $y = ax + b$ whose graph would go through the points $(1, 2)$ and $(-1, -6)$.

You began by finding several pairs of values for a and b for which the graph went through $(1, 2)$. You then looked for a relationship between a and b for those pairs.

You probably reached this conclusion.

> The line $y = ax + b$ goes through $(1, 2)$ if and only if the coefficients a and b fit the equation $a + b = 2$.

For example, the values $a = 7, b = -5$ fit this equation, and the line $y = 7x - 5$ goes through $(1, 2)$.

In the case of the point $(1, 2)$, the relationship between a and b is a simple one. In this assignment, you have a similar task, but you will be using points for which the relationship may be somewhat harder to find.

A Line Through (3, 4) and (5, 1)

1. As with the other points you've considered, the diagram shown here illustrates that there are infinitely many functions of the form $y = ax + b$ whose graphs go through $(3, 4)$.

   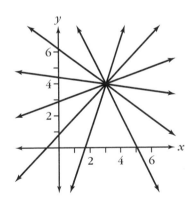

   a. Find an equation involving a and b which guarantees that the line $y = ax + b$ goes through the point $(3, 4)$.

   b. Find a pair of numbers for a and b that fit the equation you found in Question 1a. Check whether the resulting line $y = ax + b$ actually does go through the point $(3, 4)$.

Continued on next page

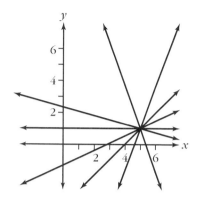

2. The diagram at the left shows some of the lines through (5, 1).

   a. Find an equation involving a and b which guarantees that the line $y = ax + b$ goes through the point (5, 1).

   b. Find a pair of numbers for a and b that fit the equation you found in Question 2a. Check whether the resulting line $y = ax + b$ actually does go through the point (5, 1).

3. The diagrams accompanying Questions 1 and 2 show some of the lines through (3, 4) and some of the lines through (5, 1). There is one line (not shown in either diagram) that goes through both points.

   a. Use the equations involving a and b from Questions 1a and 2a to find a line of the form $y = ax + b$ that goes through both (3, 4) and (5, 1).

   b. Verify that your answer is correct.

A Line Through (4, −1) and (−2, 7)

4. Use the method of Questions 1 through 3 to find a line of the form $y = ax + b$ that goes through both (4, −1) and (−2, 7).

Ages, Coins, and Fund-Raising

1. Pat is half as old as Quiana. Quiana is three years younger than Russell. Russell is nine years older than Pat.

   How old are Pat, Quiana, and Russell?

2. Uncle Ralph has 18 coins in his pocket. Each coin is either a quarter, a dime, or a nickel. The number of quarters and dimes combined is the same as the number of nickels. He has $2.10 worth of coins in his pocket.

   How many of each type of coin does he have?

3. Sonya, Dan, and Jesse were raising money for sports programs at their school. They had a pie sale, did car washes, and sold raffle tickets.

   They charged $8 for each pie, charged $4 for each car wash, and sold the raffle tickets for $1 each. Altogether, they collected $760.

   They spent $\frac{1}{2}$ hour on each car wash and 2 hours making each pie they sold, and these two activities required a total of 65 hours. They made twice as much money from the raffle tickets as they did from the car wash.

   How many pies did they sell? How many car washes did they do? How many raffle tickets did they sell?

Saved by the Matrices!

Tom Guidici and Loren Gowdy appreciate how helpful the graphing calculator is in addressing systems of linear equations with many variables.

You've seen that solving a linear programming problem requires solving many systems of linear equations. And the unit problem has six variables! As you saw in *Homework 23: Grind It Out,* even a four-variable system can be a huge amount of work.

Fortunately, your graphing calculator can help you out. But before you can use the calculator, you will learn about **matrices,** which are basically a notational shorthand for organizing a whole bunch of numbers.

Matrix Basics

A **matrix** is a rectangular array of numbers like

$$\begin{bmatrix} 1 & -8 & 3 & -1 & -4 \\ 5 & 3 & 4 & -1 & -6 \end{bmatrix} \text{ or } \begin{bmatrix} 1 & 1 & 1 \\ 2 & 1 & -1 \\ 3 & 2 & 2 \end{bmatrix} \text{ or } \begin{bmatrix} 6 & 17 & \frac{1}{8} & -368 \end{bmatrix}$$

The plural of matrix is **matrices.** (Matrices are often written using parentheses instead of brackets. Either is correct.)

The matrix $\begin{bmatrix} 1 & -8 & 3 & -1 & -4 \\ 5 & 3 & 4 & -1 & -6 \end{bmatrix}$ has two rows and

five columns, so it is called a **2-by-5 matrix.** (A row is horizontal; a column is vertical. For instance, the pair of numbers -4 and -6 form one column of this matrix.)

The numbers 2 and 5 are called the **dimensions** of the matrix. The phrase "2-by-5" is usually represented in writing as 2×5 (just as we refer in writing to a rectangle that is 3 inches wide and 4 inches long as a "3×4 rectangle"). The first dimension of a matrix tells how many rows the matrix has, and the second dimension tells how many columns it has.

Similarly, the matrix $\begin{bmatrix} 1 & 1 & 1 \\ 2 & 1 & -1 \\ 3 & 2 & 2 \end{bmatrix}$ has three rows

and three columns, so it is a 3×3 matrix, and the matrix $\begin{bmatrix} 6 & 17 & \frac{1}{8} & -368 \end{bmatrix}$ has one row and four columns, so it is a 1×4 matrix.

A matrix with the same number of rows as columns (such as a 3×3 matrix) is called a **square matrix.** A matrix with only one row is often called a **row vector,** and a matrix with only one column is often called a **column vector.** The individual numbers in a matrix are called **entries.**

Inventing an Algebra

Matrix Basics states what a matrix is and introduces you to the standard notation and terminology of matrices. There is also an *algebra* of matrices, which means there are rules for adding and multiplying them.

The purpose of this activity is to help you discover what those rules are by using matrices in meaningful contexts.

1. A matrix could be used to keep track of students' points in a class. Each row could stand for a different student: Clarabell, Freddy, Sally, and Frashy. The first column might be for homework, the second for oral reports, and the third for POWs.

   Suppose the results for the first grading period were represented by this table.

	Homework	Reports	POWs
Clarabell	18	54	30
Freddy	35	23	52
Sally	46	15	60
Frashy	60	60	60

   A matrix representation of this information might look like this.

   $$\begin{bmatrix} 18 & 54 & 30 \\ 35 & 23 & 52 \\ 46 & 15 & 60 \\ 60 & 60 & 60 \end{bmatrix}$$

Continued on next page

Here, in table form, are the students' points in each category for the second grading period.

	Homework	**Reports**	**POWs**
Clarabell	10	60	0
Freddy	52	35	58
Sally	42	20	48
Frashy	60	60	60

a. Write these second-grading-period scores in a matrix.

b. Figure out each student's total points *in each assignment category* for the two grading periods combined, and write the totals in matrix form.

c. Congratulations! If you completed Question 1b, you have added two matrices. Based on your work, write an equation showing two matrices being added to give the matrix you got in Question 1b.

2. The Woos' bakery shop is open six days a week.

Last week, for chocolate chip cookies, they sold 30 dozen on Monday, 25 dozen on Tuesday, 27 dozen on Wednesday, 23 dozen on Thursday, 38 dozen on Friday, and 52 dozen on Saturday.

For plain cookies, they sold 30 dozen on Monday, 28 dozen on Tuesday, 20 dozen on Wednesday, 25 dozen on Thursday, 35 dozen on Friday, and 45 dozen on Saturday.

For iced cookies, they sold 45 dozen on Monday, 32 dozen on Tuesday, 40 dozen on Wednesday, 38 dozen on Thursday, 48 dozen on Friday, and 70 dozen on Saturday.

Continued on next page

a. Use a matrix to represent the Woos' sales. Let each row be a different kind of cookie and each column be a different day of the week.

b. Make up sales numbers for the Woos for a second week. Show your sales in a matrix similar to that in Question 2a.

c. Add the Woos' sales for the two weeks and show the totals in a matrix similar to those in Questions 2a and 2b.

d. Write the matrix addition equation that corresponds to your work.

3. Which of the matrix sums shown here do you think make sense? Find those sums and explain why you think the others don't make sense.

a.
$$\begin{bmatrix} 1 & 5 & 0 & -6 \\ 2 & -2 & 4 & 1 \\ 0 & 1 & -3 & 1 \end{bmatrix} + \begin{bmatrix} 8 & -4 & 0 & 3 \\ 3 & 2 & 4 & 5 \\ 1 & -3 & 3 & 6 \end{bmatrix}$$

b.
$$\begin{bmatrix} 1 & 5 & 0 & -6 \\ 2 & -2 & 4 & 1 \end{bmatrix} + \begin{bmatrix} 8 & -4 & 0 \\ 3 & 3 & 2 \\ 4 & 5 & 1 \end{bmatrix}$$

c. $\begin{bmatrix} -3 & 7 & 9 \end{bmatrix} + \begin{bmatrix} 7 & -3 & 5 \end{bmatrix}$

d. $\begin{bmatrix} 5 & -4 & 2 & 1 \end{bmatrix} + \begin{bmatrix} 4 \\ -2 \\ 7 \\ 1 \end{bmatrix}$

4. What has to be true of two matrices for it to make sense to add them together?

5. Describe a rule for adding any matrices that fit your condition from Question 4.

Fitting Quadratics

In *Homework 14: Fitting a Line* and *Homework 25: Fitting More Lines,* your task was to find a linear function through a particular pair of points. That is, you were asked to find coefficients *a* and *b* so that the line $y = ax + b$ would go through the given points.

In this assignment, you move from linear functions to another important category—the family of *quadratic functions.* A quadratic function has the form $y = ax^2 + bx + c$. In this expression, the coefficients *a, b,* and *c* can be any three numbers, not necessarily different, except that *a* cannot be zero. (If $a = 0$, the function is linear.) (*Reminder:* The graph of a quadratic equation is a shape called a *parabola.*)

As you might suppose, because a quadratic function has three coefficients, it generally takes three points on its graph to determine the function. In each of Questions 1 through 3, you will consider all the parabolas going through a particular point. Question 4 asks you to put the information from those questions together.

1. The diagram here shows some of the parabolas that go through the point $(1, 6)$.

   a. Verify that the parabola defined by the equation $y = 3x^2 + 2x + 1$ goes through $(1, 6)$.

   b. Find at least two other possible choices of values for *a, b,* and *c* so that the parabola $y = ax^2 + bx + c$ goes through the point $(1, 6)$.

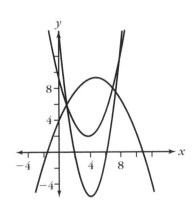

Continued on next page

c. Find an equation involving *a*, *b*, and *c* that holds true for every parabola $y = ax^2 + bx + c$ that goes through the point $(1, 6)$. (*Hint:* Substitute the values $x = 1$ and $y = 6$.)

2. Next, consider the set of parabolas that go through the point $(3, 8)$. Find an equation involving *a*, *b*, and *c* that holds true for every parabola $y = ax^2 + bx + c$ that goes through $(3, 8)$.

3. Find an equation involving *a*, *b*, and *c* that holds true for every parabola $y = ax^2 + bx + c$ that goes through $(5, 2)$.

4. a. Use the equations you found in Questions 1c, 2, and 3 to find a parabola that goes through all three points, $(1, 6)$, $(3, 8)$, and $(5, 2)$. That is, find values for *a*, *b*, and *c* so that the parabola $y = ax^2 + bx + c$ goes through all three points.

   b. Is your solution to Question 4a unique? Explain.

Flying Matrices

You've seen that there is a natural way to add matrices. Namely, if the matrices have the same dimensions, you simply add the corresponding entries. (If the matrices have different dimensions, you can't add them.)

Defining multiplication of matrices is harder, and the definition is somewhat arbitrary. The arithmetic in the questions in this activity will be the basis for deciding what might make sense in defining multiplication of matrices.

1. In *Homework 2: Heavy Flying,* you were given these facts about the materials that Linda Sue transports.

   - Charley's Chicken Feed packages its product in containers that weigh 40 pounds and are 2 cubic feet in volume.

   - Careful Calculators packages its materials in cartons that weigh 50 pounds and are 3 cubic feet in volume.

   Organize this information into a matrix and label your rows and columns to show what the numbers represent.

2. Suppose that on Monday, Linda Sue transported 500 containers of chicken feed and 200 cartons of calculators. Put those facts into a matrix.

3. Use the information in your two matrices to find out the total weight carried and the total volume used on Monday. Put those two answers into a matrix.

Continued on next page

4. Explain how you used the information in the matrices you created in Questions 1 and 2 to calculate the numbers for Question 3.

5. Suppose that on Tuesday, Linda Sue transported 400 containers of chicken feed and 300 cartons of calculators. Combine this information with the data from Question 2 to form a 2 × 2 matrix showing exactly what she carried on Monday and on Tuesday.

6. Combine the information in your answers to Questions 1 and 5 to find the total weight carried and the total volume used on Monday and on Tuesday. (Find separate totals for each day.) Put all of that information into a matrix.

7. Explain how you calculated the numbers for your matrix in Question 6.

Matrices in the Oven

The Woos' bakery provides another example for multiplying matrices. The problems in this assignment are similar to those in *Flying Matrices*.

Pay careful attention to the arithmetic involved in answering the questions.

For this assignment, you can ignore the constraints from the *More Cookies* problem, but the facts about the ingredients remain the same.

- One dozen of the plain cookies requires 1 pound of cookie dough (and no icing or chocolate chips).

- One dozen of the iced cookies requires 0.7 pounds of cookie dough and 0.4 pounds of icing (and no chocolate chips).

- One dozen of the chocolate chip cookies requires 0.9 pounds of cookie dough and 0.15 pounds of chocolate chips (and no icing).

1. Put all of this information into a matrix. Be sure to label your rows and columns.

2. Suppose that on Wednesday, the Woos made 30 dozen plain cookies, 45 dozen iced cookies, and 30 dozen chocolate chip cookies; and on Thursday, they made 28 dozen plain cookies, 32 dozen iced cookies, and 25 dozen chocolate chip cookies.

   Put all of this information into a matrix.

Continued on next page

3. Combine the information in your answers to Questions 1 and 2 to create a matrix that shows the total amount *of each ingredient* that was used on Wednesday and on Thursday.

4. Describe how you calculated the numbers for your matrix in Question 3.

Fresh Ingredients

The Woos buy their ingredients fresh each day. They shop at two markets, and the prices are slightly different at each.

It takes too much time for them to go to both markets, so each day they have to decide where to shop, depending on what they are baking that day.

The Woos' baking plan for Wednesday and Thursday is the one described in *Homework 28: Matrices in the Oven*. It can be represented by this matrix.

$$
\begin{array}{c}
 \\
\text{Wed} \\
\text{Thurs}
\end{array}
\begin{array}{ccc}
\text{plain} & \text{iced} & \begin{array}{c}\text{choc}\\\text{chip}\end{array}
\end{array}
\left[
\begin{array}{ccc}
30 & 45 & 30 \\
28 & 32 & 25
\end{array}
\right]
$$

Here, for example, the first "30" means that they will make 30 dozen plain cookies on Wednesday.

You also need the information in this *ingredient matrix*.

$$
\begin{array}{c}
 \\
\text{plain} \\
\text{iced} \\
\text{choc chip}
\end{array}
\begin{array}{ccc}
\text{dough} & \text{icing} & \begin{array}{c}\text{choc}\\\text{chips}\end{array}
\end{array}
\left[
\begin{array}{ccc}
1 & 0 & 0 \\
0.7 & 0.4 & 0 \\
0.9 & 0 & 0.15
\end{array}
\right]
$$

Here, for example, the entry "0.7" means that the Woos need 0.7 pounds of cookie dough for each dozen iced cookies.

Now, if the Woos shop at the Farmer's Market, their costs for the different components of their cookies are

cookie dough: 30¢/pound

icing: 20¢/pound

chocolate chips: 32¢/pound

Continued on next page

If they shop at the Downtown Grocery, their costs are

cookie dough: 29¢/pound

icing: 28¢/pound

chocolate chips: 22¢/pound

(The prices at the stores don't change from Wednesday to Thursday.)

The Woos want to know what it would cost to do all their Wednesday shopping at the Farmer's Market or to do all of it at the Downtown Grocery. They want similar information for Thursday.

1. Put all of the pricing information for the two markets into a single matrix. Set up your matrix in a way that will allow you to multiply matrices to get the cost information the Woos need.

2. Use your matrices to help them decide which market to shop at on Wednesday and which to shop at on Thursday.

Calculators to the Rescue

You've seen that multiplying matrices can involve a lot of cumbersome arithmetic. But even without matrices, you would still have to do the same arithmetic in order to solve problems like that in *Homework 29: Fresh Ingredients*. And this type of computation is done in businesses every day.

Fortunately, you can avoid all this arithmetic simply by entering the information as matrices in a graphing calculator and letting the calculator do the work.

1. The Woos' baking plan is given by the matrix

$$\begin{array}{c} \\ \\ \text{Wed} \\ \text{Thurs} \end{array} \begin{array}{ccc} & & \text{choc} \\ \text{plain} & \text{iced} & \text{chip} \\ \left[\begin{array}{ccc} 30 & 45 & 30 \\ 28 & 32 & 25 \end{array}\right] \end{array}$$

Give this matrix a name and enter it into your calculator.

2. The amount of each ingredient for each type of cookie is given by the matrix

$$\begin{array}{c} \\ \\ \text{plain} \\ \text{iced} \\ \text{choc chip} \end{array} \begin{array}{ccc} & & \text{choc} \\ \text{dough} & \text{icing} & \text{chips} \\ \left[\begin{array}{ccc} 1 & 0 & 0 \\ 0.7 & 0.4 & 0 \\ 0.9 & 0 & 0.15 \end{array}\right] \end{array}$$

Enter this matrix into your calculator (giving it a name different from the one you used in Question 1).

Continued on next page

3. The costs of the ingredients at each market are given by the matrix

	Frmr Mkt	Dntn Groc
dough	30	29
icing	20	28
choc chips	32	22

Enter this matrix into your calculator (giving it yet another name).

4. In *Homework 29: Fresh Ingredients,* you found a matrix showing how much all their ingredients would cost the Woos at each market on each of Wednesday and Thursday. Check that result using the graphing calculator.

Make It Simple

1. Write instructions explaining how to multiply two 3 × 3 matrices (using pencil and paper, not a graphing calculator). Make your instructions very clear.

2. Give your instructions to someone who has not learned to multiply matrices. See whether that person can use your instructions to multiply two 3 × 3 matrices that are different from the ones you used in your instructions.

3. Describe any difficulties the person may have had in following your instructions, and indicate what may have been wrong with the instructions.

4. Revise your instructions as necessary based on your experience.

Back and Forth

You have seen that a single linear equation can be written as a matrix equation. More specifically, the equation can be represented as a statement that the product of two matrices is a certain number. (Technically, the product is a 1×1 matrix, but we usually think of it as just a number.)

For example, the equation

$$5x + 3y + 7z = 10$$

states that the product of the row matrix $\begin{bmatrix} 5 & 3 & 7 \end{bmatrix}$ and

the column matrix $\begin{bmatrix} x \\ y \\ z \end{bmatrix}$ is equal to 10. Thus, the original

equation $5x + 3y + 7z = 10$ says the same thing as the matrix equation

$$\begin{bmatrix} 5 & 3 & 7 \end{bmatrix} \begin{bmatrix} x \\ y \\ z \end{bmatrix} = 10$$

Continued on next page

Now suppose you are looking at a *system* of linear equations, such as this one.

$$5x + 3y + 7z = 10$$

$$2x + y - z = 1$$

$$3x + 2y + z = 4$$

1. As a group, develop a way to write this entire system of equations as a single matrix equation. (*Hint:* Think of the numbers on the right of the equal signs as forming a column vector.)

2. Now, turn the process around by writing this matrix equation as a pair of linear equations.

$$\begin{bmatrix} 3 & -2 \\ 1 & -6 \end{bmatrix} \begin{bmatrix} u \\ v \end{bmatrix} = \begin{bmatrix} 2 \\ 1 \end{bmatrix}$$

For the rest of these problems, either turn the system of linear equations into a single matrix equation or write the matrix equation as a system of linear equations. *You do not have to solve any of these equations!*

3. $3a - 2b = 7$

   $-4a + 5b = 9$

4. $\begin{bmatrix} 1 & 0 \\ -2 & 3 \end{bmatrix} \begin{bmatrix} r \\ s \end{bmatrix} = \begin{bmatrix} 2 \\ -3 \end{bmatrix}$

5. $3c = 4$

   $-c + 2d = -5$

6. $\begin{bmatrix} 1 & -1 & 2 \\ 0 & 3 & 0 \\ 3 & -3 & 1 \end{bmatrix} \begin{bmatrix} e \\ f \\ g \end{bmatrix} = \begin{bmatrix} 2 \\ -4 \\ 1 \end{bmatrix}$

7. $3x + 2y - z = 4$

   $3y + 2z = 0$

   $5x - 3z = 1$

Matrices and Linear Systems

A system of linear equations can be expressed as a single matrix equation, which will look like

$$[A] \, [X] = [B]$$

where $[A]$ is the **coefficient matrix** of the system of linear equations and $[B]$ is a column matrix made up of the numbers on the right of the equal signs in the linear equations. (This is sometimes called the **constant term matrix.**) The matrix $[X]$ is a column matrix made up of the different individual variables in the system of linear equations.

For example, for the pair of equations

$$3a - 2b = 7$$

$$-4a + 5b = 9$$

the coefficient matrix $[A]$ is $\begin{bmatrix} 3 & -2 \\ -4 & 5 \end{bmatrix}$, the constant term matrix $[B]$ is $\begin{bmatrix} 7 \\ 9 \end{bmatrix}$, and $[X]$ is the column matrix $\begin{bmatrix} a \\ b \end{bmatrix}$.

Solving the pair of equations is the same as finding values for the entries a and b so that

$$\begin{bmatrix} 3 & -2 \\ -4 & 5 \end{bmatrix} \begin{bmatrix} a \\ b \end{bmatrix} = \begin{bmatrix} 7 \\ 9 \end{bmatrix}$$

In other words, any system of linear equations can be expressed as a matrix equation. Similarly, an appropriate matrix equation $[A] \, [X] = [B]$ (where $[X]$ is a matrix of variables) can be interpreted as a system of linear equations.

Solving the
Simplest

1. Solve each of these matrix equations. You will probably want to turn each one into a system of linear equations.

a. $\begin{bmatrix} 1 & 2 \\ 3 & 4 \end{bmatrix} \begin{bmatrix} w \\ z \end{bmatrix} = \begin{bmatrix} 6 \\ 16 \end{bmatrix}$

b. $\begin{bmatrix} 1 & 3 \\ 0 & 2 \end{bmatrix} \begin{bmatrix} r \\ s \end{bmatrix} = \begin{bmatrix} 7 \\ 2 \end{bmatrix}$

c. $\begin{bmatrix} 2 & 0 \\ 0 & 3 \end{bmatrix} \begin{bmatrix} u \\ v \end{bmatrix} = \begin{bmatrix} 8 \\ 15 \end{bmatrix}$

2. Compare the examples in Questions 1a through 1c and decide which coefficient matrix led to the most easily solved system of linear equations.

3. Find the 2×2 coefficient matrix that will give the system of linear equations that is the absolutely easiest to solve. Explain your choice.

Things We Take for Granted

We often take for granted all sorts of details about mathematics. For instance, properties like $8 \cdot 5 = 5 \cdot 8$ seem so natural and obvious that we sometimes don't even think about them.

In this assignment, you will consider two properties that are true for numbers and explore whether similar properties hold true for matrices. Here, you should consider only 2×2 matrices.

1. The Commutative Property of Multiplication

The **commutative property** of multiplication for numbers is the property illustrated by the example $8 \cdot 5 = 5 \cdot 8$. More generally, according to this property, you get the same answer if you change the order of the quantities you are multiplying. We can express this property in symbols by the equation $ab = ba$.

Does a similar property hold true for multiplication of matrices? See if you can find a counterexample.

2. The Associative Property of Multiplication

According to the **associative property** of multiplication for numbers, regrouping the factors in a product does not change the result. For instance, we have $(3 \cdot 4) \cdot 5 = 3 \cdot (4 \cdot 5)$. The left side is $12 \cdot 5$, and the right side is $3 \cdot 20$, so both sides are equal to 60.

Does a similar property hold true for multiplication of matrices? See if you can find a counterexample.

Finding an Inverse

You have seen that you can solve a matrix equation like

$$\begin{bmatrix} 1 & 2 \\ 3 & 5 \end{bmatrix} \begin{bmatrix} w \\ z \end{bmatrix} = \begin{bmatrix} 2 \\ 1 \end{bmatrix}$$

by first finding a matrix $[C]$ that fits the equation

$$[C] \begin{bmatrix} 1 & 2 \\ 3 & 5 \end{bmatrix} = \begin{bmatrix} 1 & 0 \\ 0 & 1 \end{bmatrix}$$

If there is such a matrix $[C]$, it is called the **multiplicative inverse** of $\begin{bmatrix} 1 & 2 \\ 3 & 5 \end{bmatrix}$.

To look for this inverse, suppose that $[C]$ is the matrix $\begin{bmatrix} r & s \\ t & u \end{bmatrix}$, so the equation defining $[C]$ becomes

$$\begin{bmatrix} r & s \\ t & u \end{bmatrix} \begin{bmatrix} 1 & 2 \\ 3 & 5 \end{bmatrix} = \begin{bmatrix} 1 & 0 \\ 0 & 1 \end{bmatrix}$$

1. Multiply out the product $\begin{bmatrix} r & s \\ t & u \end{bmatrix} \begin{bmatrix} 1 & 2 \\ 3 & 5 \end{bmatrix}$ to get a matrix with entries in terms of r, s, t, and u.

2. Use the fact that the product in Question 1 is equal to $\begin{bmatrix} 1 & 0 \\ 0 & 1 \end{bmatrix}$ to get a system of linear equations involving r, s, t, and u.

3. Solve the equations from Question 2 to find the values of r, s, t, and u.

4. a. Use the results from Question 3 to write the matrix $[C]$.
   b. Check your work by finding the product $[C] \begin{bmatrix} 1 & 2 \\ 3 & 5 \end{bmatrix}$.

Inverses and Equations

1. You know that some systems of linear equations have unique solutions, some have no solutions, and some have infinitely many solutions. For each of the systems here, either find the unique solution or explain why there is not a unique solution.

   a. $x + 2y = 4$

      $3x + 4y = 8$

   b. $x + 2y = 2$

      $3x + 4y = 1$

   c. $x + 2y = 4$

      $2x + 4y = 8$

   d. $x + 2y = 2$

      $2x + 4y = 1$

2. The matrices in Questions 2a and 2b are each the coefficient matrix for two of the systems of equations in Question 1. For each of these matrices, either find the inverse or explain why there is no inverse.

   a. $\begin{bmatrix} 1 & 2 \\ 3 & 4 \end{bmatrix}$

   b. $\begin{bmatrix} 1 & 2 \\ 2 & 4 \end{bmatrix}$

3. Explain how your results in Question 2 are related to those in Question 1.

4. In general, which 2 × 2 matrices have inverses and which do not? What is the connection between a system of equations and whether a matrix has an inverse?

Calculators Again

You have seen that a graphing calculator can be used to multiply matrices. Graphing calculators have another wonderful use: They can calculate the multiplicative inverse of a matrix when the matrix is invertible (as long as the dimensions of the matrix are not too large for the calculator's capacity). And it's easy to do this once you have the matrix in the calculator's memory.

Try to solve these linear systems without doing any arithmetic, letting the graphing calculator do all the hard work for you. You should check your solutions, at least for the first system, to make sure you are doing the process correctly.

1. $5d + 2e = 11$

   $d + e = 4$

2. $2r + 3s - t = 3$

   $r - 2s + 4t = 2$

   $4r - s + 7t = 8$

3. $4w + x + 2y - 3z = -16$

   $-3w + x - y + 4z = 20$

   $-w + 2x + 5y + z = -4$

   $5w + 4x + 3y - z = -10$

4. $a + b + c + d + e + f = 30$

   $2a + 3b - 6c + 4d - e + f = 8$

   $5a + 4b + 3c - d + 5e - 2f = 34$

   $2a - 3b + 8c - 6d + e + 4f = 38$

   $6a + 2b + 7c - 5d - 3e - 2f = -42$

   $-5a + 8b - 5c + 3d - 9e + 4f = -18$

Fitting Mia's Bird Houses

Do you remember Mia and her bird houses (from the Year 1 unit *The Pit and the Pendulum*)? Perhaps not, but here's the information from that situation.

Mia and her friends had spent the semester building bird houses, and now they were painting them. After one hour, they had painted two bird houses, and after three hours, they had painted six bird houses. Also, after five hours, they had painted eight bird houses.

1. Plot the data about bird house painting, using *number of hours* for the *x*-axis and *number of bird houses* for the *y*-axis.

2. Explain why there is no linear function that fits the data perfectly.

3. Find a quadratic function that does fit the data perfectly. That is, find specific numbers for *a, b,* and *c* so that all three data points from the bird-house situation fit the equation $y = ax^2 + bx + c$.

4. What do you think about the usefulness of the function from Question 3 in this situation?

Solving Meadows or Malls?

Jon Honn and Rodolfo Contreras make sure the list of combinations each developed is complete before they begin to solve the unit problem.

Congratulations! You are now ready to solve the unit problem.

It's not going to be easy, because there are so many constraints and so many variables, but careful work and a few shortcuts can help you complete the task.

This final portion of the unit also includes preparation of unit portfolios. Because this unit involves so many ideas, your work on the unit portfolio is spread out over several assignments.

Getting Ready for *Meadows or Malls?*

About a year or two ago (it may seem), you started working on a problem called *Meadows or Malls?* You now have all the tools to solve that problem, although it still will take some work to answer the main question in that problem.

As you have seen, the *Meadows or Malls?* problem has 12 constraints, of which four are equations and eight are inequalities.

For your convenience, here they are again.

$$\text{I} \qquad G_R + G_D = 300$$

$$\text{II} \qquad A_R + A_D = 100$$

$$\text{III} \qquad M_R + M_D = 150$$

$$\text{IV} \quad G_D + A_D + M_D \geq 300$$

$$\text{V} \qquad A_R + M_R \leq 200$$

$$\text{VI} \qquad A_R + G_D = 100$$

$$\text{VII} \qquad G_R \geq 0$$

$$\text{VIII} \qquad A_R \geq 0$$

$$\text{IX} \qquad M_R \geq 0$$

$$\text{X} \qquad G_D \geq 0$$

$$\text{XI} \qquad A_D \geq 0$$

$$\text{XII} \qquad M_D \geq 0$$

Continued on next page

That gives a lot of combinations to check to find corner points for the feasible region. Your task in this assignment is to list all the combinations you need to check. You should refer to the constraints by number in listing your combinations.

As you do so:

* Remember that the four equations must be part of every combination.

* Look for ways to reduce your list (without actually solving any of the systems). For instance, it is possible to prove from the constraints that certain of the variables can't be zero. Once you do that, you can eliminate some of constraints VII through XII from consideration.

Meadows or Malls?
Revisited

River City has three parcels of land to work with.

- 300 acres of farm land willed to the city by Mr. Goodfellow

- 100 acres from the U.S. government from a closed army base

- 150 acres of land formerly leased for mining

The city needs to decide how much of each parcel to use for recreation and how much to use for development, based on several constraints.

Your Assignment

Imagine that your group is a consulting team and that the city manager has come to you for help. Not only should you give her an answer, but you should try to convince her that you have the best possible answer, so that she will pick your group in the future when the city needs help again.

Your assignment is to prepare a group report for the city manager. Your report should include three parts.

- An answer to the city's dilemma

- An explanation for the city manager that will convince her that your solution will cost the least

- Any graphs, charts, equations, or diagrams that are needed as part of your explanation

As part of your work on this assignment, you will probably want to review what you already know about the problem based on your notes and previous assignments.

Beginning Portfolios—Part I

This unit has involved several closely related ideas.

• Graphing linear equations in three variables

• Solving systems of linear equations in three variables

• Finding intersections of planes in 3-space

1. Summarize how these ideas are related. In particular, focus on these two questions and how they are connected.

   • What are the possible results from solving a system of three linear equations in three variables?

   • What are the possible results of the intersection of three planes in 3-space?

2. Select activities from the unit that were important in developing your understanding of the ideas you discussed in Question 1, and explain why you made the selections you did.

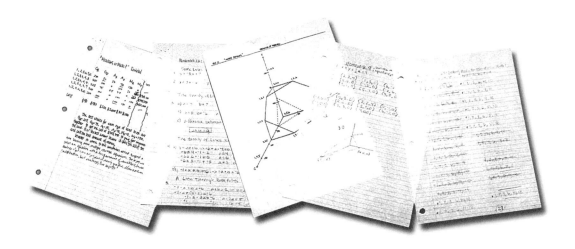

Beginning Portfolios—Part II

In this unit, you have used matrices both to represent information and to solve linear equations.

1. Summarize what you have learned about matrices. You should answer these questions in your summary.

   • What is a matrix?

   • How are matrices used to solve linear equations?

2. Select activities from the unit that were important in developing your understanding of the ideas you discussed in Question 1, and explain why you made the selections you did.

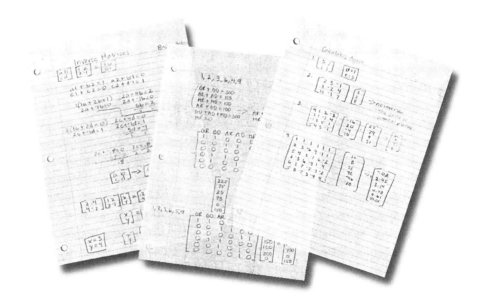

Meadows or Malls? Portfolio

Now that *Meadows or Malls?* is completed, it is time to put together your portfolio for the unit. Compiling this portfolio has three parts:

• Writing a cover letter in which you summarize the unit

• Choosing papers to include from your work in this unit

• Discussing your personal mathematical growth in this unit

Cover Letter for *Meadows or Malls?*

Look back over *Meadows or Malls?* and describe the central problem and the main mathematical ideas of the unit. This description should give an overview of how the key ideas were developed and how they were used to solve the central problem.

In compiling your portfolio, you will select some activities that you think were important in developing the key ideas of this unit. Your cover letter should include an explanation of why you selected the particular items. (For ideas discussed in *Homework 36: Beginning Portfolios—Part I* and *Homework 37: Beginning Portfolios— Part II*, you can simply refer to your work on those assignments.)

Continued on next page

Selecting Papers from *Meadows or Malls?*

Your portfolio for *Meadows or Malls?* should contain

* *"Meadows or Malls?" Revisited*

* *Homework 36: Beginning Portfolios—Part I* and *Homework 37: Beginning Portfolios—Part II*

  These two earlier portfolio assignments and the activities you discussed in them should be included as part of your cover letter.

* *Just the Plane Facts*

* An assignment on solving systems of linear equations that does not use matrices

* An assignment in which you learned concepts that allowed you to solve linear programming problems in more than two variables

* A Problem of the Week

  Select one of the POWs you completed in this unit (*That's Entertainment!, SubDivvy,* or *Crack the Code*).

Personal Growth

Your cover letter for *Meadows or Malls?* describes how the mathematical ideas develop in the unit. As part of your portfolio, write about your personal development during this unit. You may want to address this question.

> *How did your experiences in the Year 2 unit "Cookies" affect your work in "Meadows or Malls?"?*

You should include here any other thoughts you might like to share with a reader of your portfolio.

Appendix

Supplemental Problems

The supplemental problems in *Meadows or Malls?* touch on both algebraic and geometric ideas, as well as principles of linear programming. Here are some examples.

- *Embellishing the Plane Facts* asks you to find equations to illustrate some of your conclusions from *Just the Plane Facts.*

- *Producing Programming Problems—More Variables* asks you to create a linear programming problem involving at least four variables.

- *Determining the Determinant* asks you to investigate the concept of a *determinant,* which is a useful tool in deciding whether a matrix is invertible.

How Many Regions?

Any line in the coordinate plane will divide the plane into two regions, one on either side of the line. (The line itself is not considered a region.) Each of these regions can be represented by an inequality.

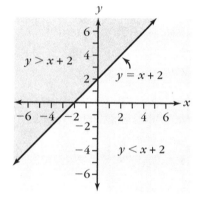

For example, the accompanying diagram shows the line defined by the equation $y = x + 2$. The line itself contains all the points that fit the equation, such as $(-3, -1)$ and $(2, 4)$.

The darkly-shaded region above the line consists of those points that fit the inequality $y > x + 2$, such as $(0, 3)$ and $(-4, 1)$. The lightly-shaded region below the line consists of those points that fit the inequality $y < x + 2$, such as $(3, 4)$ and $(-2, -2)$.

Your task here is to investigate what happens if you start with more than one line. Specifically, how many regions might you get, and how can you describe the different regions using inequalities?

1. Begin with the case of two lines.

    a. What are the possibilities for the number of regions you get when you draw two lines in the plane?

    b. For each possibility in Question 1a, give a specific pair of equations you could use for the lines, and describe how to represent each resulting region using inequalities. (Some regions may require more than one inequality.)

Continued on next page

c. Explain why you think your answer to Question 1a includes all of the possibilities.

2. Now do the same thing for the case of three lines and then for the case of four lines. Be sure to give specific examples for each possibility you describe and explain why you think you have covered all the possibilities.

The Eternal Triangle

Greg, Krys, and Juranso have decided to do a musical love story based loosely on the life of Pythagoras. Krys will design the sets. Greg and Juranso will both perform in the musical, but Juranso will write the script and Greg will write the music.

The three have agreed that the play will be a mixture of straight acting scenes and musical scenes, but they need to decide how many of each to include.

Due to time pressures, Greg, Krys, and Juranso have to limit the amount of time they can put into the project. Krys can design at most 16 sets (one set per scene, no matter what kind of scene it is). Greg and Juranso can each spend at most 36 hours on the play. Greg figures that it will take him an hour for each acting scene but three hours for each musical scene (because he has to write the music). For Juranso, it's the opposite. Because he's developing the script, he figures that the acting scenes will take him three hours each and the musical scenes will require only one hour each.

Of course, the trio wants to maximize the number of people who will attend their performance. Juranso does a lot of acting, so they figure that Greg's musical scenes will be more of a special draw. They have estimated that 20 people will show up for each musical scene they include and 10 people will show up for each acting scene they include.

Continued on next page

How many of each type of scene should they include in their play to maximize the number of people who attend?

Note: You can interpret an answer with fractions as representing a scene that is partly music and partly straight acting, so you need not limit yourself to whole numbers.

The Music Business

Rebecca, Noel, and Keenzia have decided to start a music distribution business. They will buy tapes and CDs in bulk at a discount and sell them to students, teachers, and staff at their school.

To purchase the music at the special bulk price, they need to spend at least $3,000 a month. The tapes cost them $5 apiece and the CDs $9.

They've gotten mixed opinions about what portion of their purchase should be tapes and what portion should be CDs. At this point, all they've decided is that the number of CDs should be at least half but at most three times the number of tapes.

Aside from the time spent in planning and purchasing, the partners will need to spend time on sales. Based on previous experience, they estimate that it will take an average of 15 minutes of work to sell each tape and 20 minutes to sell each CD. Together, the group can devote a total of up to 240 hours to sales.

After all their costs are considered, they make $4 profit on each CD they sell and $3 on each tape.

Assuming they sell everything they buy (and they will, because they are shrewd businesspeople), how many CDs and how many tapes should they buy to maximize their profit?

Special Planes

You know that the graph of a linear equation in three variables is a plane. In this assignment, you will find equations for planes that fit some specific conditions.

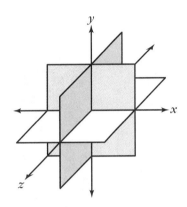

1. a. Find an example of a linear equation whose graph is a plane that includes the z-axis. (*Hint:* What is true about the coordinates of all points on the z-axis?)

   b. Find an example of a linear equation whose graph differs from that in Question 1a but still includes the z-axis.

2. a. Find an example of a linear equation whose graph includes the points $(0, 0, 0)$ and $(1, 1, 0)$.

   b. Find an example of a linear equation whose graph differs from that in Question 2a but still includes the points $(0, 0, 0)$ and $(1, 1, 0)$.

3. There are many planes whose graph includes both $(0, 0, 0)$ and $(1, 1, 0)$.

   a. In what kind of set do all of these planes intersect?

   b. What points besides $(0, 0, 0)$ and $(1, 1, 0)$ must be in the set where all of these planes intersect?

4. a. Find an example of a linear equation whose graph includes the points $(2, -1, 4)$.

   b. Find an example of a linear equation whose graph includes both $(2, -1, 4)$ and $(1, 1, 0)$.

Embellishing the Plane Facts

In *Just the Plane Facts*, you were asked to describe the possible ways in which two or more planes might intersect. You were also asked to explain each case using a diagram or a model.

In this activity, you should describe each case by giving equations of specific planes that create the given type of intersection.

1. First consider the case of two planes.

   a. Describe the different ways in which two planes can intersect. (This is a repeat of Question 2 of *Just the Plane Facts*.)

   b. For each kind of intersection, give the equations of two planes that intersect in that way. Do not use the coordinate planes for either of the two planes.

   c. How can you tell by looking at the equations for two planes how the planes will intersect?

2. Now consider the case of three planes.

   a. Describe the different ways in which three planes can intersect.

   b. For each kind of intersection, give the equations of three planes that intersect in that way. Do not use the coordinate planes for any of the three planes.

A Linear Medley

Linear equations and systems of equations arise in a wide variety of situations. Examine the situations given here, express each situation in terms of linear equations, and then try to answer the questions by solving the equations.

If a problem does not have a solution, or does not give enough information to answer the questions, propose a way to change the problem so that it will have a unique solution.

1. Hound Dog Busline charges passengers $50 to ride to Nashville plus $5 for each piece of luggage. Grand Ol' Opry Busline charges $70 for the trip but only $3 per piece of luggage.

   a. Find an expression for how much Hound Dog Busline charges if a passenger brings b pieces of luggage.

   b. Find an expression for how much Grand Ol' Opry Busline charges if a passenger brings b pieces of luggage.

   c. For what number of pieces of luggage carried by a passenger do both bus companies charge the same amount? What is the charge?

2. The length of a certain rectangle is nine times its width, and the perimeter of the rectangle is 200 meters. What are the dimensions of this rectangle?

Continued on next page

3. When Nancy sold 8 pounds of tomatoes and 5 pounds of apples, she made $12.10. When she sold 12 pounds of tomatoes and 9 pounds of apples, she made $20.10. How much does Nancy charge per pound for tomatoes and for apples?

4. Six hundred people attended the city basketball championship. Two types of tickets were sold, adult tickets and student tickets. A total of $2,200 was collected at the gate. How much did each type of ticket cost?

5. Rancher Gonzales hired some workers to put up a fence around her ranch. On the first day, she hired four experienced carpenters and six apprentices, and they completed 420 feet of fencing. The next day, she hired five experienced carpenters and three apprentices, and they completed 390 feet of fencing.

   For simplicity, assume that the workers all work independently, so that the amount of fencing completed is simply the sum of the amounts completed by each individual. Also assume that each experienced carpenter does the same amount of work and that each apprentice does the same amount of work.

   Based on these assumptions, how much fencing does each experienced carpenter finish per day? How much does each apprentice finish per day?

The General Two-Variable System

In the Year 2 unit *Solve It!,* you saw that every linear equation in one variable can be solved using basic ideas about equivalent equations.

The standard linear equation has the form $ax + b = c$. You can get from $ax + b = c$ to a solution for x in terms of the other variables using this sequence of equations.

$$ax + b = c$$

$$ax = c - b$$

$$x = \frac{c - b}{a}$$

Your task in this activity is to develop a similar solution to the general system of two linear equations in two variables.

Such a system is shown here, with the coefficients and constant terms represented by the variables $a, b, c, d, e,$ and f. You should treat the variables x and y as the "unknowns."

$$ax + by = c$$

$$dx + ey = f$$

1. Find a general solution to this system of linear equations. That is, solve for x and y in terms of $a, b, c, d, e,$ and f.

2. Discuss whether your solution makes sense for all values of the variables $a, b, c, d, e,$ and f, and how this is related to the concepts of *inconsistent* and *dependent* systems.

Playing Forever

1. The high school baseball team has seven excellent outfielders: Al, Brett, Carl, Duane, Ethan, Felipe, and Griswold. Unfortunately, only three can start a given game.

   What is the most games that the team can play before they have to repeat the same starting group of three outfielders? (It doesn't matter which player is at which outfield position—simply consider which three are chosen and list all possible combinations.)

2. The basketball team has nine excellent players: Henrietta, Inez, Jacinda, Katherine, Louise, Madeleine, Nancy, Oriana, and Paulette. Unfortunately, only five can start a given game.

   What is the most games that the team can play before they have to repeat the same starting group? List all possible combinations.

The Shortest Game

In the game SubDivvy (from *POW 6: SubDivvy*), there are often many ways to get from the starting number to 1.

For example, if the starting number is 10, the game can proceed in several ways, including the two shown below. The first of these paths takes four steps, while the second takes five steps.

$$
\begin{array}{r}
10 \\
-5 \\
\hline
5 \\
-1 \\
\hline
4 \\
-2 \\
\hline
2 \\
-1 \\
\hline
1
\end{array}
\qquad
\begin{array}{r}
10 \\
-1 \\
\hline
9 \\
-3 \\
\hline
6 \\
-3 \\
\hline
3 \\
-1 \\
\hline
2 \\
-1 \\
\hline
1
\end{array}
$$

Is the shortest path to 1 always achieved by subtracting the largest possible divisor at each step?

See what you can find out about shortest paths in SubDivvy.

Producing Programming Problems—More Variables

In the Year 2 unit *Cookies,* you invented your own linear programming problem, involving two variables. Your task in this problem is to invent a linear programming problem involving four or more variables.

Here are the key ingredients you need to have in your problem.

- Four or more variables

- Something to be maximized or minimized that is a *linear function* of those variables

- Some *linear constraints* involving your variables (Some of these constraints can be equations instead of inequalities.)

Once you have written your problem, you must solve it.

Your Own Three-Variable Problem

In *Homework 26: Ages, Coins, and Fund-Raising,* you examined three problems, each of which could be represented by a system of three linear equations in three variables.

Your task in this assignment is to make up a problem of your own that can be represented that way and to solve the problem.

Fitting a Plane

In *Homework 14: Fitting a Line* and *Homework 25: Fitting More Lines,* your task was to find a linear function through a particular pair of points. That is, you were asked to find coefficients a and b so that the line $y = ax + b$ would go through the given points.

This activity adds another dimension to this task—literally. Instead of finding the equation of a line through two points, your task will be to find the equation of a plane through three points.

Consider functions in which z is written as a linear expression in terms of x and y. That is, consider functions defined by equations of the form $z = ax + by + c$, where a, b, and c are any three numbers. The graph of any such equation is a plane.

Continued on next page

Comment: A linear equation involving only x and y, such as $2x - 3y = 7$, can be graphed in 3-space, and its graph is a plane (just as an equation like $x = 3$ can be graphed in the xy-plane, and its graph is a line). Thus, the form $z = ax + by + c$ does not represent the most general plane.

1. Suppose you want a plane that goes through the point $(3, 2, 1)$.

   a. Show that the graph of the equation $z = 2x - 4y + 3$ goes through this point.

   b. Find a condition on a, b, and c which guarantees that the graph of the equation $z = ax + by + c$ goes through $(3, 2, 1)$.

2. Find a condition on a, b, and c which guarantees that the graph of the equation $z = ax + by + c$ goes through $(1, -2, 5)$.

3. Find a condition on a, b, and c which guarantees that the graph of the equation $z = ax + by + c$ goes through $(2, -1, 6)$.

4. Find values of a, b, and c so that the graph of the equation $z = ax + by + c$ goes through all three points: $(3, 2, 1)$, $(1, -2, 5)$, and $(2, -1, 6)$.

5. Can you pick *any* three points and then find an equation of the form $z = ax + by + c$ whose graph goes through all three points?

Surfer's Shirts

1. Anna is responsible for ordering the special T-shirts for the annual Cross Town Race. The T-shirts come in two sizes—small and large. A small T-shirt costs $8 for the blank shirt itself and $2 to print a design on it. A blank large T-shirt costs $10, and it costs $2.50 to print the design. Anna will need to itemize the printing costs separately from the cost of the blank shirts.

   Suppose Anna orders S small shirts and L large shirts, with designs. Set up matrices with all of the necessary information and write an expression using the matrices that will give Anna the total cost for the blank T-shirts and the total cost for printing (in terms of S and L).

2. Ming's latest surfing competition was conducted in stages called "heats." Ming is using her three classic moves—the off-the-lip, the cutback, and the tube ride.

In this competition, off-the-lips are worth 4 points each, cutbacks are worth 6 points each, and tube rides are worth 10 points each.

• In heat 1, Ming did 5 off-the-lips, 3 cutbacks, and 2 tube rides.

• In heat 2, Ming did 7 off-the-lips, 2 cutbacks, and 1 tube ride.

• In heat 3, Ming did 3 off-the-lips, 4 cutbacks, and 3 tube rides.

a. Suppose Ming wants to know how many points she scored in each heat. Set up matrices and write a matrix expression that will give Ming this information.

b. Suppose instead that Ming wants to know the total number of points she scored (in the three heats combined) for each type of move. Set up matrices and write a matrix expression that will give Ming this information.

PROBLEM

An Associative Proof

In *Homework 32: Things We Take for Granted,* you investigated whether matrix multiplication is commutative or associative. This activity follows up on your work in that assignment.

1. Consider *only* 2×2 matrices, and prove that multiplication of such matrices is associative.

2. a. Is matrix addition commutative?

   b. Is matrix addition associative?

   Justify your answers.

When Can You Find an Inverse?

In *Homework 33: Inverses and Equations,* you saw that some 2×2 matrices have an inverse for multiplication and others do not.

In this problem, your task is to investigate the existence of matrix inverses more fully.

1. Find out which 2×2 matrices have inverses, and explain your answer. (*Hint:* Think about the connection between whether a matrix has an inverse and the graphs of certain equations related to the matrix. Use the geometry of these graphs to answer the question.)

2. Which of these 3×3 matrices have inverses? Explain your answers.

a. $\begin{bmatrix} 1 & 2 & 1 \\ 0 & 2 & -1 \\ 2 & 4 & 2 \end{bmatrix}$
c. $\begin{bmatrix} 1 & -1 & 2 \\ 0 & 3 & 0 \\ 1 & 2 & 2 \end{bmatrix}$

b. $\begin{bmatrix} 1 & -1 & 2 \\ 0 & 3 & 0 \\ 3 & -3 & 1 \end{bmatrix}$
d. $\begin{bmatrix} 1 & 2 & 1 \\ 0 & 2 & -1 \\ 2 & 6 & 2 \end{bmatrix}$

3. Based on your work in Question 2 and other examples of your own, what can you say about when a 3×3 matrix has an inverse and when it does not?

SUPPLEMENTAL PROBLEM

Determining the Determinant

If a system of linear equations has the same number of equations as variables, then "usually" it will have a unique solution. But in some cases, the system will have no solution (an *inconsistent* system) or have infinitely many solutions (a *dependent* system).

Whether a system has a unique solution depends on the coefficients of the variables. As you may have seen in *The General Two-Variable System,* the system

$$ax + by = c$$

$$dx + ey = f$$

will have a unique solution whenever a certain expression involving *a, b, d,* and *e* is not zero. When that expression is zero, the system will be either dependent or inconsistent, depending on the values of *c* and *f*.

This special expression involving the coefficients is called the **determinant** of the matrix $\begin{bmatrix} a & b \\ d & e \end{bmatrix}$.

In fact, determinants are defined for square matrices of all sizes and can be used to solve systems of linear equations.

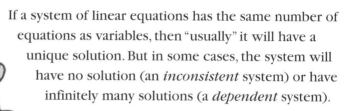

Continued on next page

Your Task

Your task in this assignment is to learn more about determinants and to write a report about what you learn.

Your report should begin with the definition of the determinant for 2×2 matrices and explain how determinants can be used to solve two-variable systems of equations like the one shown in this activity.

Discuss how determinants are used in general to solve systems of linear equations and what the relationship is between the determinant of a matrix and the invertibility of the matrix. Your report should go beyond the 2×2 case and include the definition of the determinant for at least the case of a 3×3 matrix.

Cracking Another Code

```
A B        D E
× C       + F G
D E        H I
```

The pair of arithmetic problems shown at the left uses a single code in which letters have been substituted for numbers (as in *POW 7: Crack the Code*). As in that POW, any solution must follow these rules.

- If a letter is used more than once, it stands for the same number each time it is used.

- Different letters always stand for different single-digit numbers.

- A letter standing for 0 never starts a number with more than one digit. For example, the expression 03 cannot be used (but 507, 80, and just plain 0 are all allowed).

Your job is to crack the code. Keep in mind that the multiplication problem and the addition problem use the same code.

You must not only find all the solutions (if there are any) but also prove your answer.

Adapted from a problem in the *Oregon Mathematics Teacher,* January-February, 1989.

Small World, Isn't It?

As the World Grows

Based on information in the book how long will it take until the population reaches 1.6 × 10

Lisa Newton rephrases the unit's central problem in her own words.

How many people are there in the world today? What about a century or two ago? What about in the future?

The central problem of this unit involves the analysis of world population trends. In the opening days of the unit, you will study population data since 1650, with the goal of determining how long it would take until people were "squashed up against one another."

Small World, Isn't It?

Year	Estimated Population
1650	470,000,000
1750	694,000,000
1850	1,091,000,000
1900	1,570,000,000
1950	2,510,000,000
1960	3,030,000,000
1970	3,680,000,000
1980	4,480,000,000
1985	4,870,000,000
1990	5,290,000,000
1995	5,730,000,000

Everyone knows that the world's population is increasing. The chart at the left shows the changes over the past several centuries.

If this pattern of data continued, how long do you think it would take until we were all squashed up against one another?

You may find these facts useful.

• The total surface area of the earth is approximately 196,930,000 square miles.

• Approximately 29.2% of the earth's total surface area is land.

As you consider this problem, make note of any difficulties you encounter or any issues you think need clarification.

Population and surface area data taken from *Information Please,* 1996 Almanac 49th edition Houghton-Mifflin p. 133.

The More, the Merrier?

Isn't life more interesting when there are lots of people around? Then why should people be upset about the idea of a "population explosion"? Your task on this POW is to study some aspect of this rapid population growth and to find out why at least some people are concerned.

You should then write a report on your findings, which may include your own opinions and conjectures about why things are the way they are. Graphs, drawings, and tables are often helpful.

Here are some suggestions for topics. You may choose other topics for your report.

• Population growth and the food supply

• Pros and cons of limiting family size

• Comparison of population growth in different countries

• Population growth and pollution

• Ways to cope with the population explosion

• Traffic congestion

How Many of Us Can Fit?

In the activity *Small World, Isn't It?*, you are asked when we will all get "squashed up against one another." Of course, that probably won't ever happen, but you may be curious about how many people that would require.

1. How many square miles of land surface area are there on the earth? (Use the information provided in the activity *Small World, Isn't It?*)

2. How many square feet of land area are there on the earth? (Use the fact that 1 mile is equal to 5280 feet, so 1 square mile is 5280^2 square feet, which is 27,878,400 square feet.)

3. In 1995, the world population was about 5.73 billion people. If this population were spread evenly over the land area of the earth, about how many square feet of area would each person have, on average?

4. Suppose we interpret the phrase "squashed up against one another" to mean that each person has about one square foot to call his or her own. How many people would there need to be for us to really be squashed up against one another?

Data taken from *Information Please*, 1996 Almanac 49th edition Houghton-Mifflin p. 127.

How Many More People?

Part I: The Graph

One way to get some ideas about how the world population has grown over the centuries is through a graph.

1. Choose an appropriate scale and plot the data from *Small World, Isn't It?* Show all the specific data points given in that activity and label these data points on your graph with their coordinates.

Part II: Average Increases

2. a. Find the increase in population between the years 1650 and 1900.

   b. Explain how the increase you found in Question 2a shows up on the graph.

   c. Find the average increase in population *per year* between the years 1650 and 1900.

   d. What would the portion of the graph from 1650 to 1900 look like if the population increased by the same number of people each year of this time period?

3. a. Find the increase in population between the years 1900 and 1950.

   b. Explain how the increase you found in Question 3a shows up on the graph.

Continued on next page

c. Find the average increase in population *per year* between the years 1900 and 1950.

d. What would the portion of the graph from 1900 to 1950 look like if the population increased by the same number of people each year of this time period?

Part III: Making Comparisons

4. Which interval, 1650 to 1900 or 1900 to 1950, had the greater average increase in population per year? How could you answer this question simply by looking at your graph?

Growing Up

The accompanying graph shows the average height for boys ages 0 to 6 in the United States around the middle of the twentieth century.

1. Suppose that the average amount of growth shown during the first year after birth were to continue during the second year. What would be the average height for boys on their second birthday?

2. The section of the graph for ages 3 to 6 is nearly straight. What does that mean in terms of the average growth for boys during those years?

3. a. How much does the average height for boys increase between ages 3 and 4?

   b. Express your answer for Question 3a as a percentage of the average height for boys at age 3.

4. a. How much does the average height for boys increase between ages 5 and 6?

   b. Express your answer for Question 4a as a percentage of the average height for boys at age 5.

   c. Compare your answers for Questions 4a and 4b to your answers for Questions 3a and 3b.

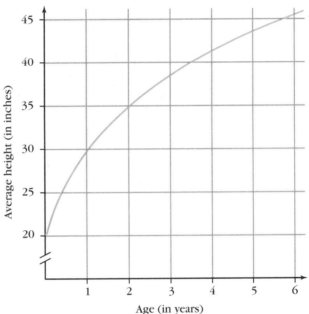

(Source: Department of Pediatrics, State University of Iowa, 1943.)

Interactive Mathematics Program

Small World, Isn't It? **287**

Average Growth

Leilani Juan and Liana DeGracia begin their investigation of growth and rates of change.

Most growth—of living things, of the economy, of organizations—is uneven, and population growth is no exception. Over the next few days, you'll look at some examples of growth and rates of change, focusing on how you can use graphs to help understand what's going on.

Story Sketches

1. This graph describes a wagon train's progress along the Overland Trail.

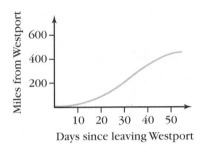

a. About how many miles per day did the wagon train go for the first 20 days? Explain how you got your answer.

b. What was the most rapid pace the wagon train achieved? Explain how you got your answer.

2. Tyler Dunkalot and his elementary school friends want to get basketball uniforms, and they are saving money so they can contribute to the purchase. One Friday afternoon, right after getting their weekly allowances, they each put some of the allowance into their piggy banks and count the savings so far.

Here's how much Tyler and his friends have that Friday (including the amount they just added) and how much each will add to savings every Friday afternoon from then on.

• Tyler has $2 now and will add 50¢ each week.

• Robin has $2 now and will add 70¢ each week.

• Mac has $4 now and will add 70¢ each week.

• Dan has $4 now and will add 30¢ each week.

Continued on next page

Interactive Mathematics Program

Draw graphs showing *accumulated savings* versus *time elapsed* for Tyler and each of his friends for a ten-week period. (Assume that they add their savings to their piggy banks each Friday and do not spend any of the saved money.)

Use the same set of axes for all four graphs, but use a different color to represent each youngster.

3. Compare your four graphs from Question 2. Describe how they are the same and how they are different.

4. For each of the youngsters, develop a formula or equation that shows how much money is in the piggy bank *n* weeks after the original count.

What a Mess!

Part I: The Mess

An oil tanker has broken up due to an explosion out at sea, and thousands of gallons of oil are spreading across the ocean. Linda Sue is flying overhead in an airplane and sees that the oil slick appears to be in the shape of a circle.

When Linda Sue first sees the oil slick, the radius of the circle is 70 meters. She flies overhead for a while and perceives that the radius is increasing at a rate of 6 meters per hour.

1. Make an In-Out table in which the *In* is the number of hours since Linda Sue first observed the oil slick and the *Out* is the radius of the oil slick after that many hours.

2. Draw a graph based on your In-Out table, and find a rule for your graph and table.

Part II: The Cleanup

Seven hours after Linda Sue first sees the oil spill with a radius of 70 meters, a cleanup operation begins. Rescue workers pump a special detergent into the center of the spill. As the detergent spreads, a circle of clean water develops inside the oil spill. The radius of this circle increases at 10 meters per hour.

3. Did the rescue team start soon enough and pump fast enough to eventually counteract the oil spill? If not, why not? If so, how many hours will it take until the spill is neutralized? (*Hint*: What was the radius of the oil spill when the cleanup operation began?)

Traveling Time

Abida has packed her bags and is ready to leave for college. She needs to catch an early train because she has a long way to travel.

Abida lives in Cincinnati, Ohio, and will be going to school in Philadelphia, Pennsylvania, 550 miles away. She is hoping to get to Philadelphia in time to see some historical landmarks. She figures that if she gets to Philadelphia by 3:00 p.m., she will have enough time to see the Liberty Bell and Independence Hall before they close for the evening.

1. If Abida catches a train leaving at 5:00 a.m., how many miles per hour must the train average for her to get there by 3:00 p.m.? (Cincinnati and Philadelphia are in the same time zone.)

2. If the 5:00 a.m. train averages 40 miles per hour for the first hour and a half, what speed must it average for the rest of the trip for Abida to make it to Philadelphia by 3:00 p.m.?

Continued on next page

3. For this question, suppose that the train actually averaged 50 miles per hour for the whole trip (which means that the trip took 11 hours altogether). That doesn't necessarily mean that the train traveled at a constant rate of 50 mph.

   Make up a scenario in which the train averaged 50 mph for the trip but traveled at least two different speeds along the way. Be specific about speeds, times, and distances.

4. Abida's train left on time at 5:00 a.m. This graph shows one possibility for how far the train traveled as a function of the time elapsed.

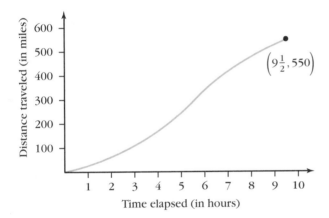

Use the graph to answer these questions.

a. Was the train's average speed faster during the first two hours of the trip or the last two hours?

b. During what one-hour period was the train's average speed the fastest?

c. If you had to pick the precise instant that the train was going the fastest, what would you choose and why?

Comparative Growth

Marvin was doing a study comparing the population growth of his hometown in the early twentieth century with its population growth in the early 1980s.

When he came across the two graphs shown here, Marvin noticed that the first graph appeared to be steeper than the second. He concluded that the population was growing faster at the beginning of the century than it was in the early 1980s.

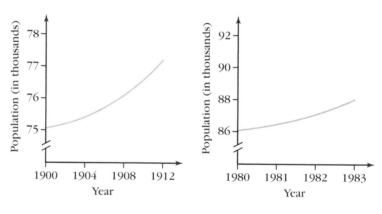

1. Use the first graph to calculate the average increase in population per year for the interval from 1900 to 1912.

2. Use the second graph to calculate the average increase in population per year for the interval from 1980 to 1983.

3. Do the results from Questions 1 and 2 support Marvin's conclusion? What does this suggest with regard to using graphs to compare rates of change?

If Looks Don't Matter, What Does?

In the activity *Comparative Growth,* you saw that you can't necessarily compare rates of growth in two graphs solely from the appearance of the graphs. In this assignment, you will look at some specific situations to decide what really matters.

1. The accompanying graph shows only two of the data points from the activity *Small World, Isn't It?*

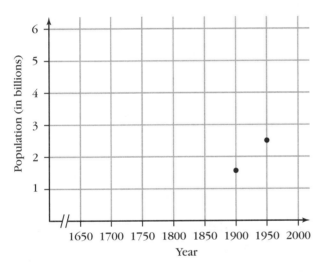

a. Use the two given points to find the average population growth per year from 1900 to 1950, and explain the process you use.

b. What would this portion of the graph look like if the population had grown by the same number of people each year?

Continued on next page

Miles from Westport

Days since leaving Westport

2. The graph at the left shows two points from the graph in Question 1 of *Homework 3: Story Sketches*. Use the graph to find the average distance traveled per day from Day 20 to Day 30, and explain the process you use.

3. Becky is a bit older than Tyler Dunkalot and his friends. The graph below shows the amount of money she had in her savings account at various times over the course of several weeks.

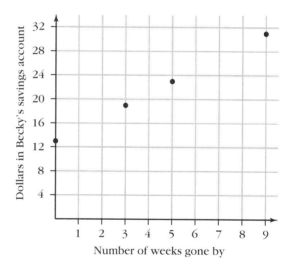

Number of weeks gone by

At what rate did the amount in Becky's savings account change per week? Explain how you got your answer from this graph.

Continued on next page

4. Find the rate of change of the function whose graph is shown here, and explain your work.

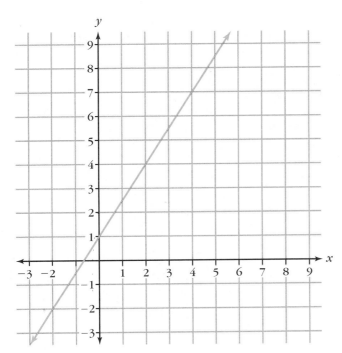

All in a Row

Niall McNamara and Melyssa Brixner explore connections between graphs and formulas.

The simplest type of growth to study is constant growth, and that leads to work with linear functions. In the next segment of the unit, you will develop the important concept of *slope*, which is the primary tool for describing the rate of change for a linear function.

You'll use this concept to develop equations for straight lines, and you'll see whether a linear model for population growth can accurately predict future trends.

Formulating the Rate

In each of the situations in *Homework 5: If Looks Don't Matter, What Does?,* you used coordinates of points on a graph to find a rate of change. In those problems, you were given specific numbers for the coordinates or could at least estimate the numerical values of the coordinates from the graph.

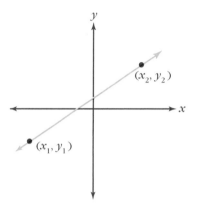

Now suppose that you have a function whose graph is a straight line and that (x_1, y_1) and (x_2, y_2) are two points on the graph. That is, instead of numerical values, you have variables representing each of the coordinates.

Find an expression for the rate of change of the function in terms of $x_1, y_1, x_2,$ and y_2.

Rates, Graphs, Slopes, and Formulas

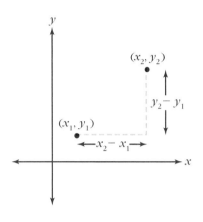

The concept of **slope** is an abstraction from the idea of a rate of change. Formally, the slope of the line connecting two points (x_1, y_1) and (x_2, y_2) is defined as the ratio

$$\frac{y_2 - y_1}{x_2 - x_1}$$

The numerator of this fraction is sometimes referred to as the **change in y** or the **rise.** The denominator is called the **change in x** or the **run.**

In these problems, you will work with both rates and slopes, exploring their connections to both graphs and formulas.

1. A jogger is moving along at a rate of 500 feet per minute. (That's about 6 miles per hour.)

   a. Use $t = 0$ as the time when the jogger starts, and plot a graph showing the distance the jogger has gone (in feet) as a function of t (in minutes).

   b. Find an equation for this function.

   c. Choose two points on your graph and use their coordinates to compute the slope of the graph.

2. A reservoir is partly filled and contains 200,000 cubic feet of water. Then water is added at a rate of 7000 cubic feet per hour.

   a. Use $t = 0$ as the time when the water begins to be added, and plot a graph showing the amount of water in the reservoir as a function of t. (You may want to "skip" part of the vertical axis as was done in the graph in *Homework 2: Growing Up.*)

Continued on next page

b. Find an equation for this function.

c. Choose two points on your graph and use their coordinates to compute the slope of the graph.

3. a. Plot the data in this In-Out table.

In	Out
3	18
5	26
10	46
16	70

b. Choose two points on your graph and use their coordinates to compute the slope of the line connecting them.

c. Find an equation to describe your graph in part a.

4. a. Choose two points on the line shown here and use their coordinates to compute the slope of the line.

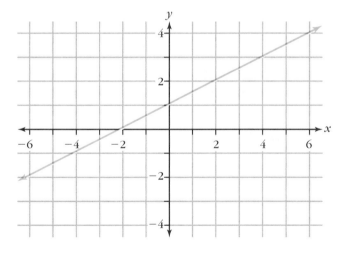

b. Find an equation for the line.

More About Tyler's Friends

In *Homework 3: Story Sketches,* you met Tyler Dunkalot and his friends, who were saving money to help buy basketball uniforms.

You may recall that two of Tyler's friends, Robin and Mac, both saved 70¢ per week, although at the start of their savings program, Robin had $2 and Mac had $4.

1. Graph both Robin's and Mac's savings as a function of the time elapsed. Treat these as *continuous* functions, as if Robin and Mac were each saving their allowance gradually throughout the week, at a constant rate. Use $t = 0$ to represent the moment when they started saving, and use the same set of axes for both graphs.

2. Find the slope of each of your graphs, and explain what you notice about the slopes.

3. Will the two graphs ever intersect? Explain your answer.

4. a. Find a formula for the amount of money each of the youngsters has at time t.

   b. How are these formulas related to your answers to Question 2?

Wake Up!

Getting going in the morning was probably hard for folks on the Overland Trail (just as it may be for you today), so coffee was a highly valued commodity.

The Cazneau family started out with a supply of 30 pounds of coffee. When they arrived at Sutter's Fort in California, after a 188-day journey, they had only 3 pounds left.

1. Draw a graph showing the amount of coffee remaining as a function of the amount of time elapsed since the start of the journey. For the sake of simplicity, assume that the Cazneaus consumed coffee at a constant rate.

2. Find the average amount of coffee consumed per day.

3. Develop an equation for the function represented by your graph in Question 1.

4. Find the slope of your graph from Question 1.

5. Suppose that at the beginning of their journey, the Cazneaus were 1600 miles from Sutter's Fort. As stated previously, their journey took a total of 188 days.

   a. How many miles per day did they travel? (For simplicity, assume that they traveled the same distance each day.)

   b. Of course, as the Cazneaus traveled, their distance from Sutter's Fort decreased. Write a formula expressing the distance remaining as a function of the number of days they'd been traveling.

   c. Make a graph of your function from Question 5b.

   d. Find the slope of your graph from Question 5c.

California, Here I Come!

According to the U.S. census, the population of California in 1850 was about 92,600. During the 1850s, with the great westward migration, the population grew substantially. In 1860, the census population was 380,000.

1. What was the average annual population increase during the 1850s (that is, from 1850 to 1860)?

2. If California's population had continued to increase after 1860 by the same annual amount as it averaged during the 1850s, what would the population have been in these years?

   a. 1900

   b. 1950

   c. 1990

3. Generalize your results from Question 2. That is, develop a formula for the population of California in the year X (based on the assumption that the population of California had continued to increase after 1860 by the same annual amount as it averaged during the 1850s).

4. According to the official U.S. census, California's population in 1990 was 29,760,021. How does this amount compare to the amount you found in Question 2c? What do you think accounts for the difference between your prediction for 1990 and the actual population?

Historical note: At the time of the Gold Rush (the 1850s), the U.S. Constitution stated that taxes and representation

Continued on next page

in Congress would be apportioned among the states "according to their respective numbers, which shall be determined by adding to the whole number of free persons, including those bound to service for a term of years, and excluding Indians not taxed, three fifths of all other persons." Thus, Native Americans were not counted at all unless they were taxed, and slaves were counted as three-fifths of a person each. The Fourteenth Amendment (1868) changed this to count everyone except "Indians not taxed."

There is still controversy today about the accuracy of the census, with some people claiming that inner-city or rural populations are undercounted.

Planning the Platforms

The Platform Display

River City is getting ready for the big Fourth of July band concert that precedes the fireworks. The concert is always a major event, but this year the band leader, Kevin, plans to make it bigger and better than ever.

Kevin wants to have each of the baton twirlers standing on an individual platform, as shown here.

The baton twirlers will toss batons up and down to one another. Kevin wants the difference in height from one platform to the next to be the same in each case.

Kevin's Decisions

Kevin has several decisions to make.

- He needs to decide on the number of platforms. (Kevin isn't sure how many of his baton twirlers will be good enough to perform by the Fourth of July.)

- He needs to decide on the height of the first platform. (This will depend on how tall the baton twirler on the first platform is, and Kevin hasn't decided who the first baton twirler will be.)

- He needs to decide on the difference in height from one platform to the next. (Kevin doesn't know yet how high the twirlers will be able to toss their batons.)

Camilla's Dilemma

Camilla is in charge of building and decorating the structure. She needs a permit from the city to build the

Continued on next page

structure, so she needs to know how high the tallest platform will be.

She also plans to hang a colorful strip of material on the front of each platform. Each strip will reach from the top of the platform to the ground. (The width of the material is the same as the width of each platform, so she needs only one strip per platform.) She needs to know the total length of material that she should buy.

Camilla is going crazy, because she can't do her job until Kevin makes his decisions.

Your Task

You are Camilla's assistant, and she has asked you to be ready to give her the information she needs as soon as Kevin makes up his mind.

Your task in this POW is to create two formulas that will allow you to do this instantly. One formula should tell you the height of the tallest platform. The other should tell you the total length of material that Camilla will need. Your formulas should give these results in terms of the number of platforms, the height of the first platform, and the difference in height between adjacent platforms.

Write-up

1. *Problem Statement:* State the mathematical essence of the problem, independent of the context of the platforms, batons twirlers, and so on.

2. *Process:* Give details of any specific examples you worked out, and explain how those examples helped you develop the formulas.

3. *Solution:* Give the two formulas and explain why they work.

4. *Evaluation*

5. *Self-assessment*

Points, Slopes, and Equations

In *Homework 8: California, Here I Come!,* you saw that knowing two data points allows you to develop a linear model for population growth. This makes geometric sense, because two points determine a straight line.

When you actually wrote the equation, you may have worked primarily with the slope (the rate of growth) and one of those points. This also makes geometric sense, because a line can also be determined by knowing one point and the "steepness" of the line (the slope).

The problems in this assignment are similar to your work in that homework, except that they do not involve population. For each problem in Part I, you are given the slope along with one point. For each problem in Part II, you are given two points. For Part II, you may want to find the slope as a first step in order to write the equation. Part III examines the special cases of horizontal and vertical lines.

Part I: Point-Slope Equations

1. Find an equation for the line with slope 5 that goes through the point $(3, 2)$.

2. Find an equation for the line with slope 10 that goes through the point $(-4, 7)$.

3. Find an equation for the line with slope -3 that goes through the point $(5, -4)$.

4. Find an equation for the line with slope $\frac{2}{3}$ that goes through the point $(4, 6)$.

Continued on next page

Part II: Two-Point Equations

5. Find an equation for the line that goes through the points $(6, 2)$ and $(8, 8)$.

6. Find an equation for the line that goes through the points $(1, 5)$ and $(3, -1)$.

7. Find an equation for the line that goes through the points $(-7, 2)$ and $(-2, 5)$.

Part III: Horizontal and Vertical Lines

8. Find an equation for the horizontal line that goes through the point $(5, 1)$. What is the slope of this line?

9. Find an equation for the vertical line that goes through the point $(2, -6)$. What is the slope of this line?

The Why of the Line

You've seen that any pair of points on a given line will lead to the same slope. But why is this so?

Consider this diagram, which shows four points—*A, B, C,* and *D*—on the same line. The diagram also shows right triangles using the segments $\overline{AB}$ and $\overline{CD}$ as their hypotenuses. The lengths of the legs of these right triangles are represented using the variables *r, s, t,* and *u,* as shown.

Use ideas from geometry to explain why the slope for the pair of points *A* and *B* must be the same as the slope for the pair of points *C* and *D.* That is, explain why the ratio $\frac{r}{s}$ must be the same as the ratio $\frac{t}{u}$.

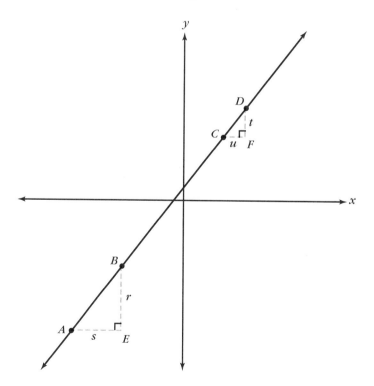

Return of the Rescue

You may recall this situation from the activity *To the Rescue* in the Year 2 unit *Solve It!*

> A helicopter is flying to drop a supply bundle to a group of firefighters who are behind the fire lines. At the moment when the helicopter crew makes the drop, the helicopter is hovering 400 feet above the ground.

The principles of physics that describe the behavior of falling objects state that when an object is falling freely, it goes faster and faster as it falls. In fact, these principles provide a specific formula describing the object's fall, which can be expressed this way.

> If an object is dropped from a height of N feet, then $h(t)$, its height off the ground (in feet) t seconds after being dropped, is given by the equation $h(t) = N - 16t^2$.

So in the case of the falling supplies, the formula is $h(t) = 400 - 16t^2$, because the supply bundle is 400 feet off the ground when it starts to fall.

1. What is $h(3)$? That is, what is the height of the supply bundle three seconds after it is dropped?

2. How far has the supply bundle fallen during those three seconds?

3. What is the average speed of the supply bundle during those three seconds?

4. How long does it take for the supply bundle to reach the ground?

Beyond Linearity

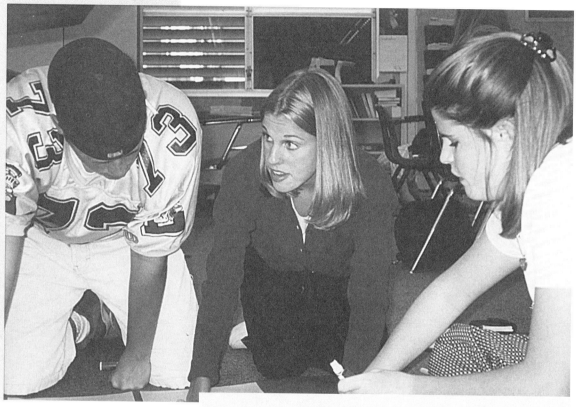

Lars Lundgren, Kim Watt, and Betsy Hooper prepare to present what they mean by "the speed at the exact moment."

Slope is an excellent concept for working with straight-line graphs. But what about rates of change that are not constant?

With the activity *The Instant of Impact,* you will begin an exploration of the meaning of *instantaneous rate of change.* Over the next week or so, you will refine this idea and explore it from several perspectives.

The Instant of Impact

As described in *Homework 10: Return of the Rescue,* a supply bundle has been dropped from a helicopter. The bundle's height off the ground *t* seconds after being dropped is given by the equation

$$h(t) = 400 - 16t^2$$

with $h(t)$ measured in feet.

Suppose that the bundle can withstand the impact of hitting the ground only for speeds up to 165 feet per second. To determine whether the bundle will survive the fall, you need to find out how fast it is traveling when it hits the ground.

Keep careful track of your computations on these questions, so you can compare results from question to question.

1. a. How far does the bundle fall during its last two seconds (that is, during the time from $t = 3$ to $t = 5$)?

   b. What is the bundle's average speed during that two-second interval?

2. a. How far does the bundle fall during the last second before it hits the ground?

   b. What is the bundle's average speed during this last second?

3. What is the bundle's average speed during the last half-second before it hits the ground?

4. What is the bundle's average speed during the last tenth of a second before it hits the ground?

5. What is the bundle's speed at the exact moment it hits the ground?

Doctor's Orders

Larry is a stunt diver. His most famous dive is off a cliff into the ocean near the town of Poco Loco.

Unfortunately, Larry injured his wrist recently, and the impact of hitting the water at high speeds could do further damage. His doctor recommends that he do no dives in which the speed of his entry into the water is greater than 60 feet per second.

The cliff at Poco Loco is 62 feet high, but Larry always begins his dive with a jump, so he actually starts his fall from a height of 64 feet. Therefore, his height above the ocean is given by the formula

$$h(t) = 64 - 16t^2$$

where t is the time, in seconds, from when he begins his fall, and $h(t)$ is his height, in feet, above the ocean.

1. How high above the ocean is Larry one second after he begins his fall?

2. What is the value of t when Larry hits the water?

3. What is Larry's average speed during the final second of his dive?

4. What is Larry's average speed during the final half-second of his dive?

5. Can Larry perform his lucky dive without violating his doctor's instructions? Explain.

Photo Finish

You may recognize this situation from the activity *Where's Speedy?* in the Year 2 unit *Solve It!*

> Speedy is the star runner for her country's track team. Among other things, she runs the last 400 meters of the 1600-meter relay race.
>
> A sports analyst studied the film of a race in which Speedy competed. The analyst came up with this formula to describe the distance Speedy had run at a given time in the race:
>
> $$m(t) = 0.1t^2 + 3t$$

In this formula, $m(t)$ gives the number of meters Speedy had run after t seconds of the race, with both time and distance measured from the beginning of her 400-meter segment of the race. (This formula might not be very accurate, but on this activity you should treat it as if it were completely correct.)

1. How long did it take Speedy to finish the race? That is, how long did it take her to run 400 meters? Explain how you found your answer.

2. A photograph was taken of Speedy at the instant she crossed the finish line. The photo shows a slight blur, so you know Speedy was going pretty fast, but you can't tell the speed at which she was going at the instant the photo was taken.

   Find Speedy's speed at that instant.

3. a. Find Speedy's speed at three other instants during the race.

   b. Was there an instant when Speedy was going exactly 10 meters per second? If so, when was that instant?

Speed and Slope

Part I: An Instantaneous Summary

You know that *average speed* can be defined by the simple formula

$$\text{average speed} = \frac{\text{distance traveled}}{\text{time elapsed}}$$

but you've seen that *instantaneous speed* is a more complicated idea.

Summarize what you have learned about how to calculate instantaneous speed from *The Instant of Impact*, from *Homework 11: Doctor's Orders*, and from *Photo Finish*.

Part II: A Linear Review

In recent activities, you have looked at how rate of change might be calculated for nonlinear situations. But you shouldn't forget how to use constant rates and the slope of a straight line, whether in the context of a real-life situation or in terms of a graph. Here is one problem of each type.

1. Ruth keeps track of rainfall in her area, by watching the level of water in a barrel outside her house. A steady rainstorm started one day, and at one point, she observed that the water level was at 420 millimeters. Three hours later, the level had increased to 438 millimeters.

   Assume that the rain continued steadily, so that the water level rose at the same rate throughout that three-hour period. Use *t* to represent the time elapsed (in hours) from Ruth's first measurement, and write a function expressing the water level in terms of *t*.

2. Find an equation for the line that goes through the points $(5, -8)$ and $(13, 4)$.

ZOOOOOOOOM

Consider the function $m(t) = 0.1t^2 + 3t$, which described the distance Speedy had run in terms of time elapsed.

Graph this function on the graphing calculator, adjusting the viewing window so that your graph includes the point $(50, 400)$. (Recall that she completed her 400-meter run in 50 seconds, so this point is on the graph.)

Then zoom in on the point $(50, 400)$ until the graph on your screen looks pretty much like a straight line.

1. a. Use the calculator's trace feature to find the coordinates of two points on this apparent straight line, and write down those two coordinate pairs.

   b. Find the slope of the line connecting those points.

2. What does the slope you found in Question 1b mean in terms of Speedy's race?

The Growth of the Oil Slick

The idea of an instantaneous rate of change doesn't apply only to speed. The questions here concern the rate of growth of the area of the oil slick (from *What a Mess!*).

You may recall that when Linda Sue first saw the circular oil slick, the radius of the circle was 70 meters. She also noticed that the radius was increasing by 6 meters per hour. This means that the radius can be described by the formula $r = 70 + 6t$ (where t is the number of hours since Linda Sue first saw the oil slick). Therefore, the area in square meters of the oil slick after t hours is given by the function

$$A(t) = \pi(70 + 6t)^2$$

1. What was the area covered by the oil slick when Linda Sue first saw it (at $t = 0$)?

In the remaining questions, express the rate of growth of the oil slick in square meters per hour.

2. a. What was the average rate at which the oil slick grew during the first two hours after Linda Sue's initial observation?

   b. What was the average rate at which the oil slick grew during the first half-hour after Linda Sue's initial observation?

   c. What was the average rate at which the oil slick grew during the 15 minutes *before* Linda Sue's initial observation? (*Suggestion:* Think of 15 minutes as one-fourth of an hour.)

3. At what rate was the oil slick growing at the instant when Linda Sue first saw it?

Speeds, Rates, and Derivatives

The derivative of a function at a point is one of the basic concepts of calculus. If a function is defined by the equation $y = f(x)$ and (a, b) is a point on the graph, then the **derivative of f at (a, b)** can be thought of in at least two ways.

- It is the slope of the line that is tangent to the curve at (a, b).

- It is the instantaneous rate at which the y-value of the function is changing as the x-value increases through $x = a$.

Note: We often refer to this as "the derivative at $x = a$" rather than as the derivative at (a, b).

This assignment gives you a chance to work with this new idea in connection with some familiar situations. Keep in mind that you can find derivatives by using smaller and smaller intervals around a particular value of a.

Continued on next page

1. The function $h(t) = 400 - 16t^2$ gives the height of the supply bundle (in feet) t seconds after it is dropped.

   a. Find the derivative of this function at the point $(3, 256)$.

   b. What does the answer to Question 1a tell you about the speed at which the supply bundle is falling?

2. The function $A(t) = \pi(70 + 6t)^2$ gives the area of the oil slick (in square meters) t hours after Linda Sue first saw it.

   a. Find the rate at which the area was growing exactly one hour after Linda Sue first saw it.

   b. Express the answer to Question 2a as a derivative.

3. *Homework 7: Wake Up!* described the Cazneau family's consumption of coffee. The function $f(d) = 30 - 0.14d$ gives a good approximation of the amount of coffee (in pounds) the Cazneau family had left after d days.

   For this assignment, you should treat this as a continuous function, rather than as a discrete function. That is, assume that d need not be a whole number.

   a. Because $f(5) = 29.3$, the graph of this function goes through the point $(5, 29.3)$. What is the derivative of the function at this point?

   b. What does the answer to Question 3a tell you about the rate at which the Cazneaus drank coffee?

   c. Pick a point on the graph of the function other than $(5, 29.3)$, and find the derivative at that point.

Zooming Free-for-All

You saw in *ZOOOOOOOOM* that if you zoom in on the calculator graph of the function $m(t) = 0.1t^2 + 3t$, the graph on the screen quickly begins to look like a straight line. (Of course, you have to take into account that on a calculator screen, even the graph of a linear function might not look perfectly straight.)

Your task in this activity is to investigate whether this phenomenon occurs for other functions as well.

1. Start with the calculator graph of the function $h(t) = 400 - 16t^2$, representing the height of the falling supply bundle. Choose a point on this graph and zoom in on that point.

   a. Does the graph begin to appear straight?

   b. If the graph does appear straight, what does the slope of that apparent straight line mean in terms of the falling supply bundle?

2. Experiment with other functions and other points. Pick a function, choose a point on its calculator graph, and zoom in on that point. (Don't worry about whether you can find a meaningful real-life situation for the function.)

   a. Does the graph begin to appear straight?

   b. If the graph does appear straight, what does a straight line with that slope through your given point represent in terms of the graph?

3. Can you think of a graph and a point on the graph so that no matter how much you might zoom in on that point, the graph would still not appear straight? You might try to sketch such a graph by hand, even if you can't find a formula for it.

On a Tangent

A *secant* for the graph of a function is the line (or line segment) connecting two points on the graph. A *tangent* is a line that "just touches" the graph at a point. This assignment explores the two concepts and their connections with derivatives.

1. Consider the function f defined by the equation $f(x) = 0.5x^2$.

   a. Sketch the graph of this function, with the scale on your x-axis going from -1 to 3. Use a full-size sheet of graph paper for this sketch so that you will be able to get enough detail in Question 1c.

   b. Label the point $(2, 2)$ on your sketch.

   c. The points listed here are also on the graph. In each case, draw the secant connecting the given point to $(2, 2)$ and find the slope of that secant.
      i. $(0, 0)$

      ii. $(1, 0.5)$

      iii. $(1.5, 1.125)$

      iv. $(1.9, 1.805)$

   d. Draw the line that is tangent to the graph at $(2, 2)$. Then estimate the slope of that line and explain your reasoning.

   e. Find the derivative of the function f at the point $(2, 2)$.

Continued on next page

2. The accompanying diagram shows the graph of a function.

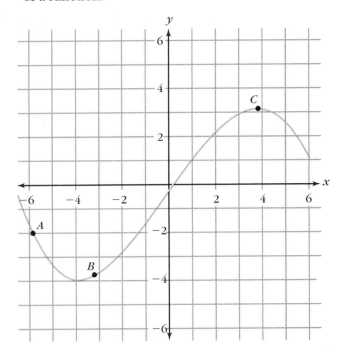

a. Make a copy of this graph.

b. Draw the tangent lines to the graph at each of the points *A*, *B*, and *C*.

c. Use your work from Question 2b to estimate the derivative of the function at each of the points *A*, *B*, and *C*.

Around King Arthur's Table

King Arthur was the ruler in Camelot who had all of those knights and a round table. He loved inviting the knights over for parties around his round table.

If there was something pleasant that the king could give to only one knight (an extra dessert, a dragon to chase, and so on), he had them play a game to determine who would get it.

The game went like this.

First, King Arthur put numbers on the chairs beginning with 1 and continuing around the table, with one chair for each knight. He had the knights sit down so that every chair was occupied. King Arthur himself remained standing.

Then King Arthur stood behind the knight in chair 1 and said, "You're In." Next, he moved to the knight in chair 2 and said, "You're Out," and that knight left his seat and went off to stand at the side of the room to watch the rest of the game. Next, he moved to the knight in chair 3 and said, "You're In." Then he said, "You're Out" to the knight in chair 4, and that knight left his seat and went to the side of the room.

The king continued around the table in this manner. When he came back around to the knight in chair 1, he said either "You're In" or "You're Out," depending on what he had said to the previous knight. (If the previous knight was "In," then the knight in chair 1 was now "Out," and vice versa.)

Continued on next page

The king kept moving around and around the table, alternately saying, "You're In" or "You're Out" to the knights who remained at the table. (If a chair was now empty, he simply skipped it.) He continued until only one knight was left sitting at the table. That knight was the winner.

Your Task

Of course, the number of knights varied from day to day, depending on who was sick, who was out chasing dragons, and so on. Sometimes there were only a handful, and sometimes there were over a hundred!

Here's the big question of the POW.

If you knew how many knights were going to be at the table, how could you quickly determine which chair to sit in so that you would win?

Your task is to develop a general rule, formula, or procedure that will predict the winning seat in terms of the number of knights present. Be sure to explain why your rule works.

Write-up

1. *Problem Statement*
2. *Process*
3. *Solution*
4. *Evaluation*
5. *Self-assessment*

What's It All About?

The idea of "the derivative of a function at a point" is a very important one in mathematics. In fact, this idea plays a key role in calculus.

You will be using this idea more in the unit. Thus, it would be a good idea for you to pull together what you know about it now, so that you will be ready to build on that knowledge.

Write down what you have learned about the idea of a derivative so far. Focus on these issues.

• What it means

• How you calculate it

• How it relates to other important ideas

Be sure to include specific examples.

A Model for Population Growth

Erika Cohen and Alex Ryane are writing equations based upon patterns they observed from the tables they completed for "Slippery Slopes."

You've seen that linear functions do not necessarily provide a good model for population growth. So what kind of function should you use?

In this section of the unit, you'll discover that for a certain family of functions, the derivative has a special property that makes it an excellent candidate to use in modeling population growth.

How Much for Broken Eggs?!!?

Do you remember a Problem of the Week called *The Broken Eggs*? (It was the first POW in Year 1.) As you may recall, it involved a farmer whose cart was hit as she was taking her eggs to market. Though she wasn't injured, her eggs got broken, and you spent a while figuring out how many eggs there were.

The cost of replacing 301 eggs may not have amounted to much then, but as prices rise, it could involve a lot of money. In this activity, you'll investigate what would happen if prices went up by the same percentage each year.

In this activity, you should assume that at the end of 1990, a dozen eggs cost 89¢ and that prices went up 5% every year. (In a situation like this, the figure of 5% is called the *rate of inflation*.)

Continued on next page

The first two questions are intended to get you started in your analysis of the situation.

1. a. How much did a dozen eggs cost at the end of 1991?

   b. How much did the price go up during 1991?

2. a. How much did a dozen eggs cost at the end of 1992?

   b. How much did the price go up during 1992?

Now gather similar information for other years, until you think you understand what's happening. Then answer these questions, assuming that the 5% inflation rate continues.

3. How much will a dozen eggs cost at the end of the year 2100? Explain your answer.

4. In what year will a dozen eggs first cost over $100?

Small but Plentiful

How Much for Broken Eggs?!!? involves growth in prices, based on a situation from a Year 1 POW. This assignment involves a type of population growth and is somewhat like *POW 1: Growth of Rat Populations,* in the unit *Fireworks.*

As you might recall, that POW was pretty complicated. You had to keep track of males and females, of different generations of rats, of when the females were ready to give birth, and so on. The situation in this assignment is much simpler.

Imagine a microscopic creature like an amoeba. Suppose that whenever one of these creatures gets to a certain size, it splits into two. Then these two each grow, and

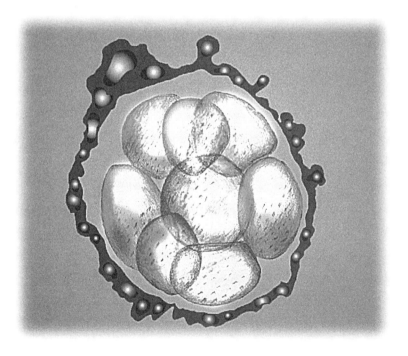

Continued on next page

when they get big enough, they each split into two, making four altogether. And so on.

Suppose further that at 12:01 a.m. on January 1 (just after midnight), there is one such tiny creature. And finally, suppose that it takes exactly 12 hours for such a creature to get big enough to split into two, with the first split taking place at 12:01 p.m. (just after noon) on January 1.

Your task is to find a general rule for figuring out the number of creatures at a given time. (*Note:* In this model, these creatures never die—they simply split into two.)

1. Begin with specific examples by figuring out how many creatures there are at each of these times.

   a. At 12:01 p.m. on January 1

   b. At 12:01 a.m. on January 2

   c. At 12:01 a.m. on January 5

   d. At 12:01 a.m. on January 31

2. Now find a general formula that tells how many creatures there are at 12:01 a.m., *d* days after the start of the experiment. (At 12:01 a.m. on January 1, $d = 0$.)

3. What will be the first day when there are over 1 million creatures?

18   The Return of Alice

In the Year 2 unit *All About Alice*, Lewis Carroll's fictional Alice could change her height by eating various kinds of special cake.

Each ounce she ate of a given type of cake multiplied her height by a particular factor, and Alice named the different kinds of cake to match their effect. For example, if the cake multiplied her height by a factor of 3, she called it "base 3 cake."

1. What would Alice's height be multiplied by if she ate each of these amounts of the particular types of cake? Write your answers using exponential expressions.

   a. 4 ounces of base 3 cake

   b. 5 ounces of base 2 cake

   c. x ounces of base 7 cake

2. Suppose Alice ate 4 ounces of base 2 cake and then 3 more ounces of the same type of cake.

   a. Use this situation to explain the equation $2^4 \cdot 2^3 = 2^7$.

   b. Explain the equation $2^4 \cdot 2^3 = 2^7$ in terms of repeated multiplication.

3. Explain the equation $\left(4^6\right)^7 = 4^{6 \cdot 7}$ in each of these ways.

   a. In a situation involving Alice

   b. In terms of repeated multiplication

Alice realized that she could express "cake questions" using exponential equations. For example, if she wanted to know how much base 2 cake to eat to multiply her height by 32, she would ask herself, "What's the solution

Continued on next page

to the equation $2^x = 32$?" She also realized that the solution to this equation could be expressed as a logarithm, namely, $\log_2 32$.

4. Find the value of $\log_2 32$ by solving the equation $2^x = 32$.

5. For each of these questions, write an exponential equation to represent the situation, find the numerical solution to the equation, and write the solution as a logarithm.

a. How much base 3 cake should Alice eat to multiply her height by 81?

b. How much base 2 cake should Alice eat to multiply her height by 128?

c. How much base 5 cake should Alice eat to multiply her height by 93? (For this example, give your numerical solution to the nearest tenth.)

Slippery Slopes

The derivatives of exponential functions show a very interesting pattern. Your task in this activity is to find the pattern.

1. Start with the exponential function defined by the equation $y = 2^x$.

   a. Your first task is to create an In-Out table like the one shown here.

x-value	y-value	Derivative

   Use these two steps to get a row of the table.

   - Pick a whole-number value for x and find the y-value that goes with it.

   - Get a good approximation for the derivative of the function at the point on the graph of the function $y = 2^x$ that is represented by your x- and y-values.

   Go through these two steps for several points to get several rows for the table.

   b. Once you have several rows for your table, study the data and write an equation expressing the derivative *in terms of the y-value.* (If necessary, develop more rows of the table.)

2. Repeat the process described in Question 1, but this time use the function whose equation is $y = 10^x$.

3. Pick a third exponential function and go through the process from Question 1 for that function.

The Forgotten Account

Tyler and his friends (from *Homework 3: Story Sketches*) had $50 left over after buying uniforms. They decided to put the money into a bank account so the next year's team would have a head start.

Well, next year's team forgot about the account, and so did the following year's team, and pretty soon, the account was completely forgotten.

Suppose the account earned 4.5% interest at the end of each year. (For simplicity, assume that the account was opened on January 1.) The interest is always added to the amount already in the account, so each year's interest is on a larger amount than the year before. (This is called *compound interest*. More specifically, the interest for this account is said to be *compounded annually* because interest is added to the account at the end of each year.)

1. How much money was in the account five years after Tyler and his friends started it?

2. Find a formula that describes the amount of money in the account after t years.

3. Write an equation that could be used to figure out how many years it would take for the account to grow to $500.

4. Solve your equation from Question 3.

5. Express the solution to the equation from Question 3 as a logarithm.

How Does It Grow?

To solve the central unit problem, you will need to find a function that grows in the same way that populations grow.

Question 1 of this assignment looks at a simple situation in order to establish some intuitive sense of what to expect from population growth.

1. Suppose a town has a population of 5000 and the population grows by 40 people in a single year. How much growth would you expect for a similar town with a population of 10,000? Explain your reasoning.

Questions 2 through 5 present two specific functions as possible models to describe population as a function of time. You will begin by getting some data about each function and its derivative.

2. First, consider the linear function $f(x) = 3x + 4$.

   a. Choose three different values for x and find $f(x)$ for each of these values.

   b. Find the derivative of the function at each of your three x-values.

Continued on next page

3. Next, consider the quadratic function $g(x) = x^2 - 9$.

   a. Choose three different values for x and find the value of the function for each of these values.

   b. Find the derivative of the function at each of your three x-values.

In Questions 4 and 5, remember that the derivative describes a rate of growth.

4. Now return to the function $f(x) = 3x + 4$ from Question 2.

   a. Describe any relationships you see between the derivative and either x or $f(x)$.

   b. Explain why the relationships you found in Question 4a are or are not appropriate to use in a mathematical representation of population growth. Consider whether those relationships seem to hold for the situation in Question 1.

5. Finally, look at the function $g(x) = x^2 - 9$ from Question 3.

   a. Describe any relationships you see between the derivative and either x or $g(x)$.

   b. Explain why the relationships you found in Question 5a are or are not appropriate to use in a mathematical representation of population growth. Consider whether those relationships seem to hold for the situation in Question 1.

The Significance of a Sign

When you are graphing a function, it's helpful to know the signs of the coordinates of the points. For instance, knowing the signs of the coordinates tells you what quadrant a point is in, and if a coordinate is 0, you know that the point is on a coordinate axis.

In this assignment, you'll explore similar issues concerning the sign of the derivative of the function.

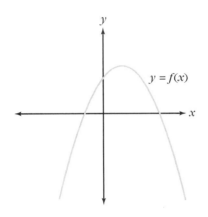

1. Make a copy of the graph at the left. Then identify where on the graph the function's derivative is positive, where the derivative is negative, and where the derivative is 0. (*Hint:* The derivative at a point on the graph can be thought of as the slope of the tangent line at that point.)

2. Sketch the graph of a function for which the derivative is positive for all values of *x*.

3. Sketch the graph of a function for which there are exactly two points where the derivative is 0.

The Sound of a Logarithm

Logarithms are a convenient concept for talking about exponents. For instance, the expression $\log_{10} 564$ represents the solution to the equation $10^x = 564$.

Logarithms are also used as the basis for certain units of measurement in science and are particularly useful when we are mainly concerned with changes in order of magnitude.

One such application concerns the measurement of noise levels. The *decibel scale* uses logarithms to describe the intensity of a sound in comparison to a particular reference value. The symbol I_0 is used to represent the intensity of a sound at the threshold of human hearing (that is, the quietest sound that humans can hear).

If I is the intensity of some other sound, the ratio of this intensity to I_0 is called the *relative intensity* of that other sound. We will represent this ratio $\frac{I}{I_0}$ by the letter R. Using this ratio, the *noise level* of that other sound, represented by N, is given by the equation

$$N = 10 \log_{10} R$$

The value of N is given in *decibels,* abbreviated as dB.

For example, suppose a sound has an intensity I that is 100 times the intensity of a sound at the threshold of human hearing. That is, suppose that the relative intensity R is 100. Because $\log_{10} 100 = 2$, this means that the sound has a noise level of $10 \cdot 2$, or 20 decibels.

Continued on next page

A sound at the threshold of human hearing, for which I is equal to I_0, has a noise level of 0 decibels, because $R = 1$, and $10 \cdot \log_{10} 1 = 10 \cdot 0 = 0$.

1. A normal conversation has a relative intensity of approximately 100,000. What is its decibel level?

2. A loud police whistle has a decibel level of approximately 90.

   a. How does its intensity compare to the threshold of human hearing?

   b. How does its intensity compare to ordinary conversation?

3. A sound intensity of approximately 10^{13} times the threshold level will cause a person's ears to hurt. What is the decibel level of such a sound?

4. a. If one sound measures 42 decibels, and the relative intensity of a second sound is three times the relative intensity of the first, what is the decibel level of the second sound?

   b. If one sound measures 60 decibels and another measures 68 decibels, how does the relative intensity of the second sound compare to the relative intensity of the first sound?

Adapted with permission from *College Algebra: A Preliminary Edition*, by Linda Kime and Judy Clark ©1996 by John Wiley and Sons. Reprinted by permission of John Wiley & Sons, Inc.

The Power of Powers

You saw in *Slippery Slopes* that certain functions have the special property that the derivative at each point is proportional to the *y*-value at that point.

For instance, in the case of the function $f(x) = 2^x$, you found that an equation very much like

$$f'(x) = 0.69 \cdot f(x)$$

appeared to hold true for all values of *x*. In the case of the function $g(x) = 10^x$, the equation was approximately

$$g'(x) = 2.30 \cdot g(x)$$

The Proportionality Property

When such a relationship between the derivative and the *y*-value holds true, we say that the function has the "proportionality property." (This is not standard terminology. We are using it here as shorthand for a complex idea.)

Continued on next page

When a function has the proportionality property, the ratio between the derivative and the y-value is called the **proportionality constant.** For instance, the numbers 0.69 and 2.30 are (approximately) the proportionality constants for the functions f and g.

Because the growth of a population is often proportional to the population itself, the proportionality property of functions like f and g makes them excellent candidates for a mathematical model of population growth.

In this assignment, you begin an exploration of which functions have the proportionality property. The exploration continues in *Homework 23: The Power of Powers, Continued.*

The Examples

For each of the two functions shown here, go through these steps.

- Estimate the value of the derivative for at least three different points on the graph.

- Based on your results, state whether you think the function has the proportionality property.

- If you think the function has the proportionality property, give an approximate value for the proportionality constant.

1. $h(x) = 2^x + 3^x$

2. $p(x) = 4.6 \cdot 2^x$

The Power of Powers, Continued

In *The Power of Powers,* you examined whether two particular functions had the proportionality property. This assignment continues the investigation of this property.

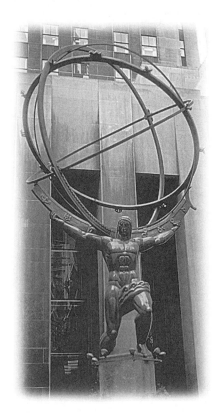

1. For each of the three functions shown here, go through these steps.

   - Estimate the value of the derivative for at least three different points on the graph.

   - Based on your results, state whether you think the function has the proportionality property.

   - If you think the function has the proportionality property, give an approximate value for the proportionality constant.

   a. $m(x) = 100 + 2^x$

   b. $k(x) = 0.83^x$

   c. $n(x) = 2^{3x}$

2. Based on your answers in Question 1 and your results from *The Power of Powers,* make some conjectures about the general form of functions that have this special property.

The Best Base

In their work with bases and exponents, Nikki Robinson and Ameilia Mitcalf discuss which might be the "best" base.

You've seen that exponential functions might be an excellent choice for modeling population growth. But what base should you use? 2? 10? Does it matter?

This portion of the unit begins with an activity in which you'll investigate whether bases are interchangeable. But with regard to derivatives, there's one that's clearly the best choice. And you'll see that this special base has a connection with a concept that at first seems completely unrelated.

A Basis for Disguise

You've seen that the derivative of an exponential function is a fixed multiple of the function's y-value.

Another useful fact is that exponential expressions can sometimes "disguise" themselves in other number bases. For example, 81^5 can also be written as 3^{20}. Here, a power of 81 is "disguised" as a power of 3. In this activity, you will explore this change-of-base idea.

1. How can you show that 81^5 and 3^{20} are equal without finding the numerical value of either expression? (*Hint:* What special relationship is there between 81 and 3?)

Continued on next page

2. Find a general rule for writing powers of 81 as powers of 3. That is, imagine that you want to put something in the box to fit the equation $81^x = 3^\square$. Explain how the number that goes in the box depends on x. (*Suggestion:* Think about how much base 3 cake would have the same effect on Alice as x ounces of base 81 cake.)

3. Reverse the roles of the two bases, 81 and 3, and find a general rule for writing powers of 3 as powers of 81. (The Alice metaphor may help here, too.)

4. Questions 1 through 3 may seem like special cases, because 81 is a whole-number power of 3.

    a. Suppose the two bases are 7 and 5. Can you find a general rule for writing 7^x as a power of 5? (*Hint:* Can you write 7 itself as a power of 5? Does the Alice metaphor help?)

    b. Examine whether there is always a general rule for writing b^x as a power of a, no matter what numbers are used for a and b. (Of course, the rule itself would have to depend on a and b.)

    Give the rule in the cases for which such a rule exists, and describe the values for a or b for which the rule would not exist.

Blue Book

Car dealers sometimes use the rule of thumb that a car loses about 30% of its value each year. Use this rule to answer Questions 1 and 2.

1. Suppose you bought a new car in December 1990 for $15,000.

   a. According to the rule of thumb, what would the car be worth at each of these times?

      i. In December 1991

      ii. In December 1995

      iii. In December 2000

   b. Develop a general formula for the value of the car *t* years after purchase.

2. Clarabell has thought about how cars lose value. She noticed that a $20,000 car will lose about $6,000 of its value the first year, while a $10,000 car will lose about $3,000 of its value the first year. She figures that the more expensive car loses more value each year, so eventually it will be worth less than the cheaper car.

   How long do you think it will take until this happens?

California and Exponents

In 1850, the population of California was about 92,600, and in 1860, it was about 380,000. In *Homework 8: California, Here I Come!*, you found a linear function that went through the two points (1850, 92,600) and (1860, 380,000).

Your task in this assignment is to find an exponential function for the same population data and then examine its accuracy for making predictions. To make the arithmetic much simpler, treat the year 1850 as $x = 0$ and the year 1860 as $x = 10$.

1. Find two numbers a and b so that the exponential function $y = a \cdot b^x$ goes through the two points (0, 92,600) and (10, 380,000). (*Hint:* Substitute the coordinates of the first point for x and y to get an equation that involves only a. Solve that equation and then use the second point and the value you found for a to find b.)

2. Use your answer to Question 1 to determine what the population of California would have been in 1990 if population growth had continued at the same relative growth rate as during the Gold Rush period. (*Hint:* If the value 0 for x represents 1850 and the value 10 for x represents 1860, what value of x represents 1990?)

3. Based on this exponential model, do you think population growth in California has slowed down or speeded up since the Gold Rush period?

Find That Base!

You know that the derivative of the exponential function $y = b^x$ is a particular constant times its y-value. As long as the base b is fixed, this proportionality constant is the same at every point on the graph, but the proportionality constant does depend on the value used for b.

Scientists prefer to pick a standard base so it will be easier to compare one function to another. Because any exponential function can be expressed in any base (as long as you stick to positive bases other than 1), they are free to pick any number for this standard base.

Because scientific work often involves derivatives, scientists have chosen for this standard base the number that makes the proportionality constant equal to 1.

Your job is to estimate this special base. In other words, estimate the value of b for which, at every point on the graph of the function $f(x) = b^x$, the derivative is equal to b^x.

Double Trouble

In inflation situations like that of *How Much for Broken Eggs?!!?*, the length of time it takes for the price to double is called the *doubling time*.

Of course, the doubling time depends on the rate of inflation. Your main task in this assignment is to investigate the relationship between these two values.

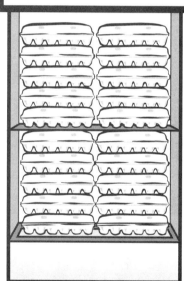

1. Consider the case of an inflation rate of 5% per year, and find its doubling time. For simplicity, you can start with a price of $1 and see how long it takes until the price gets to $2. Give your answer to the nearest hundredth of a year.

2. Choose a different inflation rate, and find the doubling time.

3. Continue with other inflation rates, and put your results in an In-Out table in which the *In* is the inflation rate and the *Out* is the doubling time.

4. a. Look for a pattern or rule that describes your In-Out table.

   b. Try to explain why your pattern works.

5. a. For each inflation rate in your table, also compute the *quadrupling time*—that is, the length of time it takes for the price to be multiplied by a factor of 4. (If you started with $1, this would be the time required to reach $4.)

   b. How does the quadrupling time compare with the doubling time? Explain your answer.

The Generous Banker

"Double Your Money in 20 Years!" read the bank's advertisement. Adam thought that sounded like a pretty good deal, but he also thought he might be able to talk his way into something even better. So he went in to speak to the banker.

"Doubling your money is like increasing it by 100%, I think," he said with a practiced uncertainty. "But what if I need my money before 20 years? Can I get a proportional part of the interest each year, just in case?"

The banker hesitated, never having studied much mathematics. "Well, that seems fair, Mr. Smith," she finally replied. "How much should you get each year?"

Adam feigned confusion and took out his calculator. "100% for 20 years . . . let's see . . . , 100 divided by 20 . . . , I guess that's 5% each year. Can you increase my account by 5% each year instead?"

The banker agreed, and so Adam deposited $1,000 in an account and left it there for the full 20 years.

1. How much was in the account 20 years later?

2. How much would have been in the account if Adam had talked the bank into giving him a proportional amount of interest, compounded every six months instead of once a year?

3. What if Adam got a proportional amount of interest, compounded every three months?

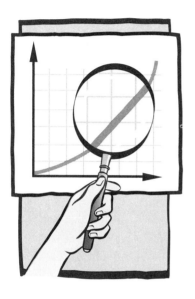

27

Comparing Derivatives

Part I: Shared Points

Here are the equations for three functions whose graphs all pass through $(0, 0)$. The three graphs also all pass through $(1, 1)$.

- $f(x) = x$
- $g(x) = x^2$
- $h(x) = x^3$

Do you think all three functions will have the same derivative at $(0, 0)$? What about at $(1, 1)$? The following questions will help you decide.

1. Graph all three functions on the same set of axes for x-values from -1 to 2. Be sure to plot enough specific points for each function (including noninteger values of x) to get accurate graphs, and pay particular care in plotting x-values between 0 and 1.

2. *Based only on your graphs,* answer each of these questions and explain your reasoning.

   a. Which of the three functions has the largest derivative at the point $(0, 0)$?

   b. Which of the three functions has the largest derivative at the point $(1, 1)$?

3. Actually find the derivative of each function at each of the common points, and compare your results with your answers to Question 2.

Continued on next page

Part II: Derivative Sketch

Suppose this is the graph of the function defined by the equation $y = f(x)$.

4. Make a copy of the graph, and show where on the graph the derivative of this function is positive, where the derivative is negative, and where the derivative is 0. Make your answers as complete as possible.

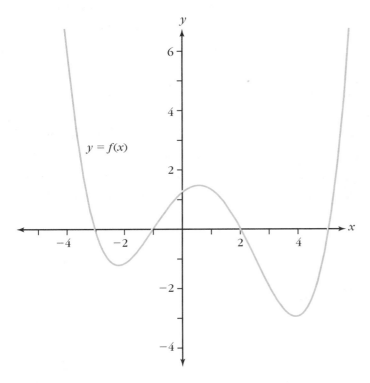

5. *Sketch* the graph of f', which is the derivative function of f. Use the same scale for the x-axis on your graph of the derivative function as you use for the graph of f itself.

28 The Limit of Their Generosity

As you saw in *The Generous Banker*, Adam deposited $1,000 in a bank. The bank had advertised that it would double his money in 20 years. But Adam persuaded the banker to increase it instead by 5% for each of the 20 years instead of increasing it by 100% all at once at the end of the 20-year term.

For a while, Adam thought he was going to get really rich due to the banker's generosity. He persuaded her to give him an appropriate fraction of the interest every six months and then persuaded her to calculate the interest every month.

Once he had gotten this far, Adam was ready to spring his ultimate request. He asked the banker to give him proportional interest every day and add it to his account.

1. Without doing any calculations, about how much do you think Adam would end up with?

2. Using your calculator, compute Adam's wealth after 20 years. (Figure 365.25 days per year.)

3. What would Adam end up with if the bank gave him proportional interest *every hour*?

California Population with e's

In *Homework 25: California and Exponents,* you used a function of the form $y = a \cdot b^x$ to get a model of the population growth of California between 1850 and 1860.

Specifically, using $x = 0$ to represent 1850 and $x = 10$ to represent 1860, you found the values of a and b so that the function $y = a \cdot b^x$ went through the points (0, 92,600) and (10, 380,000).

Your task in this assignment is similar, but now you should use e as the base of the exponential function.

1. Find values for k and c so that the exponential function $y = k \cdot e^{cx}$ goes through those two points. (*Hint:* As in the previous assignment, use the first point to get an equation involving only one of the two unknown values.)

2. Express the value you get for c in terms of a natural logarithm.

3. How are the coefficients k and c in this assignment related to the coefficients a and b in the previous assignment? (If necessary, redo Question 1 of *Homework 25: California and Exponents* to find a and b.)

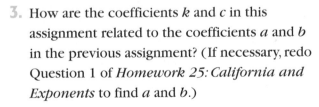

Back to the Data

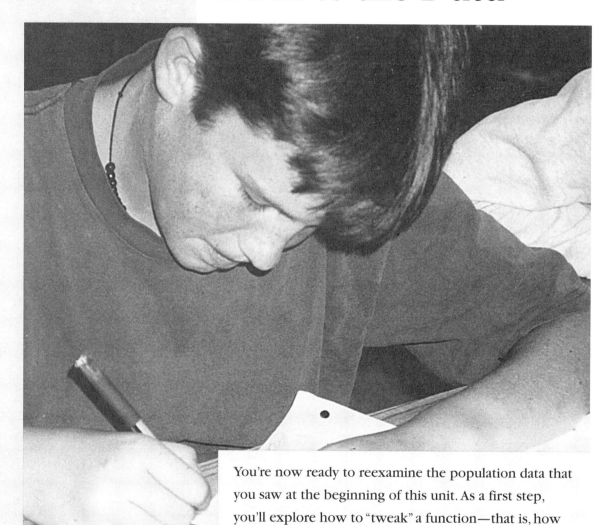

You're now ready to reexamine the population data that you saw at the beginning of this unit. As a first step, you'll explore how to "tweak" a function—that is, how to make little changes in the function so that its graph is closer to what you want.

You'll then conclude the unit by looking for a function that comes close to the initial data and using that function to predict when we will be squashed up against one another.

Which type of function is Joe Stebbins using to predict how long before the population will read $1.6 \cdot 10^{15}$?

Tweaking the Function

Suppose that you have some data points and need to fit them with a function. Suppose also that you know more or less what type of function should fit the data and that your first guess comes pretty close to fitting, but not as close as you would like.

You then need to change the function a bit—to adjust it somehow to make it fit the data somewhat better.

How do you do this? This activity should help you answer that question.

Begin with the function $y = e^x$. Change it in different ways and watch how the graph is affected. For instance, you might try multiplying e^x by various coefficients, or you might adjust the exponent in some way.

Your task is to explore how the graph is changed. Here are some things to watch for.

- What makes the graph "more curvy" or "less curvy"?

- What changes the horizontal position or the vertical position of the graph?

Begin with these questions, but do not limit yourself to them. Find out whatever you can and keep track of what you learn.

30

Beginning Portfolios—Part I

Think about the examples of growth and change that you have studied in this unit, focusing on two particular kinds of functions.

- Linear functions, which have the form $y = a + bx$

- Exponential functions, which have the form $y = k \cdot e^{cx}$

Compare the two types of functions, addressing these issues.

- How does each function represent rates of growth or change?

- How does each function represent starting points or initial values?

- What kinds of situations is each function appropriate for describing or modeling? (Be more specific than simply saying "linear growth" or "exponential growth.")

Return to *Small World, Isn't It?*

Here are the numbers you saw at the beginning of the unit, which show the changes in world population over the past several centuries.

Year	Estimated Population
1650	470,000,000
1750	694,000,000
1850	1,091,000,000
1900	1,570,000,000
1950	2,510,000,000
1960	3,030,000,000
1970	3,680,000,000
1980	4,480,000,000
1985	4,870,000,000
1990	5,290,000,000
1995	5,730,000,000

As initially stated, your task was to determine, based on this data, how long it would take until people were "squashed up against one another." In this unit, that phrase has been interpreted to mean that each person has exactly 1 square foot to call her or his own. Based on estimates of the earth's surface area, this means that the population would have to reach approximately $1.6 \cdot 10^{15}$ people.

Continued on next page

Here are your tasks in this final activity.

1. Plot the population data.

2. a. Find a function that approximates your data. At least at first, you should look for a function of the form $y = k \cdot e^{cx}$. This first approximation need not be very accurate.

   b. Assuming that the population grew according to your function from step a, determine when each person would have only 1 square foot to call his or her own. That is, based on the function from step a, how long would it take for the population to reach $1.6 \cdot 10^{15}$ people?

3. Repeat steps a and b from Question 2 as often as you think is useful, looking for a better approximation. Use ideas from the activity *Tweaking the Function* to try to make whatever adjustments you think are needed.

   State your best approximating function and the estimate it gives for how long it would take for the population to reach $1.6 \cdot 10^{15}$ people.

4. Discuss whether you think the population data in the table is really exponential and whether you think it will be exponential in the future. Give reasons for your conclusions.

Beginning
Portfolios—Part II

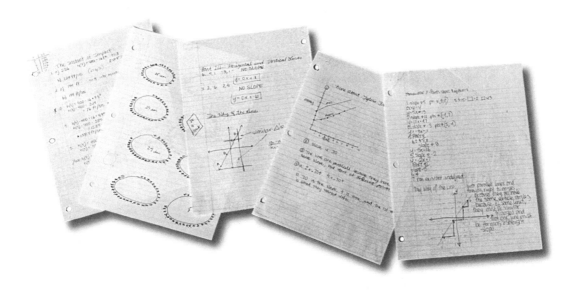

1. Much of this unit focused on exponential functions, which leads naturally into working with compound interest.

   Pick an activity from the unit that helped develop your understanding of compound interest, and describe what you learned from the assignment.

2. The beginning of this unit concentrated on linear functions. Summarize what you have learned about finding equations of straight lines, and select one or two activities that were particularly helpful to you in this area.

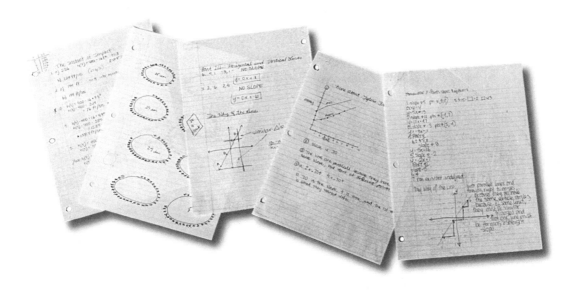

32

Small World, Isn't It? Portfolio

Now that *Small World, Isn't It?* is completed, it is time to put together your portfolio for the unit. Compiling this portfolio has three parts.

• Writing a cover letter in which you summarize the unit

• Choosing papers to include from your work in this unit

• Discussing your personal growth during the unit

Cover Letter for *Small World, Isn't It?*

Look back over *Small World, Isn't It?* and describe the central problem of the unit and the main mathematical ideas. This description should give an overview of how the key ideas were developed and how they were used to solve the central problem.

In compiling your portfolio, you will select some activities that you think were important in developing the key ideas of this unit. Your cover letter should include an explanation of why you selected the particular items.

Selecting Papers from *Small World, Isn't It?*

Your portfolio for *Small World, Isn't It?* should contain these items.

• *Homework 16: What's It All About?*

• *Homework 30: Beginning Portfolios—Part I*

• *Homework 31: Beginning Portfolios—Part II*

Include the activities from the unit that you selected as part of this assignment.

Continued on next page

- Other key activities

  Include two or three other activities that you think were important in developing the key ideas of this unit.

- A Problem of the Week

  Select one of the POWs you completed during this unit (*The More the Merrier?, Planning the Platforms,* or *Around King Arthur's Table*).

Personal Growth

Small World, Isn't It? focused on various kinds of growth. For this part of your portfolio, write about your own growth during the unit. You might want to specifically address this issue.

> *What changes or growth have you noticed during Year 3 in your ability to work well in groups?*

You should include here any other thoughts about your experiences with this unit that you want to share with a reader of your portfolio.

Supplemental Problems

The supplemental problems for *Small World, Isn't It?* continue the unit's areas of emphasis—rates of change and linear and exponential functions—although other topics appear as well. Here are some examples.

- *Solving for Slope* and *The Slope's the Thing* give additional perspectives on how to find the slope for a linear equation.

- *Deriving Derivatives* looks at developing general formulas for derivatives.

- *Dr. Doubleday's Base* and *Investigating Constants* examine the role of the parameters in two different forms of the general exponential function.

- *Summing the Sequences—Parts I and II* are follow-ups to *POW 9: Planning the Platforms*.

Solving for Slope

You've seen that in an equation like $y = 3x + 5$, the coefficient of x (in this case, 3) is the slope of the graph.

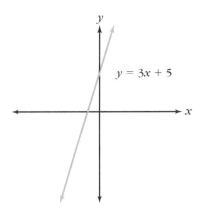

In this activity, you will examine linear equations that do not have this form.

1. Begin by examining these specific examples. In each case, solve the equation for y in terms of x to determine the slope.

   a. $3y - 2x = 12$ c. $5x - 2y = 10$

   b. $x + 4y = -8$ d. $-6y + 7x = -2$

2. Now consider the general linear equation in the standard form

   $$Ax + By = C$$

   a. Develop an expression for the slope in terms of A, B, and C.

   b. Consider each of these questions. Based on examples, describe how to answer them simply by looking at A, B, and C.

   • Is the line rising or falling as it goes to the right?

   • For lines rising to the right, is the line steeper than $y = x$?

   • For lines falling to the right, is the line steeper than $y = -x$?

   Explain not only how your method works, but also why it works.

Slope and Slant

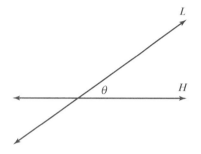

One way to describe the "steepness" or "slant" of a line is to measure the angle formed between that line and a horizontal line. This angle is called the **angle of inclination** of the line.

For instance, the diagram here shows a line L and a horizontal line H. The angle labeled θ (the Greek letter "theta") is the angle of inclination of line L.

You've been working with lines that are the graphs of linear equations. In the context of the coordinate system, the angle of inclination of a line is the angle formed between that line and the positive direction of the x-axis. You might expect to find some relationship between the slope of such a line and its angle of inclination.

Finding such a relationship is complicated by the fact that the steepness of the graph is affected by the scales on the axes. In this activity, you will eliminate that complication by assuming that the vertical and horizontal axes have the same scale.

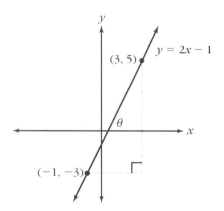

1. This diagram shows the graph of the equation $y = 2x - 1$ and two points, $(-1, -3)$ and $(3, 5)$, that fit this equation. The diagram also shows an angle of inclination θ for the line and a right triangle with $(-1, -3)$ and $(3, 5)$ as two of its vertices.

   a. Find the slope of the line $y = 2x - 1$.

   b. Use trigonometry and the right triangle to find a relationship between the slope of this line and its angle of inclination.

Continued on next page

c. Use your work from part b to find the measure of angle θ.

d. Carefully draw the line through $(-1, -3)$ and $(3, 5)$ on graph paper, using the same scale for the vertical and horizontal axes. Then measure the angle of inclination and check if it matches your result from part c.

2. Use the ideas from Question 1 to answer these questions (again making the assumption that the vertical and horizontal axes have the same scale).

   a. What is the angle of inclination for a line whose slope is 1?

   b. What is the slope of a line whose angle of inclination is 30 degrees?

3. State a general principle, using trigonometry, relating the slope of the line to its angle of inclination.

   Note: So far, we have defined the trigonometric functions only for acute angles in right triangles. Therefore, in Question 3, assume that the line has an angle of inclination between 0 and 90 degrees. (You will see how to define the trigonometric functions for arbitrary angles in the Year 4 unit *High Dive.*)

PROBLEM

Predicting Parallels

When a linear equation is written to express y in terms of x, the coefficient of x is equal to the slope of the graph. For example, the graph of $y = 3x + 5$ has slope 3. This makes it easy to recognize when two equations have graphs that are parallel, because they have the same coefficient for x.

According to this principle, the graphs of the equations $y = 3x + 5$ and $y = 3x + 9$ should be parallel. That is, they should not have any points in common. The first task in this activity is to prove this fact.

1. Show that the equations $y = 3x + 5$ and $y = 3x + 9$ cannot have any common solutions. That is, show that there is no point that is on the graphs of both equations.

But what about lines that are not in "$y =$" form? Is there a simple way to recognize such lines in the standard form $Ax + By = C$ are parallel? Begin by answering Questions 2 and 3, and then try to generalize your results.

2. a. Draw the graph of the equation $4x - 3y = 24$.

   b. Choose a point *not* on the graph, and draw a line through that point parallel to your graph from part a.

   c. Find the equation of the line you drew in part b.

3. Graph the equation $8x - 6y = 24$, and compare it with the graphs from Question 2.

The Generalization

4. Based on Questions 2 and 3, and from other equations you might examine, what general principles can you state for determining at a glance whether two linear equations in standard form have parallel graphs?

The Slope's the Thing

You know that two points determine a straight line, so knowing the coordinates of two points on a line is enough information to get an equation for that line. This activity looks at a systematic way to get the equation from that information, based on slope.

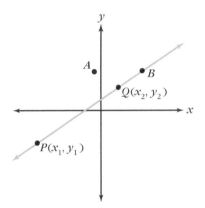

Let's call the two given points P and Q. The method is based on these two statements.

- If a point is *not* on that line (for instance, point A in the diagram), then the slope of the line connecting that point to P will be *different* from the slope of the line through P and Q.

- If a point *is* on that line (for instance, point B), then the slope of the line connecting that point to P will be *the same* as the slope of the line through P and Q.

1. Suppose that P has coordinates (x_1, y_1), that Q has coordinates (x_2, y_2), and that R is another point in the plane, with coordinates (x, y).

   a. Write an expression for the slope of the line through P and Q.

   b. Write an expression for the slope of the line through P and R.

   c. Combine parts a and b to get an equation stating that these two slopes are equal.

2. Apply this method to find the equation of the line through $(1, 5)$ and $(-2, -1)$.

3. Use similar triangles to prove the two statements on which this method is based.

Speedy's Speed by Algebra

In *Photo Finish,* you met your old friend Speedy the track star, who runs the last 400 meters of a 1600-meter relay race.

Based on a film of one of her races, an analyst came up with the function $m(t) = 0.1t^2 + 3t$ to describe how far Speedy had run after t seconds of her segment of the race. The equation $m(50) = 400$ shows that Speedy crossed the finish line after exactly 50 seconds.

In *Photo Finish,* you found Speedy's average speed for small time intervals near the end of the race and used those average speeds to get an estimate for her speed at the instant when she crossed the finish line. You may wonder how accurate or reliable that estimate is. That is, you may be wondering this:

> *How fast was Speedy really going at the instant when she crossed the finish line?*

This assignment describes an algebraic approach to answering this question.

1. First, use steps a through c to write out in detail the computation involved in finding Speedy's average speed for the last tenth of a second at the end of the race.

    a. Find out how far Speedy had run after 49.9 seconds. That is, compute $m(49.9)$.

    b. Find out how far Speedy ran during the last tenth of a second. That is, find the difference between $m(49.9)$ and 400.

Continued on next page

c. Find Speedy's average speed during the last tenth of a second of the race. That is, divide the distance you found in Question 1b by the length of the time interval, which is 0.1 seconds.

2. Now use the same process as in Question 1, but substitute the last h seconds for the last tenth of a second. That is, instead of working with the time interval from $t = 49.9$ to $t = 50$, as in Question 1, work with the time from $t = 50 - h$ to $t = 50$. Steps 2a through 2c will guide you through this process.

   a. Find out how far Speedy had run after $50 - h$ seconds. That is, find $m(50 - h)$. (Your answer should be an expression in terms of h.)

   b. Find out how far Speedy ran during the last h seconds. That is, write an expression (in terms of h) for the difference between $m(50 - h)$ and 400.

   c. Divide the distance you found in Question 2b by the length of the time interval, which is h seconds.

   d. Confirm your expression in Question 2c by substituting 0.1 for h. Does that give the same answer you got in Question 1c?

3. Your result for Question 2c should be an algebraic expression in terms of h. This expression gives Speedy's average speed during the last h seconds of the race.

   a. Simplify this expression as much as you can.

   b. What happens to your expression in Question 3a as h gets smaller and smaller?

   c. What does your result in Question 3b mean in terms of Speedy's instantaneous speed?

4. Does your work in Questions 1 through 3 give you further confidence in your results from *Photo Finish*? Explain your response.

Potential Disaster

Construction workers have partially ruptured a natural gas pipeline in a research building. The pipeline's protective inner membrane has been pushed out through the opening, forming a sphere-shaped balloon on the outside of the pipeline.

Emergency crews are confident that they can patch the hole in the pipe but see no way to push the balloon back into the pipe. They decide that they must cut the balloon off from the pipe and then quickly patch the hole.

An electrical wire nearby poses a serious danger, because if the wire and balloon come in contact with each other, the gas in the balloon will be ignited and the balloon will explode, causing massive damage. Gas is flowing into the balloon so that its volume is growing at a constant rate.

The balloon was discovered 30 minutes after the rupture. In those 30 minutes, the balloon had grown to a diameter of 1 foot. The balloon will come in contact with the wire if its diameter reaches 2 feet.

It is now 20 minutes since the balloon was discovered, and the building's manager is in a panic. The manager thinks that the balloon will explode in only 10 more minutes. But the engineer in charge of the emergency crew seems rather calm.

1. a. Why do you suppose the manager thinks they have only 10 minutes left before the balloon explodes?

   b. What is wrong with the manager's reasoning?

2. How much time do they really have? (The volume of a sphere of diameter d is given by the expression $\frac{1}{6}\pi d^3$.)

Proving the Tangent

In *Homework 15: On a Tangent,* you examined the graph of the function $f(x) = 0.5x^2$ near the point $(2, 2)$ on the graph. You were asked to use a series of secant lines through $(2, 2)$ to estimate the slope of the tangent line at that point, which seemed to be equal to 2.

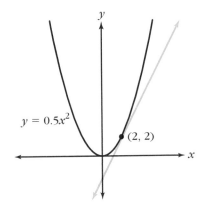

1. Use this estimate of the derivative to write the equation of the tangent line. That is, write the equation of the line whose slope is 2 and that goes through the point $(2, 2)$.

2. Prove that your estimate of the derivative is correct by showing that $(2, 2)$ is the only point where the line you found in Question 1 meets the graph of the function $f(x) = 0.5x^2$. (*Hint:* Show that your equation from Question 1 and the equation $y = 0.5x^2$ have only one solution in common.)

PROBLEM

Summing the Sequences—Part I

In *POW 9: Planning the Platform,* Camilla needed to find the sum of a sequence of numbers in which each term differed from the previous term by the same amount.

For instance, suppose that the first platform had been 28 inches tall, that the difference in height between adjacent platforms had been 8 inches, and that there had been 5 platforms altogether. Then she would have needed to find the sum

$$28 + 36 + 44 + 52 + 60$$

A sequence such as 28, 36, 44, and so on, in which the difference between terms is constant, is called an **arithmetic sequence.** (In this context, the word "arithmetic" is an adjective and is pronounced "a-rith-*met*-ic," with the emphasis on the third syllable.)

The first number in an arithmetic sequence is called the **initial term,** and the amount added to get each successive term is called the **difference.** For instance, in our example, the initial term is 28 and the difference is 8.

1. a. Find an expression in terms of *n* for the *n*th term of the arithmetic sequence whose initial term is 28 and whose difference is 8.

   b. Find an expression in terms of *n* for the sum of the first *n* terms of this sequence.

Continued on next page

Interactive Mathematics Program

If we use *a* to represent the initial term and *d* to represent the difference, then the general arithmetic sequence has the terms $a, a + d, a + 2d, a + 3d$, and so on.

2. Find an expression in terms of *a*, *d*, and *n* for the *n*th term of the general arithmetic sequence.

3. Find an expression in terms of *a*, *d*, and *n* for the sum of the first *n* terms of the general arithmetic sequence. Give your answer as an algebraic expression in closed form—that is, without the use of summation or ellipsis (...) notation.

4. Apply your expression from Question 3 to find the sum of the first 50 terms of the arithmetic sequence 15, 21, 27, 33, and so on.

Summing the Sequences—Part II

In *Summing the Sequences—Part I,* you examined arithmetic sequences, which have a constant difference between terms.

If instead we require a constant *ratio* between terms, we get another important category of sequences, the **geometric sequence.** For instance, the sequence 8, 24, 72, 216, and so on, in which each term is three times the previous term, is an example of a geometric sequence. Here, 8 is the initial term and 3 is the ratio.

1. a. Find an expression in terms of n for the nth term of the geometric sequence whose initial term is 8 and whose ratio is 3.

   b. Find an expression in terms of n for the sum of the first n terms of this sequence.

   Hint: Compare the sum of the first n terms of this sequence with the sum of the first n terms of the sequence 24, 72, 216, and so on. The second sum is three times the first (because each term is three times as big). What do you get if you subtract the first sum from the second? (Think about terms that cancel out. You may want to look at specific values of n.)

If we use a to represent the initial term and r to represent the ratio, then the general geometric sequence has the terms a, ar, ar^2, ar^3, and so on.

Continued on next page

2. Find an expression in terms of a, r, and n for the nth term of the general geometric sequence.

3. Find an expression in terms of a, r, and n for the sum of the first n terms of the general geometric sequence. Give your answer as an algebraic expression in closed form—that is, without the use of summation or ellipsis (. . .) notation. (Try to generalize the hint from Question 1b.)

4. Apply your expression from Question 3 to find the sum of the first 20 terms of the sequence 3, 6, 12, 24, and so on.

5. Consider the case of the geometric sequence with $a = 1$ and $r = \frac{1}{2}$.

    a. Write an expression (in terms of n) for the sum of the first n terms of this sequence. (Use your work from Question 3.)

    b. Find the sum of the first ten terms of this sequence by actually adding the terms, and use it to verify your answer from Question 5a.

    c. What happens to your expression from Question 5a as n gets bigger? Does that fit your intuitive idea? Explain.

6. (Extra challenge) How can you generalize Question 5 to the case in which the ratio r is any number between 0 and 1?

PROBLEM

A Little Shakes a Lot

One important use of logarithms (at least in some places) is the *Richter scale,* which is a numerical way of describing the magnitude of an earthquake.

Somewhat simplified, the formula used to get the Richter scale number of an earthquake is

$$R = \log_{10} a$$

where R is the Richter scale number and a is the amplitude or amount of the ground motion, as measured on a seismograph.

Continued on next page

In order to give intuitive meaning to Richter scale numbers, you need to have some points of reference. For example, an earthquake that measures 4.0 on the Richter scale is barely perceptible outside its immediate center. In contrast, the great San Francisco earthquake of 1906 measured 8.3 on the Richter scale.

1. These Richter scale numbers make it sound as if the 1906 earthquake was only about twice as big as an earthquake that can hardly be felt. But, in fact, that isn't the case at all. Show this by answering these questions.

   a. How many times as much ground motion does an 8.3 quake have compared to a 4.0 quake?

   b. What Richter scale measurement would represent a quake that has twice the ground motion of one that measures 4.0 on the Richter scale?

   c. What Richter scale measurement would represent a quake that has half the ground motion of one that measures 8.3 on the Richter scale?

2. The 1989 Loma Prieta earthquake in California was measured at about 7.1 on the Richter scale. In numerical terms, how did the amount of its ground motion compare to that of the 1906 earthquake?

Looking at Logarithms

Logarithms are defined in terms of exponential equations. For instance, $\log_b a$ is defined as the value of x that fits the equation $b^x = a$.

Because of this relationship between logarithms and exponents, there is a principle about logarithms corresponding to every principle about exponents. Your task in this activity is to develop these principles for logarithms. Throughout the activity, b represents a positive number other than 1.

1. The additive law of exponents states

$$b^x \cdot b^y = b^{x+y}$$

Your first task is to find a corresponding principle for logarithms. Start with the specific questions in Questions 1a and 1b.

a. What is $\log_2 2^5$? What is $\log_2 2^9$? What is $\log_2 (2^5 \cdot 2^9)$?

b. Find approximate values for $\log_3 8$, $\log_3 7$, and $\log_3 56$. What relationship do you see among these three logarithms?

c. Generalize your results from Questions 1a and 1b to get a formula for $\log_b (rs)$ in terms of $\log_b r$ and $\log_b s$.

d. Use the additive law of exponents to prove your general result. (*Hint:* Think of r as b^x and s as b^y.)

Continued on next page

2. Another principle for exponents states

$$(b^x)^n = b^{xn}$$

Again, your task is to find a corresponding principle for logarithms by first looking at specific questions.

a. How does $\log_5 (5^7)^6$ compare to $\log_5 5^7$?

b. Find approximate values for $\log_3 17$ and $\log_3 17^4$. What relationship do you see between these two logarithms?

c. Generalize your results from Questions 2a and 2b to get a formula for $\log_b (r^n)$ in terms of $\log_b r$ and n.

d. Use the principle $(b^x)^n = b^{xn}$ to prove your general result. (*Hint:* Again, think of r as b^x.)

3. The range, or set of possible outputs, for the function $y = b^x$ consists of all positive numbers. That is, as x varies over all possible values, y can be any positive number. What does this say about the domain, or set of possible inputs, of the function defined by the equation $f(u) = \log_b u$? That is, what numbers can be used for u in this function?

4. a. What is the domain for the function $y = b^x$?

b. What does your answer to Question 4a say about the range of the function defined by the equation $g(v) = \log_b v$?

PROBLEM

Finding a Function

In *Homework 21: The Significance of a Sign*, you were asked to sketch the graph of one function for which the derivative is positive for all values of x and another function for which the derivative is zero at exactly two points. This activity continues that theme.

1. Sketch the graph of a function f that fits both of these conditions.

   • $f'(x)$ is positive for all values of x between -2 and 3

   • $f'(x)$ is negative if $x < -2$ or $x > 3$

2. Sketch the graph of a function $g(x)$ that fits all of these conditions.

   • $g'(x)$ is zero for exactly three values of x

   • $g(x)$ is positive between $x = -1$ and $x = 4$

   • $g(x)$ is negative if $x > 4$ or $x < -1$

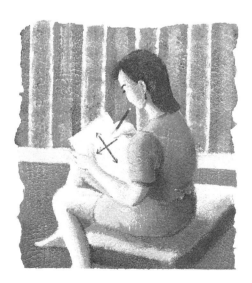

Deriving Derivatives

By looking at the derivative of a function at many of its points, you can sometimes find a rule for its derivative at any point.

In this activity, you will be looking for a rule that allows you to find quickly the derivative of a function of the form $y = ax^n$. (The functions defined by the equations $y = 2x^2$, $y = x^3$, and $y = -3x^6$ are all examples of this type of function.)

Suggestion: Start with a specific function of this form, make a table of values for its derivative, and find a rule for this table. You might then try other functions that use the same exponent and look for a generalization for functions with that exponent. (*Reminder:* This exponent is called the *degree* of the function.)

Once you have a rule for functions of a particular degree, try a different degree and then try to generalize.

The Reality of Compounding

You saw in *The Generous Banker* that getting 5% annual interest, compounded each year for 20 years, is not the same as doubling your money in 20 years.

1. If interest is compounded annually, what rate of interest should the bank give each year in order for money to double in 20 years?

2. Suppose that the bank compounds interest quarterly. What quarterly rate will double the value of an account in 20 years?

SUPPLEMENTAL
PROBLEM

Transcendental Numbers

In *Orchard Hideout,* you worked with the number π, which can be defined as the ratio between the circumference and diameter of a circle. In this unit, you were introduced to the number e. Both π and e are examples of **transcendental numbers.**

What is a transcendental number? Your task in this assignment is to find out about this category of numbers. You may want to start your investigation at the library. Then write a report explaining what you learned about transcendental numbers and their history.

Dr. Doubleday's Base

You have seen that for any positive number b, the derivative of the exponential function $y = b^x$ is a proportionality constant times its y-value.

For example, you found that if the base b is equal to 2, then the proportionality constant is approximately 0.69. In other words, for the function $y = 2^x$, the derivative at a point $(x, 2^x)$ on the graph is approximately $0.69 \cdot 2^x$.

You have also seen that there is a special base, called e, for which this proportionality constant is the number 1. In other words, for the function $y = e^x$, the derivative at any point on the graph is equal to the y-value at that point.

While it is convenient for scientists to use e as the base, Dr. Doubleday would like a base for which the proportionality constant is 2. (We don't know why.) In other words, the doctor would like to find an exponential function whose derivative at every point of its graph is equal to twice its y-value at that point.

1. Determine what base Dr. Doubleday should use. That is, find a number b such that for every point (x, b^x) on the graph of the function $f(x) = b^x$, the derivative is equal to $2 \cdot b^x$. (You will only be able to estimate b. Try to get its value to the nearest hundredth.)

2. Look for a relationship between your answer to Question 1 and the number e.

Investigating Constants

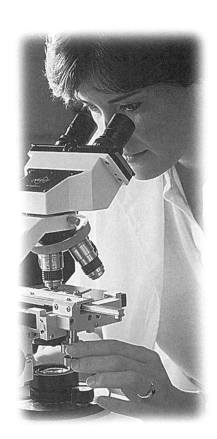

1. You've seen that the general exponential function can be written in the form $y = k \cdot e^{cx}$, where k and c can be any two nonzero numbers. (What happens if k or c is zero?)

   You also know that any such function has the proportionality property. That is, the derivative at any point on the graph is proportional to the y-value at that point.

   Investigate how the value of the proportionality constant depends on the value of the parameters k and c.

2. The general exponential function can also be written in the form $y = k \cdot b^x$, where k is some nonzero number and b is a positive number other than 1. (What happens if b is equal to 1?) In this form, too, the function has the proportionality property.

   Investigate how the value of the proportionality constant depends on the value of the parameters k and b.

Pennant Fever

Play Ball!

Brian Pusztai, Darcy O'Hanlon, Shannon Guziel, and Shannon Frattone set out to determine the probability that their team will win the pennant.

The central problem in this unit involves two baseball teams in a pennant race. Your main task will be to find each team's probability of winning.

The opening days of the unit give you a chance to speculate about the problem. Over the course of the unit, you will occasionally leave the central problem to explore a variety of other situations, including the chance of finding two people in a room with the same birthday.

Race for the Pennant!

It's almost the end of the baseball season, and only two teams still have a chance to win the pennant—the Good Guys and the Bad Guys. Here are their records for the season so far.

Team	Games won	Games lost	Games left
Good Guys	96	59	7
Bad Guys	93	62	7

The Good Guys and the Bad Guys will not be playing against each other in any of their remaining games.

The central problem of this unit is to find out the probability that the Good Guys will win the pennant.

1. First, study the possibilities for each of the two teams.

   a. What is the best record the Good Guys could have at the end of the season? That is, what is the most wins and fewest losses they could end up with?

   b. What is the worst record the Good Guys could have at the end of the season?

   c. What is the best record the Bad Guys could have at the end of the season?

   d. What is the worst record the Bad Guys could have at the end of the season?

Continued on next page

2. a. Discuss with your group what you think is the most likely outcome for each of these two teams in their remaining seven games.

   b. Make your own decision on part a, and state reasons to support your conclusion.

3. a. Discuss with your group the Good Guys' probability of winning the pennant. Try to come to agreement on the likelihood that they will win.

   b. Give your best guess right now of this probability, and explain your thinking. Be sure to state any assumptions you make.

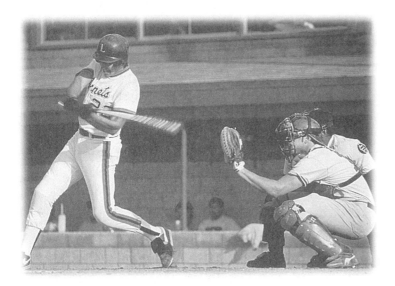

Happy Birthday!

The seven-day week is used throughout the world, and many cultures have sayings about how the day of the week on which a person is born might affect that individual's personality. Often people use as role models specific individuals born on the same day of the week they were born.

Here are some famous people born on each of the days of the week:

Sunday:	Louis Armstrong (Aug 4, 1901)
	Amelia Earhart (July 24, 1898)
	Whoopi Goldberg (Nov 13, 1949)
	Katharine Hepburn (May 12, 1907)
	Michael Jordan (Feb 17, 1963)
Monday:	Henry "Hank" Aaron (Feb 5, 1934)
	Michelangelo Buonarroti (Mar 6, 1475)
	Bill Clinton (Aug 19, 1946)
	Jodie Foster (Nov 19, 1962)
	Kristi Yamaguchi (July 12, 1971)
Tuesday:	Dr. Martin Luther King Jr. (Jan 15, 1929)
	Golda Meir (May 3, 1898)
	Marilyn Monroe (June 1, 1926)
	Michelle Pfeiffer (Apr 29, 1958)
	Mao Tse-tung (Dec 26, 1893)
Wednesday:	Maya Angelou (Apr 4, 1928)
	Corazon Aquino (Jan 25, 1933)
	Anwar Sadat (Dec 25, 1918)
	Dr. Seuss (Mar 2, 1904)
	Bishop Desmond Tutu (Oct 7, 1931)
Thursday:	Louisa May Alcott (Nov 29, 1832)
	Marie "Madame" Curie (Nov 7, 1867)
	Nelson Mandela (July 18, 1918)
	Stephen Spielberg (Dec 18, 1947)
	Laura Ingalls Wilder (Feb 7, 1867)

Continued on next page

Friday: Fidel Castro (Aug 13, 1926)
           Madeleine L'Engle (Nov 29, 1918)
           Jesse Owens (Sept 12, 1913)
           Jerry Seinfeld (Apr 29, 1955)
           Oprah Winfrey (Jan 29, 1954)

Saturday: Mahatma Gandhi (Oct 2, 1869)
           Madonna (Aug 16, 1958)
           Eleanor Roosevelt (Oct 11, 1884)
           Mother Teresa (Aug 27, 1910)
           Booker T. Washington (Apr 5, 1856)

This raises an interesting question:

Do you know what day of the week you were born on? And how would you figure it out if you didn't know?

Your POW is to develop a system for finding out the day of the week on which someone was born, based on the date when the person was born. You should go through these three steps.

1. Use only a calendar for the current month and the "Basic Information About Calendars" below to figure out what day of the week you were born on. Do not look at calendars for any other month of this year or at any calendars for other years.

2. Develop general directions so that someone else could apply the method you used in Question 1 to determine the day of the week on which he or she was born.

3. Have someone try to use the directions you created in Question 2, and have that person tell you how well your directions worked. Based on this feedback, make changes to correct or clarify your directions.

Basic Information About Calendars

Except for February, the number of days in each month is the same every year. The month of February gets an extra

Continued on next page

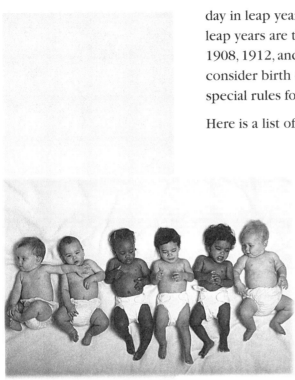

day in leap years. For the period between 1900 and 1999, leap years are those years that are multiples of 4—1904, 1908, 1912, and so on. (For this POW, you should only consider birth dates between 1900 and 1999. There are special rules for years that are multiples of 100.)

Here is a list of the number of days in each month.

- January: 31 days
- February: 28 days (but 29 in leap years)
- March: 31 days
- April: 30 days
- May: 31 days
- June: 30 days
- July: 31 days
- August: 31 days
- September: 30 days
- October: 31 days
- November: 30 days
- December: 31 days

Write-up

1. *Process*

2. *Solution:* Describe how you determined the day of the week on which you were born, and give the general directions you created. Also describe the experience of having someone else use your directions. If you modified the directions based on that person's feedback, include a description of the changes you made.

3. *Evaluation*

4. *Self-assessment*

Playing with Probabilities

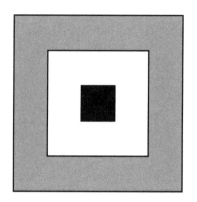

1. Suppose someone throws a dart at the target shown here, and assume that the dart will hit the target, with all points equally likely to be hit.

   What is the probability that a given dart will land in the black area? In the white area? In the gray area? Explain your answers.

2. Draw an area diagram that represents a situation with three outcomes. One outcome should have a probability of $\frac{1}{5}$, the second should have a probability of .7, and the third should have a probability of . . . , well, you figure out the probability of the third outcome.

   Explain how you found the third probability and how your diagram represents these probabilities.

3. Make up a situation with three outcomes that would have the probabilities in Question 2.

4. Ms. Hernandez and her twins are in front of a gum ball machine that contains red, blue, and purple gum balls. Twenty-five percent of the gum balls are red, 60 percent are blue, and the remaining nine gum balls are purple.

   How many of the gum balls are red and how many are blue? Explain why you feel sure you have the correct answer.

New Year's Day

To get you going on your POW, this assignment asks you to determine what day of the week each of these special events fell on during the calendar year *previous to* the current year.

Don't forget to take into account whether either the current year or the previous year was a leap year.

1. New Year's Day (January 1)

2. Valentine's Day (February 14)

3. Your birthday

Explain each of your answers. As in the POW, determine these days of the week without consulting any calendar except for the current month.

Trees and Baseball

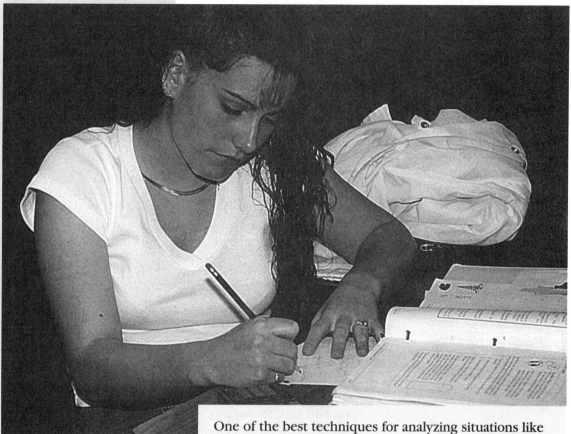

Tiffany Parysek uses tree diagrams to aid her in finding and explaining probability outcomes for different situations.

One of the best techniques for analyzing situations like the baseball problem is the tree diagram. (You may recall using tree diagrams in the Year 1 unit *The Game of Pig*.)

Over the next several days, you'll apply this technique to several situations. You'll also get your first definitive probability results about particular possible outcomes of the baseball pennant race.

Choosing for Chores

Part I: Wash or Dry?

Scott and Letitia are brother and sister. After dinner, they had to do the dishes, with one washing and the other drying.

They were having trouble deciding who would do which task, so they came up with a method for deciding based on probability.

Letitia grabbed some spoons and put them in a bag. Some had purple handles and others had green handles. Scott had to pick two of them. If the handles were the same color, Scott would wash. If they were different colors, he would dry.

It turned out that there were two purple spoons and three green ones. What was the probability that Scott would wash the dishes? Explain your answer.

Part II: Allowance Choices

Scott and Letitia's parents want to encourage them to learn more about probability, so they gave Scott and Letitia two choices for how to get paid for their chores.

- Choice 1: They can get $4.
- Choice 2: They can pick two bills out of a bag that contains four $1 bills and one $5 bill.

Which choice would you take? Explain your reasoning carefully.

Baseball Probabilities

Willie is one of the star hitters for the Good Guys. Every time he comes up to bat, he has one chance in three of getting a hit. (In standard baseball terminology, we would say his batting average is .333.)

1. Suppose Willie comes up to bat twice in a certain game.

   a. What is the probability that he'll get a hit both times?

   b. What is the probability that he won't get a hit either time?

   c. Use your answers to Questions 1a and 1b to find the probability that he will get exactly one hit.

2. Now suppose that in another game, he comes up to bat three times.

   a. What is the probability that he'll get a hit all three times?

   b. What is the probability that he won't get any hits?

   c. Use your answers to Questions 2a and 2b to find the probability that the number of hits will be either 1 or 2.

4   Possible Outcomes

The Good Guys and the Bad Guys can each achieve many different records their final seven games. For instance, they could both win the rest of their games, or one team could win the rest of its games while the other team loses the rest of its.

1. List the possible records that the Good Guys might have for their final seven games.

2. List the possible records that the Bad Guys might have for their final seven games.

3. a. How many combinations of records are there for the two teams? (For instance, one combination is that the Good Guys win six games and lose one while the Bad Guys win three games and lose four.)

   b. Make a table or other display showing all the possible combinations of records. Indicate in your display which team ends up winning the pennant in each case.

How Likely Is All Wins?

For the rest of this unit, you should use .62 as the probability that the Good Guys will win any given game and .6 as the probability that the Bad Guys will win any given game. (These values come from the teams' current percentages of winning games. Remember that the two teams do not play against each other.)

1. Find the probability that the Good Guys will win all seven of their remaining games. Justify your conclusion with a tree diagram or area diagram.

2. Find the probability that the Bad Guys will win all seven of their remaining games.

3. What is the probability that both teams will finish the season this way? That is, find the probability that both the Good Guys *and* the Bad Guys will win all seven of their remaining games.

Go for the Gold!

This is your lucky week. You received an invitation to be a contestant on the television game show *Go for the Gold!* You'll have a chance to win big money if you accept the invitation, but the *Go for the Gold!* producers require a nonreturnable fee of $100 for the right to play their game.

Here's how the game works:

> You are given a jar containing two white cubes and one gold cube. You choose a cube without looking (so each cube is equally likely). If you get the gold cube, you are shown another jar. If you don't get the gold cube, you are out.

> The second jar contains four white cubes and one gold cube. Again, you choose one cube from the jar without looking. If you get the gold cube from this jar, you win $1,000. If not, you get nothing.

1. a. What is the probability that you will pick the gold cubes from both jars and win the $1,000 prize? Use both an area diagram and a tree diagram to justify your results.

   b. Pick a section of your area diagram from Question 1a, and explain what path of your tree diagram it corresponds to.

2. If you win the game (by picking the two gold cubes), you get $1,000. But you have to pay $100 simply to play the game.

   Do you accept the show's offer to be a contestant? Explain your decision.

Diagrams, Baseball, and Losing 'em All

1. a. Compare the process of calculating probabilities using the two approaches of area diagrams and tree diagrams. Describe the advantages and disadvantages of each, using specific examples to illustrate.

b. When might you be better off using no diagram at all?

2. Where do you stand on solving the unit problem? That is, what parts of the problem have been solved and what remains to be figured out?

3. What is the probability that the season will end up with both the Good Guys and the Bad Guys losing all seven of their remaining games?

The Birthday Problem

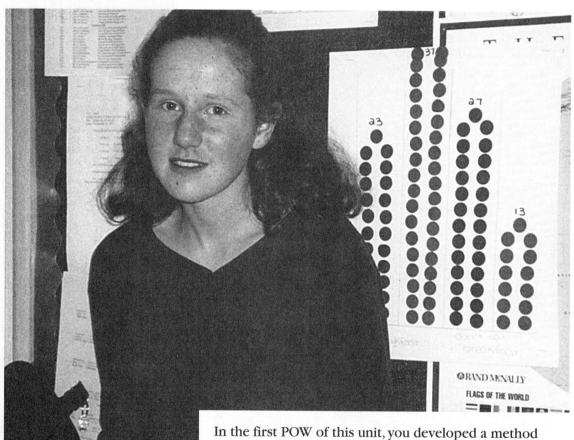

Sheila Roberts explains to her classmates what the probability is that there would be at least one birthday match in a group the size of their class.

In the first POW of this unit, you developed a method for finding the day of the week on which someone was born. Beginning with *Homework 7: Day-of-the-Week Matches,* you now begin a sequence of activities that continue this "birthday" theme. You may find the answer to the final problem in this sequence quite surprising.

Before starting those problems, though, you will work on an activity that relates to the new POW.

Let's Make a Deal

Congratulations! You've been invited to be part of the audience for the television show *Let's Make a Deal*. Then, miracle of miracles, you are selected to be a contestant on the show!

Let's review how the game works.

> You are shown three doors, labeled A, B, and C. Behind one of the doors is a brand new car of your dreams. Behind the other two doors are worthless prizes.

> You select a door. The host of the game then opens one of the other doors. Because the host knows where the car is, he makes sure to open a door that reveals a worthless prize.

> You now have to make a choice: You can either stay with the door you originally selected or switch to the remaining closed door.

> You win whatever is behind the door you choose at this time.

Here's the big question for you (and for this POW).

> *Are your chances of winning the car better if you stay with your original choice, or are they better if you switch to the remaining closed door, or are they equally likely with the two strategies?*

More precisely, your task is to find the probability of getting the car for each of the two strategies. Write a careful explanation of how you found these probabilities.

Continued on next page

Write-up

1. *Problem Statement*

2. *Process:* Include a description of how you and your partner did the simulation in *Simulate a Deal,* give the results of your simulation, and discuss how that activity contributed to your understanding of the problem.

3. *Solution:* Give the probability of winning for each strategy, including an explanation of how you found the probabilities.

4. *Extensions*

5. *Self-assessment*

Adapted with permission from the *Mathematics Teacher,* © April, 1991 by the National Council of Teachers of Mathematics.

Simulate a Deal

In *POW 12: Let's Make a Deal,* you need to decide
whether to switch to the remaining closed door or stay
with your original choice.

In this activity, you will simulate the
problem. That is, you will use each
of the two strategies (*switch* or
stay) a number of times and see
what happens.

You should work with a
partner on this assignment.

1. First, try the strategy in
   which you always
   switch your guess after
   being shown the open
   door. One of you should
   play the game show host
   and the other should
   play the contestant. Come
   up with some way of
   acting out the situation as
   realistically as possible.

   Play the game ten times using this strategy, keeping
   track of how many times the contestant wins.

2. Then try the strategy in which you always stay with
   your original door. You and your partner should
   switch roles this time. Again, play the game ten times
   using this strategy, keeping track of how many times
   the contestant wins.

Day-of-the-Week Matches

7

POW 11: Happy Birthday! involved the day of the week on which a person is born. This assignment is the first of several assignments connecting that theme to probability.

In this activity, you should assume that each of the seven possibilities—Sunday through Saturday—is equally likely.

1. Is there a group size for which you would be certain that at least two people in the group were born on the same day of the week? What's the smallest such group size? Explain your answer.

2. If you pick two people at random, what is the probability that they were born on different days of the week? What is the probability that they were born on the same day of the week? Justify your answers.

3. If you pick three people at random, what is the probability that all three were born on different days of the week? What is the probability that at least two of the three were born on the same day of the week? Justify your answers.

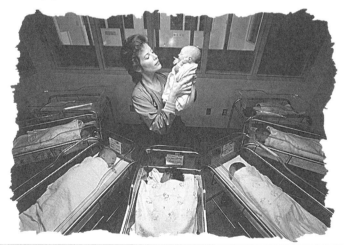

"Day-of-the-Week Matches" Continued

In *Homework 7: Day-of-the-Week Matches,* you found the probability that two people were born on the same day of the week and then the probability for three people.

You also found that if there were at least eight people, the probability would be 1, because you would be certain of a match.

There is only one question for this assignment.

> *What is the minimum number of people you need so that the probability of having at least one day-of-the-week match is greater than $\frac{1}{2}$?*

(As before, assume that each day of the week is equally likely.)

Be sure to explain your answer. (Because the probability for two people and the probability for three people were both less than $\frac{1}{2}$, you know that you need more than three people. You also know that the number needed can't be more than eight.)

Hint: It may be easier to figure out the probability that a group of people were all born on *different* days of the week than to figure out the probability that at least two were born on the *same* day of the week.

Monthly Matches

You've been working on problems involving the probability that two people are born on the same day of the week. In this assignment, you move from days of the week to months of the year.

Although the months do not all have the same length, you should make the simplifying assumption in this assignment that each month is equally likely as the birth month for a person chosen at random.

1. What is the smallest number of people you need for the probability to be 100 percent that at least two of them were born in the same month?

2. If you pick a person at random, what is the probability that you and that person were born in the same month?

3. If you have a group of three people chosen at random, what is the probability that at least two of them have the same birth month? What is the probability for a four-person group?

4. How many people would you need in a randomly chosen group for the probability of a month-of-birth match within the group to be greater than $\frac{1}{2}$?

The Real Birthday Problem

You've been working on day-of-the-week matches and month-of-the-year matches. Now you're ready to solve a very famous problem known simply as "the birthday problem."

What is the minimum number of people you need so that the probability of having at least one birthday match is greater than $\frac{1}{2}$?

For this problem, you should ignore leap year; that is, you should assume that a year has 365 days. You should also assume that each of these 365 days of the year is equally likely as a person's birthday.

1. Before doing any computation or analysis, make a guess about the answer to the birthday problem and write it down.

2. Now do the necessary analysis to find the answer, and explain your work.

10

Six for the Defense

Marcia has always wanted to be a defense attorney. She is very excited because her civics teacher has just announced that the class will soon begin a four-day unit on the court system.

The class will act out a different famous court case each day. At the beginning of each class, the teacher will decide on the role for each student using a die. If the die comes up 6, then the student will be one of the defense attorneys for that case. If the die comes up 1 through 5, the student will play some other role.

1. Make a tree or area diagram for the situation that will help Marcia analyze how often she is likely to be a defense attorney over the four days.

2. What is the probability that Marcia will be a defense attorney every day of the unit?

3. What is the probability that Marcia will never get to be a defense attorney during the unit?

4. On the third day of the unit, the class will be acting out a case with which Marcia is very familiar. What she'd like best is to be a defense attorney on that day and have other roles for the other three cases. What is the probability that she will get her wish?

5. What is the probability that Marcia will be a defense attorney exactly once during the four days? Explain your answer.

Baseball and Counting

Mike Holcombe is clearly confident that the list method has resulted in his finding all possible combinations.

The unit now returns briefly to the central problem, as you find the probabilities for a few more cases.

You then begin an important section of the unit involving sophisticated ways to count. (Among other things, you'll be counting the number of different ways to create ice cream cones.) As part of this section of the unit, you'll apply the counting techniques to some more baseball outcomes.

And If You Don't Win 'em All?

Sometimes you can "win 'em all," but usually you can't.

The Good Guys would like to win all of their remaining seven games, but winning six out of seven wouldn't be so bad either. The Bad Guys would probably also be pretty happy to win six out of seven.

1. Find the probability that the Good Guys will win the first six of their remaining games and then lose the seventh game.

2. Find the probability that the Good Guys will win exactly six out of their seven remaining games.
(*Hint:* Question 1 involves only one of several ways that the Good Guys can compile a record of six wins and one loss in their remaining games.)

3. Find the probability that the Bad Guys will win exactly six out of their seven remaining games.

But Don't Lose 'em All, Either

The activity *And If You Don't Win 'em All?* involves the "next-to-best" scenario for each of the two teams, in which they win six games and lose just one. In this assignment, you examine the "next-to-worst" scenario.

1. Find the probability that the Good Guys will win the first of their remaining games and then lose the remaining six.

2. Find the probability that the Good Guys will win exactly one out of their seven remaining games.

3. Find the probability that the Bad Guys will win exactly one out of their seven remaining games.

The Good and the Bad

You have found a great deal of information about the probability of the Good Guys and the Bad Guys getting certain records.

For instance, you know the probability that the Good Guys will win six games and lose one, and you know the probability that the Bad Guys will win six games and lose one. But what is the probability that both of these things will happen? And for what other combinations can you find the probability?

Use the information you have so far on the probabilities of individual records for the Good Guys and Bad Guys to complete as much of the chart of probability combinations as possible.

Top That Pizza!

Jonathan delivers pizza several evenings a week. He doesn't get paid very much, but he does get a free pizza for dinner every night he works.

He gets bored with the same old kind of pizza every night, and in fact he likes variety. The pizza shop he works for has five different toppings that he likes—pineapple, sausage, mushrooms, onions, and anchovies.

1. If Jonathan always has exactly *two* of these five toppings on his pizza, how many nights can he work without repeating a combination? Explain your answer.

2. Now Jonathan's sister Johanna has come to work there as well. She likes the same toppings as her brother, but she always wants to get exactly *three* of the five toppings on her pizzas. How many nights can she work without repeating a combination? Explain your answer.

3. How does the answer to Question 1 relate to the answer to Question 2? Explain why this relationship holds.

Double Scoops

After Jonathan finishes delivering pizza, he always treats himself to a two-scoop bowl of ice cream at the shop next to the pizza store. The ice cream shop serves 24 different flavors of ice cream.

1. How many different combinations of two scoops of ice cream can Jonathan create? (He always insists on getting two different flavors for his two scoops.)

2. Next, Jonathan's sister Johanna enters the scene. She likes her ice cream on a cone, and it's important to her which scoop is on top. After all, she says, eating chocolate and then vanilla is a different taste experience from eating vanilla and then chocolate. Like her brother, she always wants two different flavors.

   How many different two-scoop ice cream cones can Johanna create?

Triple Scoops

Poor Johanna! She had to have her tonsils out and was stuck at home with a sore throat. But fortunately, one of the things she could eat easily was ice cream. She decided she deserved a special treat.

Her boyfriend Joshua was coming over, so she asked him to get her a three-scoop cone. She told Joshua that he would probably find her brother Jonathan eating a bowl of ice cream at the ice cream shop and that Joshua should get her the same flavors that Jonathan had.

Well, sure enough, there was Jonathan, eating a three-scoop bowl of ice cream. He had one scoop each of pistachio, boysenberry, and chocolate, so Joshua knew he should use those three flavors.

Unfortunately, neither Jonathan nor Joshua had any idea what order Johanna would want her scoops in. Joshua knew she was fussy about this, and he really wanted her to get what she wanted.

1. Joshua decided to get Johanna all possible cones made up of those three flavors. How many different cones did he buy for her?

2. Joshua realized he was lucky that Johanna hadn't asked for a four-scoop cone. If she had told him she wanted a four-scoop cone with pistachio, boysenberry, chocolate, and butter pecan (without specifying the order of the flavors), how many different cones would he have had to bring her?

More Cones for Johanna

After Johanna recovered from her tonsillectomy, she continued to eat three-scoop ice cream cones. In fact, she thought it would be fun to try every possible three-scoop cone the shop had to offer.

1. If Johanna had 1 three-scoop cone every day, how many days could she go before she would have to repeat? (Remember that the ice cream shop has 24 flavors.)

2. Suppose instead that she had a different four-scoop cone each day. How long would it take for her to try them all?

3. Find a rule for determining the number of different cones in terms of the number of scoops on the cone. (Continue to base your work on the 24-flavor ice cream shop. Of course, your rule won't work for more than 24 scoops.)

4. One day, while visiting relatives in another town, Johanna went into a different ice cream shop. She figured out that there were 156 possible two-scoop cones that could be made from the flavors at this shop. How many different flavors did this shop offer?

Cones from Bowls, Bowls from Cones

In *Homework 13: Triple Scoops,* you saw that there are many different ice cream cones that can be made from the scoops in a given bowl of ice cream. (The number of such cones depends on the number of scoops involved.)

The questions in this assignment continue that theme. (*Note:* You do not need to figure out the number of flavors at each ice cream shop.)

1. At Mookie's Ice Cream Mart, you can make 465 different two-scoop bowls of ice cream. How many different two-scoop ice cream cones can you make there? (*Hint:* If there was only one possible two-scoop bowl, how many different two-scoop cones would be possible?)

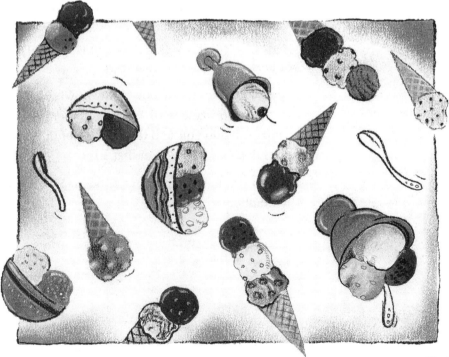

Continued on next page

---

2. At the Chilly Ice Cream Parlor, you can make 220 different three-scoop bowls of ice cream. How many different three-scoop ice cream cones can you make there?

3. a. At the Tasty Ice Cream Shop, you can make 210 different four-scoop bowls of ice cream. How many different four-scoop ice cream cones can you make there?

   b. At Eric's Creamery, you can make 3024 different four-scoop ice cream cones. How many different four-scoop bowls of ice cream can you make there? (*Careful:* This question and Question 4b reverse the situation in the other problems.)

4. a. If you go to Spud's Finest, you can make 792 different five-scoop bowls of ice cream. How many different five-scoop ice cream cones can you make there?

   b. If you visit Ice Cream by Midge, you can make 55,440 different five-scoop ice cream cones. How many different five-scoop bowls of ice cream can you make there?

5. a. In general, if you know how many bowls of ice cream can be made with a given number of scoops, how do you find the number of different cones that can be made of that size?

   b. How do you find the number of bowls if you know the number of cones?

Bowls for Jonathan

In *Homework 14: Cones from Bowls, Bowls from Cones,* you considered several ice cream shops. In some of the problems, you found the number of distinct bowls of ice cream of a particular size in terms of the number of distinct cones of that size.

Apply the principles from that assignment to these questions. In this activity, Johanna and Jonathan return to their favorite ice cream shop, so there are 24 flavors to choose from.

1. How many different three-scoop bowls of ice cream are there?

2. How many different four-scoop bowls of ice cream are there?

15   At the Olympics

1. The nation of Panacea has decided to participate in the 400-meter race in the next Olympics. They have ten runners of equal ability. They must choose three of these runners to represent them at the Olympics.

   How many different three-person teams are there to choose from?

2. There will be ten finalists in the Olympics gymnastics competition. One of these ten will win the gold medal, one will win the silver, and one will win the bronze.

   After the competition, a plaque will be made listing the three winners in order. Use the fact that there were ten contestants in this competition to determine the number of possibilities for the sequence of names on this plaque.

3. Compare Questions 1 and 2. Which question is like an ice cream cone problem and which one is like an ice cream bowl problem? How can you find the answer to one question from the answer to the other?

Fair Spoons

The Original Problem

In Part I of *Choosing for Chores,* Scott and Letitia determined who would wash the dishes and who would dry by having Scott pull two spoons out of a bag.

The bag contained two purple spoons and three green ones. If the two spoons Scott pulled out were the same color, then Scott washed and Letitia dried. If the two were different colors, then Letitia washed and Scott dried.

The New Problem

Letitia decided she didn't like that system, because it turned out that she washed the dishes about 60 percent of the time. Scott thought that if they found the right number of spoons of each color to put in the bag, they could make the probability of a match equal to 50 percent. But Scott wasn't sure what the right numbers would be, and neither was Letitia.

What do you think? Find out as much about their choices as you can—don't merely find the simplest answer. Assume that plenty of spoons of both colors are available. As you work, keep track of the probability of a match in cases that do not come out to 50 percent.

Continued on next page

Write-up

1. *Problem Statement*

2. *Process*

3. *Solution:* Give the percentage of matches for all the specific examples you examined, and give all the combinations you found that led to matches exactly 50 percent of the time. Explain how you found the percentages in each case, and describe any patterns you see in the combinations that give matches 50 percent of the time.

4. *Self-assessment*

Which Is Which?

Permutations and Combinations

In recent assignments, you have been carefully examining two types of counting problems. Mathematicians use the terms **permutations** and **combinations** to refer to these two types of problems.

We use the notation $_nP_r$ in connection with permutation problems and the notation $_nC_r$ in connection with combination problems. In both cases, the variable n stands for the size of the group you are choosing from, and the variable r stands for the number of things you are picking from that group.

The numbers $_nC_r$ are called **combinatorial coefficients.** (There is no standard term for the numbers $_nP_r$.)

Your Task

In this assignment, you need to review the assignments you have done so far in this unit.

1. Identify three specific problems you believe are combination problems and three specific problems you believe are permutation problems.

2. Explain why you think the problems are the type you say they are.

3. Express the answers to the questions in each problem using the notations $_nP_r$ and $_nC_r$.

Formulas for $_nP_r$ and $_nC_r$

You have seen that many of the problems in this unit involve the concepts of *combinations* and *permutations*.

In *Homework 16: Which Is Which?*, you looked at how to apply these concepts and the notations $_nP_r$ and $_nC_r$ to problems from earlier in the unit. Your task in this activity is to find formulas for $_nP_r$ and $_nC_r$.

1. Find formulas for these specific cases of $_nP_r$, giving each answer as an expression in terms of n. (You may want to think about specific situations to which these cases apply.)

   a. $_nP_1$

   b. $_nP_2$

   c. $_nP_3$

2. Find a general formula for $_nP_r$ in terms of n and r.

Next, think about the relationship between permutations and combinations in specific situations. For example, for a given number of flavors, what is the relationship between the number of three-scoop bowls of ice cream and the number of three-scoop ice cream cones?

3. Develop a general equation expressing the relationship between $_nP_r$ and $_nC_r$.

4. Combine your results from Questions 2 and 3 to get a formula for $_nC_r$ in terms of n and r.

Who's on First?

The Good Guys have a terrific team. In fact, the team is so good that its manager, Sammy Lagrange, is sure that it will win the pennant and then go on to play in the World Series.

In the World Series, the first team to win four games is declared world champion. (American baseball has always assumed that its best team is the best in the world.)

Sammy is already planning ahead, but one drawback of having such a good team is that it's often hard to make decisions.

1. When the Good Guys get to the World Series, Sammy will have to pick four different pitchers, one for each of the first four games of the Series. (He isn't thinking beyond four games, because he expects the Good Guys to win four World Series games in a row and be declared the champions.)

   Sammy has seven excellent pitchers to choose from. To prepare properly, the pitchers need to know which game, if any, they will pitch, so Sammy not only has to determine which four pitchers to use but who will pitch in which game.

   He decides to resolve the situation by putting all possible sequences of four pitchers on slips of paper. He'll then pick one of these slips out of a hat to settle the pitching order.

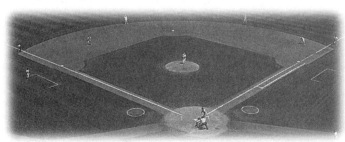

Continued on next page

How many slips of paper does Sammy need? (The answer is not seven! Sammy isn't doing this the easy way. Remember that each slip of paper shows a sequence with the names of four pitchers in order.)

And that's only the pitchers! For the rest of the team, Sammy is only thinking as far as the first game, but he still has choices to make.

2. To begin with, Sammy needs to choose his outfield—a left fielder, a center fielder, and a right fielder. He has five good outfielders to choose from, and he needs to decide which outfielder plays which position.

How many ways are there for Sammy to fill these positions for the first game?

3. And then there's the infield. Sammy needs a first baseman, a second baseman, a shortstop, and a third baseman. He has six highly qualified infielders, all very versatile and all able to play any of these four positions.

How many possibilities must he consider in filling the infield positions for the first game?

4. Fortunately, Sammy knows who his best catcher is. That player will complete his nine-player team for the first game (a pitcher, three outfielders, four infielders, and the catcher).

Considering all that's going on, how many different possibilities are there altogether for who will play each position for the Good Guys in the first game?

5. Finally, once Sammy has decided on his nine players, he has to choose a batting order. That is, he needs to decide which one of the nine players bats first, bats second, bats third, and so on.

How many ways are there to arrange his starting nine players in the batting order in the first game?

Five for Seven

It's time to return to the central unit problem about the Good Guys and Bad Guys. There are still many possible outcomes whose probabilities you have not yet figured out.

This activity looks at a few of those cases. You may find that you can apply what you learned about pizza and ice cream to the baseball pennant race.

1. What is the probability that the Good Guys will win five and lose two of their remaining seven games? Explain your answer.

2. What is the probability that the Bad Guys will win two and lose five of their remaining seven games? Explain your answer.

3. What is the probability that the outcomes from Questions 1 and 2 will both happen? That is, what is the probability that the Good Guys will win five and lose two *and* the Bad Guys will win two and lose five?

18

More Five for Sevens

In *Five for Seven,* you found two probabilities that are important in solving the unit problem.

- The probability that the Good Guys will win five and lose two of their remaining seven games

- The probability that the Bad Guys will win two and lose five of their remaining seven games

1. Find each of these similar probabilities.

    a. The probability that the Good Guys will win two and lose five of their remaining seven games

    b. The probability that the Bad Guys will win five and lose two of their remaining seven games

In *Five for Seven,* you also found the probability of both events happening, that is, the probability that the Good Guys will win five and lose two *and* the Bad Guys will win two and lose five. This probability represents only one of the 64 cells in the chart of possible records for the two teams.

2. Enter the values from Question 1 in your chart, and find the probabilities for all the cells that involve either two wins or five wins for each team.

Combinatorial Reasoning

Sara Mills computes by hand the number of ways pennant contenders can win or lose their remaining games.

There are many situations besides baseball and ice cream for which combinatorial coefficients can be helpful. Because probability involves counting cases, these special numbers play a role in a wide variety of probability problems.

In the next section of the unit, you'll see how to use both permutations and combinations, along with principles of statistical reasoning such as the null hypothesis, to find probabilities and to make decisions.

What's for Dinner?

Lai Yee is trying to earn money to buy a motor scooter. His parents want to encourage him to take care of his own expenses, and so they have told him they will pay him to put dinner on the table four nights a week (Sunday, Tuesday, Thursday, and Saturday). They agree to pay him $20 a week for his work, in addition to reimbursing him for the cost of the food.

Because Lai Yee has never done any cooking before, his parents are afraid they will just get the same one or two meals over and over again. So they decide that he must submit his planned menu for each week in advance, showing the four meals for that week. They tell him that his menus must obey two rules.

• No weekly menu can contain two of the same meal.

• Each weekly menu must be different from all previous weekly menus.

Continued on next page

Lai Yee is clever. After some research, he finds that there are seven meals in his town that he can buy already prepared. That way, he won't have to learn to cook. These meals are Chinese noodles, pasta, tacos, tuna salad, hamburgers, sushi, and roasted chicken.

1. How much money can Lai Yee earn before he has to learn to cook something? Express your answer using the notation $_nP_r$ or $_nC_r$ appropriately, and also find the actual numerical answer. Explain how you got your answer.

2. It turns out there was a misunderstanding between Lai Yee and his parents. He thought that he could use the same set of four meals for more than one weekly menu if he simply presented the four meals in a different order. His parents say otherwise. To them, "different weekly menu" means "a different set of four meals."

    Whichever way you interpreted Question 1, now answer the question using the other interpretation. Again, express your answer using the notation $_nP_r$ or $_nC_r$ appropriately, and also find the actual numerical answer.

3. What if Lai Yee cut back to three meals per week? How many weeks could he go under his interpretation? Under his parents' interpretation?

19

All or Nothing

In most cases, the formulas for the combinatorial and permutation coefficients are pretty clear, but in some special cases, it helps to have a situation to give concrete meaning to these numbers.

1. You found that there are 21 different sequences by which the Good Guys can win exactly five of their remaining seven games. In other words, the combinatorial coefficient $\binom{7}{5}$ is equal to 21. (*Reminder:* The notation $\binom{n}{r}$ means the same thing as $_nC_r$.)

   Use the pennant race situation to determine the numerical value of the combinatorial coefficient $\binom{7}{0}$. Explain your reasoning.

2. You found that there are ten different pizza combinations that Jonathan can create if he chooses three toppings for his pizza out of the five that he likes. In other words, the combinatorial coefficient $\binom{5}{3}$ is equal to 10.

   Use the pizza situation to determine the numerical value of the combinatorial coefficient $\binom{5}{5}$. Explain your reasoning.

3. Use either Jonathan's or Johanna's ice cream preferences to determine the numerical values of $_{24}P_0$ and $\binom{24}{0}$. Explain your reasoning.

4. Use any of the situations in Questions 1 through 3, or some other situation that you make up, to determine the numerical values of $_nP_1$ and $\binom{n}{1}$. Explain your reasoning.

The Perfect Group

At last, in his third year of high school, Julio has lucked out. He is finally part of what he considers the perfect four-person group. This is the group he would have chosen for himself on the first day of his first year of high school if he'd had a chance.

Each time new groups were formed, he kept wishing for this group. He'd sometimes get one or two members of this ideal group, but he never got all three.

So how lucky was Julio? Begin with these assumptions.

- There are 32 students in Julio's class.

- This 32-person class has been together throughout high school so far.

- New groups are created randomly every two weeks.

- Groups always have four students in them.

1. First *guess* the probability of Julio getting his perfect group in three years. (Resist the temptation to do any arithmetic yet—simply give your intuitive idea about what the chances were.)

2. Now actually find this probability. You will need to make some further assumptions to do so. State those assumptions clearly.

And a Fortune, Too!

Do you remember the very economical king from the Year 1 POWs *Eight Bags of Gold* and *Twelve Bags of Gold* (in the unit *The Pit and the Pendulum*)? Well, he's still around, and despite his economical nature, he has only five bags of gold now.

One reason he has less gold is that his old pan-balance scale broke down and he decided to buy a new scale. His advisor found an antique scale, the kind in which you put in a penny and are told your weight. Unfortunately, this scale doesn't let you compare weights, but it does give very precise measurements.

The king was very excited about another feature of the scale. With each weight, he also got a slip of paper that predicted his fortune. But he didn't pay attention to the fact that he was spending a penny every time he used it. He used up a lot of pennies before he suddenly realized that his fortune of gold had dwindled to five bags.

The King's New Problem

Now, as before, the king has given one bag of gold to each of the five people he trusts the most in his kingdom. And, as before, rumors have drifted back to the king that one of these five trusted caretakers is not to be trusted. According to rumor, this person is asking a counterfeiter to make phony gold.

Continued on next page

The king has brought in the local counterfeiter for questioning, to find out who hired her to double-cross him. (She's the same counterfeiter from *Twelve Bags of Gold,* and she still lives near the palace.)

She admitted being involved, but as in previous interrogations, she refused to name the traitor. She wouldn't even say whether the counterfeit gold she was making was heavier or lighter than real gold. All the king learned from her was that one of the five bags had counterfeit gold and that this bag weighed a different amount from the others.

Your Challenge

The king wants to know two things.

- Which bag weighs a different amount

- Exactly how much that bag weighs

And, of course, he wants to learn these things economically, using the least number of pennies possible. (He has suddenly started to economize.)

The court mathematician says it can be done with only three pennies. No one else can see how it could be done with so few weighings. Anyone can do it with five pennies. Some say they can do it with four pennies. But three pennies? Can you figure it out?

Write-up

1. *Problem Statement*

2. *Process*

3. *Solution:* You might get only a partial solution to this problem. If so, explain what cases your solution covers and where you got stuck.

4. *Self-assessment*

Feasible Combinations

In *Meadows or Malls?*, you generalized ideas about graphs and inequalities to solve linear programming problems in several variables.

One important principle in that unit is that you can find the corner points for a feasible region by examining certain systems of linear equations. If the set of constraints uses n variables, then each system you examine should contain n linear equations.

In this assignment, you'll apply ideas from this unit to see how many linear systems one might have to consider to solve linear programming problems.

1. The central problem from *Meadows or Malls?* involved six variables, which were labeled G_R, A_R, M_R, G_D, A_D, and M_D. The situation was described by these 12 constraints.

I	$G_R + G_D = 300$	VII	$G_R \geq 0$
II	$A_R + A_D = 100$	VIII	$A_R \geq 0$
III	$M_R + M_D = 150$	IX	$M_R \geq 0$
IV	$G_D + A_D + M_D \geq 300$	X	$G_D \geq 0$
V	$A_R + M_R \leq 200$	XI	$A_D \geq 0$
VI	$A_R + G_D = 100$	XII	$M_D \geq 0$

Each of the inequalities in this list has a corresponding linear equation. For instance, the inequality $G_D + A_D + M_D \geq 300$ corresponds to the linear equation $G_D + A_D + M_D = 300$.

Continued on next page

So the 12 constraints lead to 12 linear equations. Because the *Meadows or Malls?* problem involves six variables, every corner point for the feasible region is the solution to a system that consists of 6 of these 12 equations.

a. How many 6-equation systems can be formed from the 12 equations? (Of course, some of these systems do not actually lead to a corner point of the feasible region.)

If any of the constraints in a linear programming problem are actually equations, then all corner points have to fit those equations. Therefore, in your search for corner points, you can restrict yourself to linear systems that include those equations.

b. In the *Meadows or Malls?* problem, four of the constraints are equations. Suppose you only examine six-equation systems that include these four equations. That is, you only examine systems consisting of the four constraint equations together with two of the eight equations that correspond to constraint inequalities.

How many systems will you need to consider?

2. Suppose a linear programming problem has eight variables and 20 constraints, and that three of the constraints are equations.

How many linear systems would you need to consider? (Again, some of these systems might not actually lead to a corner point of the feasible region.)

About Bias

At Jackson High School, a 15-member schoolwide committee handles many decisions. The committee consists of ten adults and five students. Principal Fifer has been asked to select a special subcommittee of six people out of this group of 15.

Students are furious because they just learned that the subcommittee consists entirely of adults. They feel that the principal stacked the subcommittee with adults and didn't consider students. Principal Fifer, however, claims that the subcommittee was chosen randomly.

The students have decided to present their case to the school board.

1. As part of their presentation, they want to tell the school board the probability of getting only adults if the principal had selected six people at random from the committee of 15. Find this probability, giving your answer both as a number and as an expression using the notation $_nP_r$ or $_nC_r$ appropriately.

2. Do you think the principal stacked the committee? Explain your answer.

Binomial Powers

You've seen that combinatorial coefficients can be helpful in finding probabilities like those involved in the unit problem. As you know, these numbers are also known as *binomial coefficients*.

(*Reminder:* A **binomial** is an expression that is the sum of two terms, each of which is a product of numbers and variables. For example, $3x + 2y$, $5 - z$, $-3xy + 15zw$, and $7x^3 + 3xy^2$ are all binomials.)

A little later in this unit, you'll see what binomials have to do with the combinatorial coefficients $_nC_r$. In preparation for that discussion, your task in this assignment is to simplify certain powers of binomials, writing each expression as a sum of terms, without parentheses.

The diagram to the right illustrates Question 1. You may find similar diagrams helpful on Questions 2 through 6 (and perhaps even for Question 7).

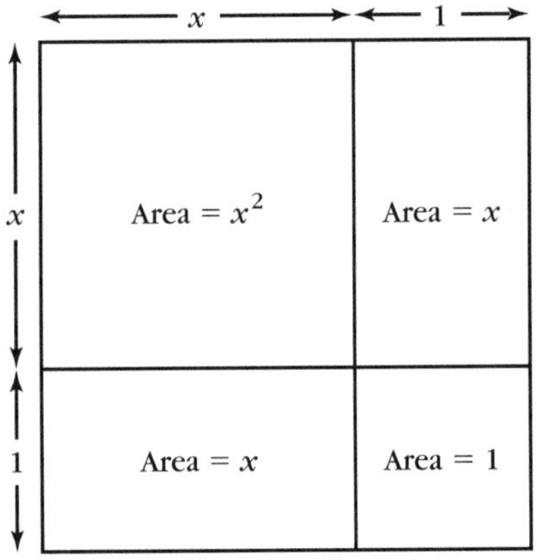

1. $(x + 1)^2$

2. $(a + b)^2$

3. $(r - 7)^2$

4. $(5g + 1)^2$

5. $(K + 4L)^2$

6. $(3y - 8)^2$

7. $(a + b)^3$

Continued on next page

While you're simplifying algebraic expressions, go ahead and simplify these (which are not powers of binomials).

8. $x^2(2x^3 + 3x - 6)$

9. $(x^2 + 3)(x^2 - 2x + 4)$

Complete the square for each of these expressions; that is, in each case, find a number for c so that the expression is the square of a binomial.

10. $x^2 + 8x + c$

11. $x^2 - 13x + c$

Don't Stand for It

In a very small town, there is a small factory with ten workers. All ten go out for lunch every day, and they all go out at the same time, but no one else in the small town goes out for lunch.

There are two lunch spots in town. Every day, each worker chooses to eat at one of these places, with the two lunch spots equally likely. Both establishments provide only counter seating (no tables).

One owner has ten stools at her counter just in case all ten workers come to her place on the same day. The other owner realizes that it is unlikely that all ten will come on the same day. He figures it's okay for business as long as he isn't short of stools more than an average of once a month. Because there are typically 20 workdays per month, he decides to have enough stools so that the chance of running short on any given day is less than 5 percent.

How many stools should he provide? Justify your answer.

Adapted from a problem in *Introduction to Finite Mathematics*, Kemeny, Snell, and Thompson, © 1957, Prentice-Hall, Inc.

Stop! Don't Walk!

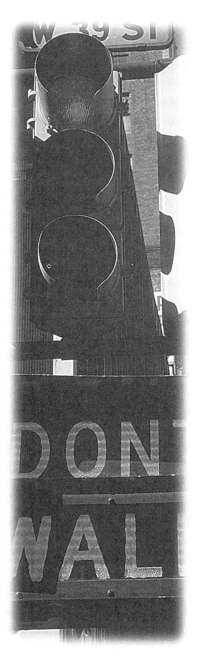

Patience Walker always walks to school, although the time of day varies. She feels that one of the stop lights on her way to school has it in for her. It always seems to be red when she approaches its corner, no matter what time of day it is. She thinks it happens too often to be a coincidence.

Patience is actually not a very patient person, so she is anxious to get to the bottom of this.

She phones the Department of Public Works and is told that within the traffic light's timing cycle, the light is set to be red 60 percent of the time. Patience finds this difficult to believe and asks the DPW to investigate the light. The DPW representative tells her that they have little time for such trivial matters and asks her to come back when she has some hard evidence.

1. Patience keeps track of the light for five days (one school week). Sure enough, the light is red on her way to school each and every one of those days.

   If the information from the DPW is correct, what is the probability of that happening? Explain your answer. (Assume that Patience is equally likely to arrive at the light at any point during its cycle.)

2. Patience is afraid that the DPW won't be convinced by a five-day survey, so she keeps track for two more school weeks, for a total of 15 days. She finds the light to be red on 13 out of the 15 days.

   She's ready to confront the DPW. If the light is really red exactly 60 percent of the time during each cycle, what is the probability that Patience would find it red 13 or more times out of 15?

Pascal's Triangle

In creating Pascal's triangle, Maile Martin, Jeanette Austria, and Kahala Neil find many patterns.

Pascal's triangle is an array of numbers that displays many interesting patterns and relationships. (The array is named for a French mathematician who did important work in the theory of probability, but this arrangement of numbers was studied long before his time.)

Over the next several days, you'll investigate how the array is formed and see some of its many applications.

Pascal's Triangle

```
              1
            1   1
          1   2   1
        1   3   3   1
      1   4   6   4   1
    1   5  10  10   5   1
  ?   ?   ?   ?   ?   ?   ?
?   ?   ?   ?   ?   ?   ?   ?
```

The triangular arrangement shown here is the beginning of a pattern of numbers commonly called **Pascal's triangle.** Although only six completed rows are shown here, the pattern can be extended indefinitely.

This number pattern is named in honor of the French mathematician Blaise Pascal (1623–1662), who developed the beginnings of the modern theory of probability.

Though Pascal was a distinguished mathematician, he was also famous as a physicist, geometer, and religious philosopher. Among other things, he invented the first digital calculator. A commonly used computer language is named for him as well. (*Note:* Pascal was certainly not the first person to work with this numerical pattern. In fact, the pattern has been found in use as early as around 1300 CE, in a book of Chinese prints.)

1. Find a pattern in Pascal's triangle that will allow you to extend it to more rows. Then use this pattern to extend Pascal's triangle to at least ten rows altogether. (Save this extended version of Pascal's triangle, because you will need it for the rest of the unit.)

2. Find other patterns in the triangle. Describe each new pattern you find in words and with examples.

Hi, There!

There is a classic mathematics problem, called the *handshake problem*, which goes like this.

> *There are n people in a room. Everyone shakes hands exactly once with everyone else. How many handshakes are there?*

(When two people shake hands, that counts as one handshake.)

1. Find the answer to the handshake problem for the case $n = 3$, for $n = 5$, for $n = 10$, and for two other specific cases of your choice.

2. Look for a pattern in your answers, or find a general formula for n people.

3. Explain how this problem appears to be related to Pascal's triangle.

4. How is this problem related to the combinatorial coefficients? (*Reminder:* The combinatorial coefficient $_nC_r$ tells you how many different bowls of ice cream you can make with r scoops, of different flavors, if there are n flavors altogether.)

25

Pascal and the Coefficients

```
                1
             1     1
          1     2     1
       1     3     3     1
    1     4     6     4     1
 1     5    [10]   10    5     1
?     ?     ?     ?     ?     ?     ?
?     ?     ?     ?     ?     ?     ?     ?
```

It turns out that the entries in Pascal's triangle are combinatorial coefficients. In fact, this is the main reason Pascal's triangle is important in mathematics.

It is standard practice to refer to the top row of Pascal's triangle as "row 0," the next row as "row 1," and so on. Similarly, we refer to the first number in each row as "entry 0," the next as "entry 1," and so on. The reason for using this numbering system is that it connects the position of a number to its meaning as a combinatorial coefficient.

For example, according to this system, the boxed number 10 shown above is entry 2 of row 5 of Pascal's triangle. This fits with the fact that 10 is equal to the combinatorial coefficient $\binom{5}{2}$, which tells you how many different bowls of ice cream you can make with two scoops (of different flavors) if there are five flavors altogether.

In general, it can be proved that entry r of row n is the combinatorial coefficient $\binom{n}{r}$. For instance, the row 1 4 6 4 1 is row 4, and it consists of the combinatorial coefficients $\binom{4}{0}, \binom{4}{1}, \binom{4}{2}, \binom{4}{3}$, and $\binom{4}{4}$.

Continued on next page

1. Check that $\binom{4}{0}, \binom{4}{1}, \binom{4}{2}, \binom{4}{3}$, and $\binom{4}{4}$ do have the numerical values $1, 4, 6, 4$, and 1, and explain the values in terms of bowls of ice cream.

2. Use the connection between Pascal's triangle and combinatorial coefficients to find these numerical values.

   a. $\binom{6}{5}$

   b. $\binom{7}{4}$

   c. $\binom{9}{5}$

   d. $\binom{10}{6}$

3. One feature of Pascal's triangle is that each row begins and ends with the number 1. In terms of combinatorial coefficients, this means that $\binom{n}{0}$ and $\binom{n}{n}$ are both equal to 1, for any value of n.

   Explain this feature of Pascal's triangle in terms of bowls of ice cream or using some other model for combinatorial coefficients.

Combinations, Pascal's Way

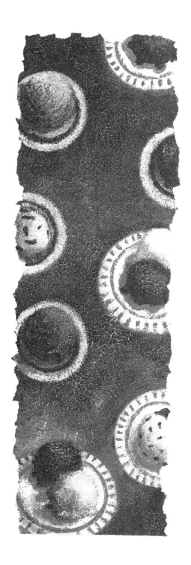

In the activity *Pascal's Triangle,* you explored and looked for patterns and relationships within that special array of numbers. You now know that the numbers in Pascal's triangle are actually combinatorial coefficients.

Your task in this activity is to examine the patterns and relationships within Pascal's triangle in light of the connection between Pascal's triangle and combinatorial coefficients.

For each pattern or relationship you found in Pascal's triangle, do two things.

- Express the pattern or relationship in terms of combinatorial coefficients.

- Explain the pattern or relationship based on the meaning of combinatorial coefficients (for example, by using the "bowls of ice cream" model for $_nC_r$).

Binomials and Pascal—Part I

In *Homework 22: Binomial Powers,* you found powers of
some binomials. In this assignment, you look at powers of
a special binomial and examine how the coefficients in the
expansion are related to Pascal's triangle.

1. Expand and simplify each of these expressions,
   combining terms and writing each result as a sum
   without parentheses.

   a. $(a + b)^2$

   b. $(a + b)^3$

   c. $(a + b)^4$

   d. $(a + b)^5$

2. Examine the coefficients in your results from
   Question 1. How are these coefficients related to
   Pascal's triangle?

Blaise Pascal (1623–1662).

Binomials and Pascal—Part II

In *Homework 26: Binomials and Pascal—Part I,* you examined powers of the binomial $a + b$, expanding expressions of the form $(a + b)^n$.

In each case, the coefficients form a row of Pascal's triangle. That is, they are numbers of the form $\binom{n}{r}$.

In this assignment, your task is to use the connection between the coefficients and Pascal's triangle to find the expansions for powers of some other binomials.

1. Find the expansion of $(a + b)^{10}$. Using your insights from the previous assignment and your copy of Pascal's triangle, write the expansion as a sum of terms with powers of a and b and with appropriate coefficients from Pascal's triangle.

2. Find the expansion of $(a + 2)^5$. [*Suggestion:* Write the expansion of $(a + b)^5$ and then substitute 2 for b.]

3. Find the expansion of $(x - 1)^4$. [Be careful about signs. It might help to think of $x - 1$ as $x + (-1)$.]

A Pascal Portfolio

Write a summary of what you know about Pascal's triangle. Include these elements.

• How to create Pascal's triangle

• How to use Pascal's triangle to find combinatorial coefficients

• Properties of Pascal's triangle and explanations of these properties in terms of combinatorial coefficients

• Why the numbers in Pascal's triangle are called *binomial coefficient*s

Another portrait of Blaise Pascal.

The Baseball Finale

Jeff Kirilov records the probability of one of several possible outcomes for the teams competing in the pennant race.

After many digressions, it's now time to solve the central problem of the unit. Remember, in this unit as in baseball, it's not over till it's over.

"Race for the Pennant!" Revisited

Time is running out, and the season will soon be over. Here's your last chance to figure out the probability that the Good Guys will win the pennant.

Once again, here are the records of the two teams.

Team	Games won	Games lost	Games left
Good Guys	96	59	7
Bad Guys	93	62	7

Recall these key facts and assumptions.

• The Good Guys and Bad Guys do not play against each other.

• In each game the Good Guys play, their probability of winning is .62.

• In each game the Bad Guys play, their probability of winning is .6.

Determine the probability that the Good Guys will win the pennant. Also determine the probability that the teams will be tied when they each finish their remaining seven games.

Graphing the Games

You've seen that there are eight possible overall outcomes for the Good Guys' final seven games. They can win all seven, they can win six and lose one, and so on, down to losing all seven. You've also seen that these eight outcomes are not equally likely.

1. Make a bar graph showing the probabilities for the eight possible overall outcomes. Keep in mind that in each game they play, the Good Guys' probability of winning is .62.

The Bad Guys are almost as good a team as the Good Guys. For each remaining game, their probability of winning is .6. If you made a bar graph showing the probability of each overall outcome, it would not be much different from the graph for the Good Guys.

A fair coin, on the other hand, has a probability of .5 of coming up heads. Suppose you flipped a fair coin seven times and recorded the results. As with the baseball problem, there are eight possible overall outcomes (seven heads and no tails, six heads and one tail, and so on, down to no heads and seven tails).

2. Make a bar graph showing the probabilities for the eight possible overall outcomes for seven flips of a fair coin.

3. Discuss the similarities and differences between your two graphs.

Binomial Probabilities

In the central unit problem, the Good Guys play a series of seven games. For each game, the result is either a win or a loss and their probability of winning is .62.

In a sequence of seven flips of a fair coin, the result of each flip is either heads or tails, and the probability of heads is .5 for each flip.

Although the probabilities are different in the two examples, the situations share two key features.

• There is some "event" with two possible outcomes.

• The "event" is repeated some number of times, but the probabilities of the two outcomes do not change. (That is, each occurrence of the event is *independent* of the previous occurrences.)

Continued on next page

The probabilities associated with such a situation define the **binomial distribution.** Just as there are many variations of the normal distribution, with different means and standard deviations, so there are also many variations of the binomial distribution, depending on the probabilities for the two outcomes and the number of times the event is repeated.

1. The Good Guys are thinking about next year. Suppose their outcome for next season follows a binomial distribution. Specifically, assume that as in the unit problem, they have a probability of .62 of winning each time they play a game.

   If their season consists of 162 games, what is the probability that they will win exactly 100 games? Express your answer using a combinatorial coefficient. (You do not need to get a numerical value for the probability.)

2. Now consider the general case of the binomial distribution. As with the baseball and coin flip examples, the event in question must have two outcomes. The two outcomes are generically referred to as **success** and **failure,** and each repetition of the event is called a **trial.** (For instance, in the central unit problem, the *event* is a single game, *success* means winning the game, *failure* means losing the game, and the part of the Good Guys' season under consideration involves seven *trials.*)

   Suppose the probability of success is p and the event is repeated n times. What is the probability of getting exactly r successes out of the n trials? (*Hints:* What is the probability of failure on each trial? How many failures will there be if there are r successes?)

Pennant Fever Portfolio

Now that *Pennant Fever* is completed, it is time to put together your portfolio for the unit. Compiling this portfolio has these three parts.

- Writing a cover letter in which you summarize the unit

- Choosing papers to include from your work in this unit

- Discussing your personal mathematical growth in this unit

Cover Letter for *Pennant Fever*

Look back over *Pennant Fever* and describe the central problem of the unit and the main mathematical ideas. This description should give an overview of how the key ideas like combinations, permutations, and Pascal's triangle were developed and how they were used to solve the central problem. Also include ideas that were not directly part of the unit problem, such as the birthday problem and the binomial theorem.

As part of the compilation of your portfolio, you will select some activities that you think were important in developing the key ideas of this unit. Your cover letter should include an explanation of why you selected the particular items.

Continued on next page

Selecting Papers from *Pennant Fever*

Your portfolio for *Pennant Fever* should include these items.

- *Homework 6: Diagrams, Baseball, and Losing 'em All*

- *Homework 16: Which Is Which?*

  Include in your portfolio the activities you discussed as part of this assignment.

- *Homework 28: A Pascal Portfolio*

- *"Race for the Pennant!" Revisited*

- *Homework 30: Binomial Probabilities*

- An activity illustrating the use or meaning of the binomial theorem.

- A Problem of the Week

  Select one of the POWs you completed in this unit (*Happy Birthday!, Let's Make a Deal, Fair Spoons,* or *And a Fortune, Too!*).

- Other key activities

  Identify two concepts that you think were important in this unit. For each concept, choose one or two activities that helped your understanding improve, and explain how the activity helped.

Personal Growth

Your cover letter for *Pennant Fever* describes how the mathematical ideas develop in the unit. As part of your portfolio, write about your personal development during this unit, and include a summary of your mathematical development over the course of Year 3. Also include here any other thoughts you might like to share with a reader of your portfolio.

Supplemental Problems

Probability and counting techniques form the heart of this unit, and many of the supplemental problems continue those themes. Others follow up on ideas from the POWs. Here are some examples.

- *Programming a Deal* and *Simulation Evaluation* build on the activity *Simulate a Deal*.

- *Determining Dunkalot's Druthers* is a baseball probability problem quite similar to the central unit problem.

- *Sleeping In* and *My Dog's Smarter Than Yours* are probability problems involving the combinatorial coefficients.

Putting Things Together

You saw in *Homework 4: Possible Outcomes* that the Good Guys can end up with any of eight possible records for their final seven games, from seven wins and no losses to no wins and seven losses. Similarly, there are eight different possibilities for the Bad Guys' final seven games.

In *Homework 4: Possible Outcomes,* you were asked to use this information to find the number of possible combinations of records for the two teams.

Here are some other problems involving finding the number of possibilities by making combinations from different lists.

1. The school cafeteria offers three choices of main dish (tacos, burgers, and tuna salad), four choices of beverage (milk, iced tea, soda, and apple juice), and two choices for dessert (brownies and pineapple). If you must choose one main dish, one beverage, and one dessert, how many options do you have in creating your meal?

2. You're planning your weekend and have decided to go to the movies Friday night, a concert Saturday night, and a sports event Sunday afternoon. There are five good movies showing, four excellent bands performing, and six local teams playing. How many different entertainment plans are there available to you?

Continued on next page

3. You are going to be away for 60 days and are planning what clothes to bring along. For each day, you will need a shirt, a pair of pants, a pair of shoes, and a hat. You don't mind wearing an individual item more than once, but you refuse to wear the exact same outfit on two different days.

You realize that if you brought one shirt, one pair of pants, one pair of shoes, and 60 hats, you could simply change hats each day to create exactly 60 different outfits, but that doesn't seem very interesting. (Besides, all those hats would be pretty bulky.)

a. How many different shirts, pairs of pants, pairs of shoes, and hats should you bring? Find several possibilities that will lead to exactly 60 different possible outfits.

b. Find a combination that will require as few total items as possible.

4. What do Questions 1 through 3 have in common? Formulate some general principles for dealing with situations like this.

Ring the Bells!

After your experience with *Go for the Gold!,* you've decided that television game shows could be lots of fun. You apply and are accepted to be a contestant on *Ring the Bells!* You find out that you must pay a fee of $200 to be on the show.

The show involves two buttons that are connected to colored bells and buzzers through a computer that uses a random number generator.

Here's how the game works.

You begin by pushing button 1. There is a 40 percent chance that a green bell will ring, a 20 percent chance that a yellow bell will ring, and a 40 percent chance that a red buzzer will ring. If the green bell rings, you go on to button 2. If the red buzzer rings, the game is over and you lose and get no prize. But if the yellow bell rings, you get a second try with button 1.

If you push button 1 a second time, the yellow changes from a bell to a buzzer, but the probabilities stay the same. If you get red or yellow (the buzzers), the game is over and you get a consolation prize of $100. But if you get the green bell, you go on to button 2.

With button 2, there are only two possible outcomes— the green bell and the red buzzer. You have a 40 percent chance of getting the green bell and a 60 percent chance of getting the red buzzer. If you get the bell, you win $1,000, but if you get the buzzer, the game is over and you lose and get no prize.

Continued on next page

Do you accept the invitation to be on the show? (Don't forget about the $200 fee.) Show both an area diagram (or sequence of area diagrams) and a tree diagram to explain your decision.

PROBLEM

Programming a Deal

In the activity *Simulate a Deal,* you test out both the "switch" and "stay" strategies by carrying out a simulation. Like many simulations, this one can be accomplished by a calculator or computer program using a random number generator.

Your task in this activity is to write such a program. Here are two options you might consider.

- **A one-game-at-a-time program:** In this type of program, the user would decide at the start of each game which of the two strategies to test. The program would use a random number generator to decide where the car is and then allow the user to choose the initial door. The game might end with a message like, "You decided to <'switch' or 'stay'> and you ended up with <'a car' or 'a worthless prize'>." With this type of program, the user would have to keep track of the results.

- **A many-games-at-a-time program:** In this type of program, the user would decide which strategy to test and also state how many games to play. The program would then play that many games one after another, using the random number generator to decide both where the car is and what the player's initial guess is. At the end of the program, the program would give a message like, "You used the <'switch' or 'stay'> strategy <some number> times. You got the car <some number> times and got a worthless prize <some number> times."

You may come up with other variations of your own.

Simulation Evaluation

When your class compiled its results from *Simulate a Deal,* you probably concluded that the "switch" strategy was better than the "stay" strategy. But whenever you use a simulation to estimate probabilities, you should ask yourself how reliable your estimates are.

If you had no evidence about the strategies, you might take as your null hypothesis that the two strategies are equally good. Under this null hypothesis, you would expect the number of successes for the "switch" strategy to be the same as the number of successes for the "stay" strategy. (*Note:* That's *not* the same as saying that each strategy has a 50 percent chance of success.)

Your class data probably did not show the two strategies having the same rate of success. Your task in this activity is to evaluate whether the difference between your class results and the results expected under the null hypothesis just described might be due to sampling fluctuation.

Specifically, answer this question.

> *If the two strategies are actually equally good, what is the probability of getting results as far off from equal for the two strategies as your actual class results?*

Use the chi-square statistic to compare two populations—games played using the "switch" strategy and games played using the "stay" strategy. Treat the overall class results from simulations for each strategy as your sample from that population.

The Chances of Doubles

Suppose you roll a pair of ordinary dice.

1. Explain why the probability of rolling a double is $\frac{1}{6}$. (A "double" means getting the same result on both dice.)

Now suppose you roll that pair of dice and then roll them again. You have a $\frac{1}{6}$ chance of getting a double the first time, and then you also have a $\frac{1}{6}$ chance of getting a double the second time. So it might seem reasonable that the probability of getting a double on at least one of the rolls should be $\frac{1}{6} + \frac{1}{6}$.

By that reasoning, if you rolled the pair of dice three times, your probability of getting a double on at least one of the rolls should be $\frac{1}{6} + \frac{1}{6} + \frac{1}{6}$. And if you rolled the pair of dice six times, the probability would be $\frac{1}{6} + \frac{1}{6} + \frac{1}{6} + \frac{1}{6} + \frac{1}{6} + \frac{1}{6}$, which equals 1.

In other words, by this reasoning, you would be certain of getting a double on at least one of the six rolls, which is definitely not correct.

Continued on next page

2. a. Explain why the probability of getting a double on at least one of the rolls of the pair of dice is *not* simply $\frac{1}{6} + \frac{1}{6}$.

b. Find the correct probability of getting a double on at least one of the rolls of the pair of dice.

3. What is the probability of rolling a double at least once if you roll the pair of dice three times? Four times? *n* times? (*Hint:* Find the probability of rolling *n* times and never getting doubles.)

Determining
Dunkalot's Druthers

Tyler Dunkalot's team has tied for the basketball league's championship. He and the other team's captain have to choose between two options for determining the champion.

• A three-game series between the two teams, in which the first team to win two games is the champion

• A five-game series between the two teams, in which the first team to win three games is the champion

Tyler estimates that in each game the teams play, his team has a probability of .55 of winning. (That's because his team has been getting better over the season and the other team has stayed pretty much the same.)

Which of the two methods for choosing the champion (two out of three or three out of five) would you advise Tyler to push for?

Sleeping In

At Cynthia's school, there are eight class periods. Here is the schedule.

1st period: 8:00–8:50

2nd period: 9:00–9:50

3rd period: 10:00–10:50

4th period: 11:00–11:50

5th period: 12:00–12:50

6th period: 1:00–1:50

7th period: 2:00–2:50

8th period: 3:00–3:50

Each student takes five courses and has three free periods. The free periods are assigned randomly, and students do not need to report to school until the period when their first course meets.

Now Cynthia does not think that she should be expected to be coherent at 8:00 a.m. Even 9:00 a.m. is a bit early for her to be able to think clearly. She is hoping to be able to sleep late and wonders what her chances are.

1. What is the probability that Cynthia will have the first period off?

2. How lucky does Cynthia have to be to have the first *two* periods off?

3. What is the probability that Cynthia will get her dream schedule and have the first three periods free?

"Twelve Bags of Gold" Revisited

Because the king and his gold have reappeared in this unit, perhaps you want to look back at his previous adventures.

In particular, you might want to look back at the *Twelve Bags of Gold* problem, which has the reputation of being one of the hardest POWs in Year 1 of IMP. (Then again, maybe you'd rather forget this POW entirely.)

If you'd like to revisit this problem, perhaps you can improve on your previous work. Maybe you can give a clearer explanation, or a simpler solution, or .... So here's the problem (in case you forgot).

> The king now has 12 bags of gold. Of course, each of his 12 bags holds exactly the same amount of gold as each of the others, and they all weigh the same. Well ... maybe not.

> Rumor has it that one of his 12 trusted caretakers is not so trustworthy. Someone, it is rumored, is making counterfeit gold. So the king sent his assistants to find the counterfeiter. They did find her, but she wouldn't tell them who had the counterfeit gold she had made, no matter how persuasive they were.

Continued on next page

All the assistants learned from her was that one of the 12 bags had counterfeit gold and that this bag's weight was different from the others. They could not find out from her whether the different bag was heavier or lighter.

So the king needed to know two things.

- Which bag weighed a different amount from the rest?

- Was that bag heavier or lighter?

And, of course, he wanted the answer found economically. He still had only the old balance scale. He wanted the solution in two weighings, but his court mathematician said it would take three weighings. No one else could see how it could be done in so few weighings. Can you figure it out?

Find a way to determine which bag is counterfeit and whether it weighs more or less than the others. Do so using the balance scale only three times.

My Dog's Smarter Than Yours

Emiko claims that her dog is very smart. When she opens the door in the morning, he runs out and brings in a newspaper.

You don't think that sounds very unusual? Well, Emiko lives in an apartment building. There are five newspapers outside every morning, and only one is a Japanese language newspaper. That's the one that belongs to Emiko's family.

Now, Emiko doesn't claim that her dog always brings in the right newspaper, but she says he does so more often than would happen if he were picking randomly. Emiko's brother, Hiro, is skeptical. His hypothesis—the null hypothesis—is that the dog is simply picking papers at random.

Emiko and Hiro decide to do a test. They will observe the dog for five straight days. Hiro says that if the dog brings in the right paper three or more times out of five, he'll reject his null hypothesis.

If Hiro's null hypothesis is actually correct, what is the probability that he will end up rejecting it?

Defining Pascal

$$
\begin{array}{ccccccccccccc}
 & & & & & & 1 & & & & & & \\
 & & & & & 1 & & 1 & & & & & \\
 & & & & 1 & & 2 & & 1 & & & & \\
 & & & 1 & & 3 & & 3 & & 1 & & & \\
 & & 1 & & 4 & & 6 & & 4 & & 1 & & \\
 & 1 & & 5 & & 10 & & 10 & & 5 & & 1 & \\
1 & & 6 & & \boxed{15} & & 20 & & 15 & & 6 & & 1 \\
\end{array}
$$

One way to define Pascal's triangle is by stating how each row is formed from the previous row. For example, the number 15 (shown in the box) is the sum of the entries 5 and 10 just above it in the previous row. In general, each entry in a new row can be found by adding the two closest terms in the previous row.

Another approach is to define Pascal's triangle in terms of the combinatorial coefficients. To do this, we label the top row of Pascal's triangle as "row 0," the next row as "row 1," and so on. Similarly, we label the entry at the left of any row as "entry 0," the next entry as "entry 1," and so on. For example, the boxed number 15 is entry 2 of row 6.

Using this system, we can define Pascal's triangle by this statement.

> Entry r of row n of Pascal's triangle is the combinatorial coefficient $\binom{n}{r}$.

For example, entry 2 of row 6 should be $\binom{6}{2}$ and sure enough, $\binom{6}{2} = 15$. The terms 5 and 10 that add up to give the entry 15 are the combinatorial coefficients $\binom{5}{1}$ and $\binom{5}{2}$.

Continued on next page

It's important that these two ways of defining Pascal's triangle give the same result. This activity explores the relationship between the two definitions.

1. Applying both definitions to the particular case of the entries 15, 5, and 10, we get the equation

$$\binom{6}{2} = \binom{5}{1} + \binom{5}{2}$$

You can verify numerically that $15 = 10 + 5$, but your task here is to explain this equation *in terms of the meaning of combinatorial coefficients*. For example, why should the number of possible two-scoop bowls of ice cream, chosen from among six flavors, be the same as the sum of the number of one-scoop bowls chosen from among five flavors and the number of two-scoop bowls chosen from among five flavors?

2. Write a generalization of the equation displayed in Question 1. That is, write a general equation expressing the pattern for extending Pascal's triangle in terms of combinatorial coefficients.

3. Explain why your equation in Question 2 must be true for all values of n and r. This explanation should be based on the meaning of $\binom{n}{r}$ as the number of ways to select r objects from a set of n objects.

Maximum in the Middle

One of the reasons for the interest in Pascal's triangle is that combinatorial coefficients play an important role in many probability problems.

For example, the combinatorial coefficient $\binom{6}{2}$ (which is the number shown as $\boxed{15}$ at the right) gives the number of ways to flip a coin six times and get exactly two heads.

If a coin is flipped six times, it makes sense that the most likely number of heads to get is three. This matches the fact that the largest term in the last row shown here for Pascal's triangle is 20. This entry corresponds to the combinatorial coefficient $\binom{6}{3}$. [Remember that values for $\binom{n}{r}$ appear in what is actually the $(n + 1)^{\text{th}}$ row of Pascal's triangle although we refer to this as "row n."]

$$
\begin{array}{ccccccccccccc}
 & & & & & & 1 \\
 & & & & & 1 & & 1 \\
 & & & & 1 & & 2 & & 1 \\
 & & & 1 & & 3 & & 3 & & 1 \\
 & & 1 & & 4 & & 6 & & 4 & & 1 \\
 & 1 & & 5 & & 10 & & 10 & & 5 & & 1 \\
1 & & 6 & & \boxed{15} & & 20 & & 15 & & 6 & & 1
\end{array}
$$

1. First consider the case where n is even, so n is twice some other integer m. Prove that among all choices for r, the largest value of $\binom{2m}{r}$ occurs when r is equal to m. Your proof should be based on the formula for combinatorial coefficients.

2. State and prove a similar result for the case where n is odd. (*Suggestion:* Write n as $2t + 1$ for some integer t.)

The Why's of Binomial Expansion

You have expanded various expressions of the form $(a + b)^n$ and seen that the coefficients turn out to be combinatorial coefficients. In fact, this is true for every positive integer value of n, and this principle is called the **binomial theorem.**

Your goal in this activity is to see *why* combinatorial coefficients appear in these expansions.

1. Use the distributive property to expand the expression

$$(a_1 + b_1)(a_2 + b_2)(a_3 + b_3)(a_4 + b_4)$$

2. Each term in the expansion from Question 1 is a product of terms with some a's and some b's (or perhaps all a's or all b's). For instance, one of the terms is $a_1 b_2 b_3 a_4$, which has two factors that are a's and two factors that are b's.

   a. Altogether, how many terms in your expansion have two a's and two b's?

   b. What are the values of n and r for the combinatorial coefficient that best represents your answer from Question 2a? Explain your answer.

3. Use your work from Questions 1 and 2 to write a general explanation of the fact that the coefficients of $(a + b)^n$ are combinatorial coefficients.

The Binomial Theorem and Row Sums

You have seen that the coefficients in the expansion of $(a + b)^n$ are the combinatorial coefficients that form row n of Pascal's triangle. This principle is called the *binomial theorem.*

In Pascal's triangle, the sum of the entries in row n is 2^n, as illustrated below. How can you prove this property using the binomial theorem? [*Hint:* What can you substitute for a and b to make the expansion of $(a + b)^n$ equal to the sum of the entries from row n of Pascal's triangle?]

$$1 = 1$$
$$1 + 1 = 2$$
$$1 + 2 + 1 = 4$$
$$1 + 3 + 3 + 1 = 8$$
$$1 + 4 + 6 + 4 + 1 = 16$$

Glossary

This is the glossary for all five units of IMP Year 3.

Additive identity

See **identity and inverse elements.**

Additive inverse

See **identity and inverse elements.**

Adjacent interior angle

See **exterior angle.**

Alternate interior angles

See *A Geometric Summary* in *Orchard Hideout.*

Angle bisector

A line segment or ray that divides an angle into two smaller angles of equal measure.

Analytic geometry

The study of geometry using a coordinate system, in contrast to **synthetic geometry.**

Angle sum property

The principle that the sum of the angles of any triangle is exactly 180°. See also *A Geometric Summary* in *Orchard Hideout.*

Arithmetic sequence

A sequence of numbers in which the difference between successive terms is constant.

Example: The sequence 5, 8, 11, 14, … is an arithmetic sequence in which each term is 3 more than the preceding term.

Associative

An operation ∗ is associative (or has the associative property) if the equation $(a * b) * c = a * (b * c)$ holds true for all values of a, b, and c. An operation that does not have this property is called **nonassociative.**

Examples: The operation of addition is associative because for any numbers a, b, and c, $(a + b) + c = a + (b + c)$. The operation of division is nonassociative because, for example, $(12 \div 4) \div 2$ is not equal to $12 \div (4 \div 2)$.

Average rate of change

The ratio between the change in a quantity over an interval of time and the length of the time interval, used in contrast to **instantaneous rate of change.**

Example: If the population of a town grows by 15,000 people over a period of 10 years, its average rate of change is 1500 people per year. The rate of change in any given year may be higher or lower than this.

Binomial

A polynomial with exactly two terms. See **polynomial.**

Binomial coefficient

A synonym for **combinatorial coefficient.**

Binomial distribution

A probability distribution describing the result of repeated independent trials of the same event with two possible outcomes.

Suppose a particular outcome has probability p for each trial. The binomial distribution states that in n trials, the probability that this outcome occurs exactly r times is $_nC_r \cdot p^r \cdot (1 - p)^{n - r}$. (See **combinatorial coefficient** for the meaning of $_nC_r$.)

Example: Suppose a weighted coin comes up heads 70% of the time. If the coin is flipped 50 times, the probability of exactly 30 heads is $_{50}C_{30} \cdot (.7)^{30} \cdot (.3)^{20}$.

Binomial theorem

The binomial theorem states that the expression $(x + y)^n$ is the sum of all terms of the form ${}_nC_r \cdot x^r \cdot y^{n-r}$ where r goes from 0 through n. (See **combinatorial coefficient** for the meaning of ${}_nC_r$.)

Circumcenter

See **circumscribed and inscribed figures.**

Circumcircle

See **circumscribed and inscribed figures.**

Circumscribed and inscribed figures

If a circle intersects all of the vertices of a polygon, then the circle is **circumscribed** about the polygon, and the polygon is **inscribed** in the circle.

Example: In this diagram, the circle is circumscribed about triangle *ABC* and the triangle is inscribed in the circle. This circle is called the **circumcircle** of the triangle and its center is called the **circumcenter** of the triangle.

If a circle is tangent to all of the sides of a polygon, then the circle is **inscribed** in the polygon, and the polygon is **circumscribed** about the circle.

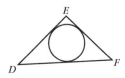

Example: In this diagram, the circle is inscribed in triangle *DEF* and the triangle is circumscribed about the circle. This circle is called the **incircle** of the triangle and its center is called the **incenter** of the triangle. (*Note:* Not all polygons have a circumcircle or incircle.)

Coefficient

Usually, a number used to multiply an algebraic expression. In some cases, a variable is used as a coefficient.

Example: In the expression $3x + 4 \sin x$, the numbers 3 and 4 are coefficients. In the expression ae^{kx}, the variables a and k can be considered coefficients.

Coefficient matrix

The matrix representing the coefficients of the variables in a system of linear equations.

Example: For the system

$$3r + 2s = 9$$
$$-5r + 4s = 16$$

the coefficient matrix is

$$\begin{bmatrix} 3 & 2 \\ -5 & 4 \end{bmatrix}$$

Column vector

A matrix that contains exactly one column.

Combination

See **combinatorial coefficient.**

Combinatorial coefficient

The number of ways of selecting a set of a given size r from a specific set of size n. This number is written as $\binom{n}{r}$ or $_nC_r$. Each way of selecting the set of size r is called a **combination.**

Combinatorial coefficients are also called *binomial coefficients,* because of their relationship to the expansion of powers of binomials (see **binomial theorem**).

Example: You can select two numbers from the set $\{1, 2, 3, 4, 5\}$ in these ways: $\{1, 2\}, \{1, 3\}, \{1, 4\}, \{1, 5\},$ $\{2, 3\}, \{2, 4\}, \{2, 5\}, \{3, 4\}, \{3, 5\},$ and $\{4, 5\}.$ Because there are exactly ten distinct ways, $_5C_2 = 10.$

See also **permutation coefficient.**

Common logarithm

A logarithm using a base of 10.

Example: The common logarithm of 100, written **$\log_{10} 100,$** is 2, because $10^2 = 100.$

Commutative An operation ∗ is commutative (or *has the commutative property*) if the equation $a * b = b * a$ holds true for all values of a and b. An operation that does not have this property is called **noncommutative.**

Examples: The operation of addition is commutative because for any numbers a and b, $a + b = b + a$. The operation of subtraction is noncommutative because, for example, $5 - 9$ is not equal to $9 - 5$.

Completing the square The technique of adding a constant term to an expression, especially a quadratic expression, in order to make it a **perfect square.**

Example: To complete the square for the expression $x^2 + 10x$, one adds 25, because $x^2 + 10x + 25$ is the perfect square $(x + 5)^2$.

Complex number Any number that can be represented in the form $a + bi$, where a and b are real numbers and i is the symbol for $\sqrt{-1}$. The number a is called the *real part* of the number and the expression bi is called the *imaginary part* of the number.

Conclusion See **"If . . . , then" statement.**

Congruent See *A Geometric Summary* in *Orchard Hideout.*

Constant term In any polynomial, a term that does not contain the variable. (If no such term appears in the expression, then the constant term is 0.) See also **polynomial.**

Example: In the polynomial $x^3 - 2x^2 + 7$, the number 7 is the constant term. In the polynomial $2x^4 + 5x$, the constant term is 0.

Constraint Informally, a limitation or restriction. In a linear programming problem, any of the conditions limiting the variables.

Continuous graph

Informally, a graph that can be drawn without lifting one's pencil, in contrast to a **discrete graph.**

Converse

See **"If . . . , then" statement.**

Coordinate plane

In the three-dimensional coordinate system, any of the three planes that includes two of the coordinate axes. (In the two-dimensional coordinate system, the term *coordinate plane* refers to the set of all points.)

Example: The *xz*-plane is the plane containing the *x*- and *z*-axes, and consists of all points whose *y*-coordinate is 0.

See also *The Three-Variable Coordinate System* in *Meadows or Malls?*

Corresponding angles

See *A Geometric Summary* in *Orchard Hideout.*

Cosine

See *A Geometric Summary* in *Orchard Hideout.*

Cubic equation, expression, or function

An equation, expression, or function involving a polynomial of degree 3. See **polynomial** and see also *Quadratics and Other Polynomials* in *Fireworks.*

Degree of a polynomial

See **polynomial.**

Dependent system of equations

See **system of equations.**

Derivative	The derivative of the function f at the point $(a, f(a))$ [written $f'(a)$] is equal to the instantaneous rate of change of f at $x = a$. The derivative at $(a, f(a))$ is also the slope of the line tangent to the graph of f at that point. *Note:* The derivative of a function does not necessarily exist at every point.

For a given function f, the derivatives at each point together define a new function, also called the derivative (or *derived function*) and represented by the symbol f'.

Dimensions of a matrix	The number of rows and columns in a matrix. See *Matrix Basics* in *Meadows or Malls?*

Example: The matrix below has dimensions 2×3 because it has two rows and three columns.

$$\begin{bmatrix} 1 & -3 & 0 \\ 5 & 6 & -4 \end{bmatrix}$$

Discrete graph	A graph consisting of isolated or unconnected points, in contrast to a **continuous graph.**
Distance formula	A formula for determining the distance between two points using the coordinates of the points. In a two-dimensional coordinate system, the distance formula states that the distance between the points (x_1, y_1) and (x_2, y_2) is $\sqrt{(x_2 - x_1)^2 + (y_2 - y_1)^2}$. This formula is based on the Pythagorean theorem.
Edge	See **polyhedron.**
Elimination method	A method of solving a system of equations in which, at each step, one variable is "eliminated" by performing various operations on the equations. This creates a new system with one less variable. The eventual goal of the method is to create an equation with only one variable.

Also called **Gaussian elimination.**

Exponential function	Informally, any function in which the variable is in the exponent. Often used specifically to refer to a function defined by an equation of the form $y = k \cdot b^{cx}$, where $k, b,$ and c are specific numbers with $b > 0$ and with k and c both nonzero.
Exterior angle	An angle formed at a vertex of a polygon but outside the polygon by extending one of the sides of the polygon. The angle of the polygon at the same vertex is called the **adjacent interior angle,** and an angle of the polygon at a different vertex is called a **nonadjacent interior angle.**

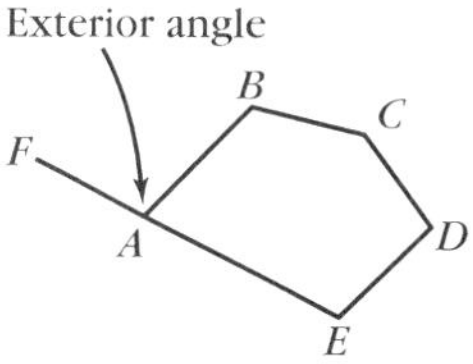

Example: The diagram shows exterior angle *BAF* for polygon *ABCDE.* Angle *BAE* is the adjacent interior angle. The angles of the polygon at *B, C, D,* and *E* are nonadjacent interior angles.

Face	See **polyhedron.**
Factorable	Usually used to refer to a polynomial with integer coefficients that can be written as the product of two polynomials of smaller degree, each of which also has integer coefficients.
	Example: The polynomial $x^2 + 4x + 3$ is factorable because it is equal to the product $(x + 1)(x + 3)$. The polynomial $x^2 + 4x + 5$ is not factorable in this sense.
Feasible region	The region consisting of all points whose coordinates satisfy a given set of constraints. A point in this set is called a **feasible point.**
First octant	See **octant.**
Gaussian elimination	See **elimination method.**

Geometric sequence	A sequence of numbers in which the ratio between successive terms is constant.

Example: The sequence $3, 6, 12, 24, \ldots$ is a geometric sequence in which each term is 2 times the preceding term.

Hypothesis	See **"If . . . , then" statement.**

Identity and inverse elements	For a given operation, an **identity element** for that operation is an element which, when combined with any element using the given operation, yields that second element as the result.

Examples: The number 0 is the identity element for addition (or the **additive identity**) because $x + 0$ and $0 + x$ are both equal to x for any number x. Similarly, the number 1 is the identity element for multiplication (or the **multiplicative identity**).

If an operation has an identity element, then an **inverse** for a given element (for that operation) is an element which, when combined with the given element, yields the identity element as the result.

Examples: The number -7 is the inverse element for 7 for the operation of addition (or the **additive inverse** of 7) because both $7 + (-7)$ and $(-7) + 7$ are equal to 0, which is the identity element for addition. Similarly, the number $\frac{1}{5}$ is the inverse for 5 for the operation of multiplication (or the **multiplicative inverse** of 5).

Identity matrix	Any square matrix that acts as the identity element for multiplication of square matrices of the same dimensions.

Example: The matrix $\begin{bmatrix} 1 & 0 & 0 \\ 0 & 1 & 0 \\ 0 & 0 & 1 \end{bmatrix}$ is the identity matrix

for 3×3 matrices.

"If ..., then ..." *statement*	A specific form of mathematical statement, saying that if one condition—the **hypothesis**—is true, then another condition—the **conclusion**—must also be true.

Example: Here is a true "If ..., then ..." statement.

> *If two angles of a triangle have equal measure, then the sides opposite these angles have equal length.*

The statement "two angles of a triangle have equal measure" is the hypothesis; the statement "the sides opposite these angles have equal length" is the conclusion.

The statement obtained from an "If ..., then ..." statement by interchanging the hypothesis and conclusion is called its **converse.**

Example: The converse of the statement used as an example for "If ..., then ..." is the statement

> *If the sides opposite two angles of a triangle have equal length, then the angles have equal measure.*

"If and only if" A phrase used to indicate that both a given "If ..., then ..." statement and its converse are true.

Example: The two statements in the glossary entry for **"If ..., then ..." statement** can be combined to create this "If and only if" statement.

> *Two angles of a triangle have equal measure if and only if the sides opposite these angles have equal length.*

Incenter See **circumscribed and inscribed figures.**

Incircle See **circumscribed and inscribed figures.**

Inconsistent equations See **system of equations.**

Independent equations	See **system of equations.**
Initial term	The first term in a sequence.
Inscribed figure	See **circumscribed and inscribed figures.**
Instantaneous rate of change	The rate at which a quantity is changing at a given instant, used in contrast to **average rate of change.** An important example is the instantaneous speed of an object. The instantaneous speed can be found from the function describing the motion of the object by evaluating the derivative of the function at the desired instant.
Inverse	See **identity and inverse elements.**
Inverse trigonometric function	Any of the functions used to find an angle when a trigonometric function of the angle is known. See *A Geometric Summary* in *Orchard Hideout.*
Invertible matrix	A matrix for which a multiplicative inverse exists. If no multiplicative inverse exists, the matrix is **noninvertible.**
Lattice point	A point in a coordinate system with integer coordinates.
Least squares method	A method of determining a function of best fit for a set of data by finding the vertical distance between the graph of a function and each data point and summing the squares of these distances.
	Generally, the goal of this method is to find the function within a given family for which the sum of the squares of the distances is as small as possible.

Limit

A process used to investigate the behavior of a function at a given point by examining the value of the function at points which are successively closer to the given value.

Example: For the function defined by the equation $f(x) = \frac{\sin x}{x}$, the limit as x approaches 0 can be found intuitively by examining the value of the function at $x = 0.1$, then 0.01, then 0.001, and so on. The notation used for this limit is

$$\lim_{x \to 0} \frac{\sin x}{x}$$

In defining this expression formally, one must also consider negative values near 0, such as $-0.1, -0.01, -0.001$, and so on, as well as positive values. *Note:* A function does not necessarily have a limit at every value of x.

Limits are especially useful in finding the derivative of a function, which is studied in detail in calculus.

Linear algebra

The branch of mathematics dealing with linear expressions and systems of linear equations.

Linear equation in n variables

Using the symbols x_1, x_2, and so on, through x_n to represent different variables, a **linear equation in *n* variables** is an equation of the form

$$a_1x_1 + a_2x_2 + \ldots + a_nx_n = c$$

where $a_1, a_1, \ldots, a_n$, and c are any numbers.

Linear programming

A problem-solving method that involves maximizing or minimizing a linear expression subject to a set of constraints that are linear equations or inequalities.

m-by-n matrix

A matrix with m rows and n columns. See *Matrix Basics* in *Meadows or Malls?*

Matrix	A rectangular array of numbers or expressions. See *Matrix Basics* in *Meadows or Malls?*
Matrix algebra	The study of operations with matrices.
Median	In a triangle, the line segment connecting a vertex to the midpoint of the opposite side.
Midline	The line segment connecting the midpoints of two sides of a triangle.
Midpoint formula	A formula for determining the midpoint of a line segment using the coordinates of the endpoints of the segment. In a two-dimensional coordinate system, the midpoint formula states that the midpoint of the segment with endpoints (x_1, y_1) and (x_2, y_2) is $\left(\frac{x_1 + x_2}{2}, \frac{y_1 + y_2}{2}\right)$.
Monomial	A polynomial with exactly one term. See **polynomial.**
Multiplicative identity	See **identity and inverse elements.**
Multiplicative inverse	See **identity and inverse elements.**
Natural logarithm	A logarithm using a base of e (where e is the special number that is approximately 2.718).
	Example: The natural logarithm of 25, written **ln 25,** is approximately 3.22, because $e^{3.22}$ is approximately 25.
Nonadjacent interior angle	See **exterior angle.**
Nonassociative	See **associative.**
Noncommutative	See **commutative.**
Noninvertible	See **invertible.**

Octant

One of the eight regions into which three-dimensional space is divided by the coordinate planes, as shown in the diagram. Points with one or more coordinates equal to zero do not belong to any of the octants.

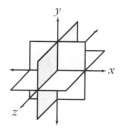

Example: The set of points (x, y, z) for which $x > 0$, $y < 0$, and $z < 0$ is one of the eight octants, and is the right-hand, lower, rear region in the diagram. The **first octant** is the set of points for which all three coordinates are positive. (The other octants are not numbered.)

See also *The Three-Variable Coordinate System* in *Meadows or Malls?*

Parabola

The type of curve that occurs as the graph of a quadratic function. The maximum or minimum point of the graph is called the **vertex** (or *turning point*) of the parabola.

Examples: The graphs of the equations $y = x^2$ and $y = -x^2 + 2x + 2$, shown here, are both parabolas. The first is described as "opening upward," and its vertex is at its minimum point, $(0, 0)$. The second is described as "opening downward," and its vertex is at its maximum point, $(1, 3)$.

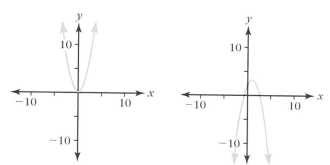

Parallel

Two lines in a plane or two planes in three-dimensional space are defined as parallel if they do not meet. See also **skew lines.**

*Pascal's
triangle*

A specific triangular array of numbers in which each entry is the sum of the entries in the preceding row that are just to its right and left. (Entries at the ends of rows are equal to 1.) The entries in Pascal's triangle are all **combinatorial coefficients.**

The array here shows the first six rows of Pascal's triangle. For example, the boxed entry $\boxed{10}$ is the sum of the entries 4 and 6 in the preceding row.

$$
\begin{array}{ccccccccccc}
& & & & & 1 & & & & & \\
& & & & 1 & & 1 & & & & \\
& & & 1 & & 2 & & 1 & & & \\
& & 1 & & 3 & & 3 & & 1 & & \\
& 1 & & 4 & & 6 & & 4 & & 1 & \\
1 & & 5 & & \boxed{10} & & 10 & & 5 & & 1
\end{array}
$$

Perfect square

A number or expression that is the square of a number or expression.

Examples: 49 and $x^2 + 8x + 16$ are perfect squares, because $49 = 7^2$ and $x^2 + 8x + 16 = (x + 4)^2$.

Permutation

Generally, an arrangement of objects in a particular order. See **permutation coefficient.**

*Permutation
coefficient*

The number of ways of selecting r distinct objects in a specific order from a specific set of size n. This number is written as $_nP_r$.

Example: You can select two distinct numbers in a particular order from the set $\{1, 2, 3\}$ in these ways: $(1, 2), (2, 1), (1, 3), (3, 1), (2, 3),$ and $(3, 2)$. Because there are exactly six distinct ways, $_3P_2 = 6$.

See also **combinatorial coefficient.**

Perpendicular bisector

The line that is perpendicular to a given line segment at that segment's midpoint.

Pigeon-hole principle

The principle that if m objects are placed in n disjoint sets, with $m > n$, then at least one of the sets must contain at least two of the objects. Often stated as, "If you place m pigeons in n pigeon holes, with $m > n$, then you have to put at least two pigeons in the same pigeon hole."

Polygon

A closed two-dimensional figure consisting of three or more line segments. The line segments that form a polygon are called its sides. The endpoints of these segments are called **vertices** (singular: **vertex**).

Examples: The figures below are all polygons.

Polyhedron

A three-dimensional figure bounded by intersecting planes. The polygonal regions formed by the intersecting planes are called the **faces** of the polyhedron, and the sides of these polygons are called the **edges** of the polyhedron. The vertices of the polygons are also called **vertices** of the polyhedron.

Example: The figure below shows a polyhedron. Polygon *ABFG* is one of its faces, segment $\overline{CD}$ is one of its edges, and point *E* is one of its vertices.

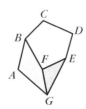

Polynomial (in a given variable)

Any expression that is a sum in which each term added is a whole-number power of the variable, multiplied by a coefficient. A **monomial** is a polynomial with just one term, a **binomial** is a polynomial with exactly two terms, and a **trinomial** is a polynomial with exactly three terms.

The **degree** of a polynomial is the highest exponent appearing with the variable.

See also *Quadratics and Other Polynomials* in *Fireworks*.

Examples: $4x^3$ is a monomial of degree 3; $3x^4 - 2x$ is a binomial of degree 4; $-2x^5 + x^2 + 7$ is a trinomial of degree 5. The constant polynomial 7 is a monomial of degree 0.

Profit line or plane

In a problem in which profit is a linear function of the variables, the line or plane representing the set of points that give a particular profit. Sometimes used generically to refer to the set of points that give a particular value for any linear function, even when the linear function does not represent profit.

Proportionality constant

A number that represents a fixed ratio between two quantities.

Example: The ratio between the circumference C and the diameter d is the same for all circles. This ratio, π, is the proportionality constant between C and d. This fact is expressed by the equation $C = \pi d$.

Proportionality property

An informal term for the property that for functions of the form $y = k \cdot b^{cx}$, the derivative of the function is proportional to the function itself.

Pythagorean theorem

The statement that in a right triangle with legs of lengths a and b and hypotenuse of length c, the lengths satisfy the equation $a^2 + b^2 = c^2$. See *A Geometric Summary* in *Orchard Hideout*.

Pythagorean triple

Any set of three positive whole numbers a, b, and c that satisfy the equation $a^2 + b^2 = c^2$.

Examples: The set 3, 4, and 5 and the set 7, 24, and 25 are each Pythagorean triples.

Quadratic equation, expression, or function

An equation, expression, or function involving a polynomial of degree 2. See **polynomial** and see also *Quadratics and Other Polynomials* in *Fireworks*.

Root of a function

A number that gives the output 0 when substituted for the variable in a function. On a graph, a root is the x-coordinate of an x-intercept.

Example: The numbers 4 and -1 are the roots of the function g defined by the equation $g(x) = x^2 - 3x - 4$, because $g(4) = 0$ and $g(-1) = 0$.

Row vector

A matrix that contains exactly one row.

Sampling with and without replacement

These terms are used to distinguish two ways in which to choose a sequence of objects from a set.

If an object that has been chosen is always restored to the set before the next object is chosen, then the process is called sampling *with* replacement.

If an object once chosen is no longer available for further selection, then the process is called sampling *without* replacement.

Secant line	A line or line segment connecting two given points on a graph.
Similar	See *A Geometric Summary* in *Orchard Hideout.*
Sine	See *A Geometric Summary* in *Orchard Hideout.*
Skew lines	In three-dimensional space, lines that do not intersect but are not parallel.
Slope of a line	Informally, the steepness of a line. The slope of a nonvertical line in the *xy*-coordinate system is defined formally as the ratio $\frac{y_2 - y_1}{x_2 - x_1}$, where (x_1, y_1) and (x_2, y_2) are any two distinct points on the line. Slope is not defined for vertical lines.
Square matrix	A matrix in which the number of rows is equal to the number of columns.
Step function	A function whose output values remain constant over each of various intervals of input values before "jumping" to a different value. The graph of a step function often looks like a series of steps.
Straight angle	An angle that measures 180°.
Substitution method	A method for solving a system of equations in which one equation is solved for one variable and the resulting expression is substituted into another equation. See *Ideas for Solving Systems* in *Meadows or Malls?*
Synthetic geometry	The study of geometry without use of a coordinate system, in contrast to **analytic geometry.**

System of equations	A set of two or more equations being considered together. If the equations have no common solution, the system is **inconsistent.** Also, if one of the equations can be removed from the system without changing the set of common solutions, that equation is **dependent** on the others, and the system as a whole is also **dependent.** If no equation is dependent on the rest, the system is **independent.** In the case of a system of linear equations with the same number of equations as variables, the system is *inconsistent* if there is no solution, *dependent* if there are infinitely many solutions, and *independent* if there is a unique solution.
Tangent of an angle	See *A Geometric Summary* in *Orchard Hideout.*
Tangent to a circle	A line that intersects a circle in exactly one point.

Example: In this diagram, the line *m* is tangent to the circle at point *P*.

Tangent to a graph	Informally, a line that "just touches" the graph of a function.
Term	See **polynomial.**
Three-dimensional coordinate system	See *The Three-Variable Coordinate System* in *Meadows or Malls?*
Three-space	The set of points in the **three-dimensional coordinate system.**
Transversal	See *A Geometric Summary* in *Orchard Hideout.*

Triangular numbers	The numbers that are obtained by finding the sum of the first n positive integers, for different values of n; that is, the numbers $1, 1 + 2, 1 + 2 + 3, 1 + 2 + 3 + 4$, and so on. These are called *triangular numbers* because they give the number of elements in triangular arrays like those shown here.

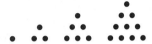

Trigonometry	The study of the relationship between any angle of a right triangle and the ratios of the sides of the triangle. See *A Geometric Summary* in *Orchard Hideout.*
Trinomial	A polynomial with exactly three terms. See **polynomial.**
Unit circle	A circle whose radius is 1 unit. A unit circle has a circumference of 2π units and an area of π square units.
Vertex	See **parabola, polygon,** and **polyhedron.**
Vertex form (of a quadratic expression)	A quadratic expression written in the form $a(x - h)^2 + k$, where a, h, and k are numbers, so named because the corresponding quadratic function has the point (h, k) as its vertex (see **parabola**).
Vertical angles	A pair of "opposite" angles formed by a pair of intersecting lines. Example: Angles u and v are vertical angles.

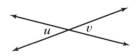

x-intercept	A point where a graph crosses the *x*-axis. Sometimes, the *x*-coordinate of that point.
y- intercept	A point where a graph crosses the *y*-axis. Sometimes, the *y*-coordinate of that point.
Zero property	The property of multiplication stating that if a product is equal to zero, then at least one of the factors must be equal to zero. Example: If $a \cdot b = 0$, then either a or b (or both) must be zero.

Interior Photography

3 Mililani High School, Diana Agor; **4** The Image Bank; **5** The Image Bank; **7** Hillary Turner, **9** PhotoDisc, The Image Bank; **10** Stock Boston; **16** Animals, Animals; **18** Los Altos High School, Judy Strauss; **27** Mendocino High School, Don Cruser, Lynne Alper; **34** The Image Bank; **35** PhotoDisc; **53** The Image Bank; **55** Laura Murray; **59** Foothill High School, Cheryl Dozier; **60** SuperStock, Inc.; **62** PhotoEdit; **64** SuperStock, Inc.; **65** Comstock ©1995; **73** PhotoDisc; **76** Foothill College, Cheryl Dozier; **82** Fresno High School, Dave Calhoun; **86** Lumina; **87** PhotoDisc; **89** Foothill High School, Cheryl Dozier; **90** SuperStock, Inc.; **93** FPG International; **95** Stock Boston; **103** Capuchino High School, Chicha Lynch; **104** SuperStock, Inc.; **106** FPG International; **112** Foothill High School, Cheryl Dozier; **116** The Image Bank; **120** PhotoDisc, PhotoDisc; **125** SuperStock, Inc.; **143** SuperStock, Inc.; **148** SuperStock, Inc.; **151** Laura Murray; **155** Kapa'a High School, Elaine Denny; **156** PhotoFile; **157** The Image Works; **159** Leo de Wys Inc. PHOTOFILE; **160** The Image Works; **165** Roosevelt High School, George Giffen; **167** Hillary Turner, **173** The Image Bank; **177** Santa Cruz High School, Kevin Drinkard, Lynne Alper; **178** PhotoDisc; **186** Hillary Turner; **187** Hillary Turner; **192** Santa Cruz High School, Kevin Drinkard; **195** Hillary Turner; **196** Hillary Turner; **197** Hillary Turner; **198** Shasta High School, Dave Robathan; **199** Hillary Turner; **200** Hillary Turner; **201** Hillary Turner; **207** Rosemead High School, Melody Martinez; **217** SuperStock, Inc.; **218** PhotoEdit; **222** Pleasant Valley High School, Mike Christensen; **223** Hillary Turner, **225** Hillary Turner; **228** FPG International; **232** Hillary Turner; **234** Tony Stone Worldwide; **236** Hillary Turner, **237** Hillary Turner, **245** Hillary Turner; **247** Santa Maria High School, Chris Paulus; **249** PhotoFile, The Image Works; **251** Hillary Turner; **252** Hillary Turner; **262** Leo de Wys Inc. PHOTOFILE; **263** PhotoDisc; **266** Comstock ©1995; **267** Hillary Turner; **270** SuperStock, Inc.; **281** Los Altos High School, Judy Strauss, Lynne Alper; **282** PhotoDisc; **283** Leo de Wys Inc. PHOTOFILE; **288** Kapa'a High School, Elaine Denny; **292** FPG International; **298** Santa Cruz High School, Kevin Drinkard, Lynne Alper, **299** Comstock ©1994; **309** Leo de Wys Inc. PHOTOFILE; **312** Lincoln High School, Lori Green; **314** Leo de Wys Inc. PHOTOFILE; **316** PhotoEdit; **319** Stock Boston; **327** Brookline High School, Terry Nowak; **328** Hillary Turner; **329** Hillary Turner; **330** SuperStock, Inc.; **335** PhotoEdit; **341** SuperStock, Inc.; **343** Comstock ©1989; **344** Santa Cruz High School, Kevin Drinkard, Lynne Alper, **345** FPG International;

347 Stock Boston; **348** SuperStock, Inc., **356** San Lorenzo Valley High School, Dennis Cavaillé, Lynne Alper; **359** PhotoDisc; **361** Hillary Turner; **367** The Image Bank; **378** SuperStock, Inc.; **383** SuperStock, Inc.; **384** SuperStock, Inc.; **387** SuperStock, Inc.; **391** Orange Glen High School, Linda Steiner; **393** PhotoEdit; **396** Comstock © 1995; **398** PhotoEdit; **399** Fresno High School, Dave Calhoun; **401** FPG International; **403** Comstock © 1995; **406** Silver Lake Regional High School, Kevin Sawyer, Lynne Alper; **410** SuperStock, Inc.; **415** Lincoln High School, Lori Green; **426** SuperStock, Inc.; **427** Hillary Turner; **428** Hillary Turner; **431** Stock Boston; **433** Stock Boston; **435** Foothill High School, Cheryl Dozier; **442** Leo de Wys Inc. PHOTOFILE; **443** The Image Works; **448** Leo de Wys Inc. PHOTOFILE; **449** Kapa'a High School, Elaine Denny; **451** PhotoDisc; **455** PhotoEdit; **457** The Image Works; **458** Lincoln High School, Lori Green; **461** SuperStock, Inc.; **466** Hillary Turner; **467** Hillary Turner; **469** Stock Boston

Cover Photography

Fireworks Image Bank; *Pennant Fever* SuperStock, Inc.; *Meadows or Malls?* SuperStock, Inc.; *Small World, Isn't It?* Hillary Turner and Richard Wheeler; *Orchard Hideout* Hillary Turner and Richard Wheeler

Front Cover Students

Small World Isn't It?, first row: Allan Duncan, Laura Holst, Alycia Brown, Neema Patel, Nick Bulgerin, Arthur Alcones, Efigenia Vasquez. Second Row: Rey Swengel, Amie Yeargan, Simone Adams, Issac Dozer, Ali Pourghadir, Kong Phan, LaQuana Lee, Charmayne Alcones. *Orchard Hideout,* from left, Sung Lee, Jordan Bromely, Trenika Fields.